W9-ABI-446

Governing Consumption

The Bucknell Studies in Eighteenth-Century Literature and Culture

The Bucknell Studies in Eighteenth-Century Literature and Culture aims to publish challenging, new eighteenth-century scholarship. Of particular interest is critical, historical, and interdisciplinary work that is interestingly and intelligently theorized, and that broadens and refines the conception of the field. At the same time, the series remains open to all theoretical perspectives and different kinds of scholarship. While the focus of the series is the literature, history, arts, and culture (including art, architecture, music, travel, and history of science, medicine, and law) of the long eighteenth century in Britain and Europe, the series is also interested in scholarship that establishes relationships with other geographies, literatures, and cultures of the period 1660–1830.

Titles in This Series

http://www.departments.bucknell.edu/univ_press

Governing Consumption

Needs and Wants, Suspended Characters,
and the "Origins" of
Eighteenth-Century English Novels

James Cruise

Lewisburg
Bucknell University Press
London: Associated University Presses

Associated University Presses
440 Forsgate Drive
Cranbury, NJ 08512

Associated University Presses
16 Barter Street
London WC1A 2AH, England

Associated University Presses
P.O. Box 338, Port Credit
Mississauga, Ontario
Canada L5G 4L8

The paper used in this publication meets the requirements of the American National Standard for Permanence of Paper for Printed Library Materials Z39.48-1984.

Library of Congress Cataloging-in-Publication Data

Cruise, James, 1949–
    Governing consumption : needs and wants, suspended characters, and the "Origins" of eighteenth-century English novels / James Cruise.
      p. cm. — (The Bucknell studies in eighteenth-century literature and culture)
    Includes bibliographical references and index.
    ISBN 0-8387-5428-7 (alk. paper)
    1. English fiction — 18th century — History and criticism.
2. Capitalism and literature — England — History — 18th century.
3. Consumption (Economics) — England — History — 18th century.
4. Authors and readers — England — History — 18th century. 5. Books and reading — England — History — 18th century. 6. Characters and characteristics in literature. 7. Consumption (Economics) in literature. 8. Suspense in literature. 9. Narration (Rhetoric)
10. Marxist criticism. I. Title. II. Series.
PR858.C25C78 1999
823'.509355 — dc21   99-23974
                                      CIP

PRINTED IN THE UNITED STATES OF AMERICA

For Ian and Peter,
and in Memory of My Father

Contents

Preface

THE HISTORY OF THIS STUDY HAS MEANT MANY THINGS TO ME AND has occupied a portion of my life that I suppose I would trade for a good Faustian bargain, but not much else. A lot has happened along the way, but I will spare readers the details. In practical terms, writing this book has made me attentive to the demands of a range of readers whose queries and criticisms have encouraged greater precision in my thinking and writing. Through this process I have also become more adept at learning when to let go and when not.

From its earliest days this project has had one broad goal: to situate the Defoe-to-Sterne episode of the eighteenth-century novel within the contexts and culture of period commerce. That design has required some fairly extensive research into the history of English commercialization, an odyssey that, though time-consuming, has been the source of enormous satisfaction. I should also mention that when I began this project I too was among those who subscribed to the dominant institutional notion of the "origins" and "rise" of the novel. But as I proceeded that idea and the reasoning behind it, while still alluring, grew less convincing in my eyes as an explanation for the advent of what we nowadays tend to think of as the novel.

As far as specific issues are concerned, the questions that organize this study deal with contribution: what did Defoe, Richardson, Fielding, and Sterne contribute to the novel? And what did the market contribute to the shape and representational form that their narratives took? The answers to these question entail an examination of both the language of the period economy and its relevance to the individual novelist. The principal terms I use to order the former are "needs and wants" and "suspense." These two elements are domesticated in the novel of moral realism and, as I believe, superintend the level of contradiction and irreconcilable claim that I see as central to this mode of writing during the half-century that followed the publication of *Robinson Crusoe*. In the second half of my study I apply the cultural contexts of the commercial economy to individual novels—the "first" novels of Defoe, Richardson, Fielding, and Sterne—and attempt to read these narratives in ways that are consistent with the terms and conditions of that economy.

9

Surely the better part of writing a preface is this one: of forgetting, at long last, the book and remembering, finally, those who have made forgetting possible. This book, as is probably the case with all books, has caused its share of spills and tumbles. But I have had the good fortune to get up and dust myself off with the help and counsel of a number of individuals—three in particular. Alan McKenzie has been a friend and colleague and probably because of the latter, not the former, he read large chunks of this project in varying states of completion. In one of our postmortems he asked, somewhat optimistically, why I had buried the word "suspense" in the middle of a chapter, hoping, I suppose, that I was creating suspense all my own, rather than merely stumbling upon a word, which is what I had done. He recommended that I give the idea greater play, and, as is evident, I have heeded his advice.

The two others I want to mention are Paul Korshin and Tom Ohlgren. Some years ago Paul was my dissertation adviser. And it was he, in one of my first courses in graduate school, who introduced me to the world of eighteenth-century books that, at the time, I had appreciated only faintly. Later, he again walked me through what was then unfamiliar ground, the old British Library, where I did much of the research for this project. If I exclude myself, no one has lived the history of this book more fully than Paul. He has encouraged me every step of the way, has helped me when I needed help, and, more than he can possibly realize, has lifted my spirits when reasons for joy were few.

A shortage of office space threw me in Tom Ohlgren's path about ten years ago. His interests in the eighteenth century gravitate to the fate of Robin Hood rather than the marriage plot or the heroic couplet. I hold none of this against him. A few years ago, as we talked in his office, he casually spoke of the *Morte d'Arthur* as a novel in Mallory's day. "How could it be?" I thought and then thought again, "Why can't it be?" Although he has read chapters and offered insightful comments about readability and clarity of argument, which occasioned even more revisions on my part, his greater and unfailing role has been that of friend.

During the research and writing of this project, my two sons were born, Ian and Peter. Having them has utterly changed my life. Each in his way is a book alive with stories, mystery, and wonder. They have taught their father, among other things, that sometimes reading and writing are not the most important things. During this same period—and at the opposite end of the great scheme of things—my father died. He, probably more than anyone else, wanted to see this book—not to read it, since he was never much for reading, but to hold it. Unfortunately, my efforts, not unlike Walter Shandy's with the *Tristrapaedia*, failed to keep pace with his life. I am deeply sorry that I could not write faster—or better—but, throughout, have persevered, which, I think, would have pleased him. It is to his memory and to his grandsons, my children, that I dedicate this book.

After the book was accepted, my wife Barbara Pierce took time out of her schedule and offered to alphabetize my bibliography. I did not relish doing that task and for that reason accepted her offer. In return I promise recompense in a form that yet remains unsettled. Her contribution, however, probably would not have been possible had Simon Varey not asked me some deceptively simple questions about my work. I am most grateful to him for requesting the answers that he did. Although there were times when I doubted whether I would ever get my project into a manageable form, once I had it in a shape that did not risk too much embarrassment I had the good fortune to make a connection with Greg Clingham, the Director of Bucknell University Press, in whom I found both an interested and receptive audience. His advocacy of my work has been generous and flattering.

Some small portions of chapter 4 that deal with *Pamela* have already appeared in print, and I wish to thank the Editors of the *Journal of English and Germanic Philology* and the University of Illinois Press for permission to reprint those passages here. For their patience and support, I would also like to acknowledge and thank the American Council of Learned Societies and the National Endowment for the Humanities, which provided grant money that enabled me to travel to London to continue my research on this project. The Purdue Research Foundation also helped in this regard. Finally, I would be remiss not to thank the staffs at the various libraries where I have worked, including staffs at the former North Library, the Van Pelt Library, the Library Company of Philadelphia, and the Krannert Library.

Governing Consumption

1

Against the Grain: An Essay on "Origins"

Few single works of modern literary scholarship can lay claim to the kind of enduring influence and authority that Ian Watt's *The Rise of the Novel* has commanded since its publication in 1957. Whole generations of students have formed their experience of the novel from the model he elaborated and have continued to read and value the novelists he grouped in his work. By any standard of scholarly measure, *The Rise of the Novel* has played a monumental role in determining the questions we ask about the eighteenth-century novel. This is not to suggest that time has stood still over the past four decades, but it is so often through Watt or with at least one eye fixed on him that we craft our responses to the genre. Obviously, we no longer think merely in terms of the "fathers of the novel," if this was one of Watt's behests, but of the "mothers of the novel" as well. Even though sound reasons may exist now to look beyond Watt, we have yet to demonstrate much of an inclination to challenge the foundational premise of his work: namely, the methodological imperium of the prehistory of the novel, that doggedly elusive "before" which would determine, once and for all, the provenance, origin(s), and rise of the novel.

The purpose of this study, however, is not just to dispute the prevailing assumptions that undergird the "before" approach to early modern fiction but also to propose an alternative to it, one grounded in the needs and wants of the period commercial culture and the broad-ranging consequences that ensued from this phenomenon. At the heart of my argument lies the deceptively simple notion of suspense, which, as I show in later chapters, stakes out the common ground between a commercial culture in search of governance and a form of narrative writing that concentrated and personalized this conflict in the "suspended" character. Although some readers may initially prefer to believe that suspense, with its ties to literary handbooks and primers, cannot carry the weight assigned to it, archival evidence will demonstrate that, long before suspense became integral to narrative fiction, it was first the principal cultural and intellectual by-product of British commercializa-

15

tion. In the final chapters of this project I employ the alliance of suspense, needs and wants, and the suspended character to challenge, in
practice, all that origins, prehistories, and the "before" imply about how
we read and conceptualize the early modern novel. As my design
throughout is to work in stages, I want to begin then with the difficulties that surround origins and prehistory as methods of analysis. By dismantling these received institutions, we can, I believe, begin to
appreciate the role and function of early modern fiction within its own
historical period.

The Persistence of and an Alternative to Origins

J. Paul Hunter's humane and probing *Before Novels* (1990), as we
might expect from its title, details what he has determined to be the
foundational prehistory of the novel. His purpose is to excavate the various cultural strata that underlie the genre and tell us something about
its origins. Mindful about how the history of the novel since the eighteenth century can addle our view of its first formulations, he writes:
"novels, especially early novels, often bear features that do not 'fit' later
conceptions of what the novel is or ought to be, and even the most sophisticated later novels often have features that embarrass readers who
bring to them rigid formal expectations." These expectations, he goes
on to explain, are predicated upon our habitual need to abstract "the
novel" from novels, for which he supplies a cautionary aphorism:
"definitions remain high-minded, novels recalcitrant."[1] This procedural
step effectively justifies the "before" approach, which Hunter anchors
in the period novel by enumerating its chief characteristics and by urging that the term "novel" is appropriate for those works we all understand it to signify, even though the usage itself was not standard until
the mid-eighteenth century.[2] From this list follows another more elaborate one, in which he examines nine features of the novel, including
credibility/probability, discursiveness, and didacticism, that distinguish
it from "other forms of fictional narrative, especially romance."[3] Between novels and romance, Hunter suggests, lies a chasm, at once profound and unbridgeable. Even more, this divide becomes the central
justification for *Before Novels*, because romance must remain segregated
from the novel for the latter to take shape, as it draws upon a dominant
culture that accounts for its origins.

In legitimizing the novel, Hunter generally avoids those obvious lures
that make antecedent forms and postdated definitions so tempting to
the ideologue. Even so, he does not question the validity of prehistory
or challenge the assumptions behind the origins of the novel, both of

which typify a long-standing pattern in twentieth-century criticism.[4] The most influential exponent of this view has of course been Watt himself, whose ranging yet intense examination of the cultural contexts of the novel serves Hunter well. If anything, his edifice is grander and even more ornate than Watt's, though we never for a moment lose sight of the original architect behind the design. Granted, much has changed since the 1950s, not the least of which is the acute awareness that has developed about the "political" nature of literary texts or text selection. With regard to the latter, Watt seems not to have twisted himself into knots over the individual novelists he chose for examination. Defoe, Richardson, and Fielding were givens whose narratives required no justification, other than that they "were no doubt affected by the changes in the reading public of their time"—or that, unlike romance writers, they did write in a way that comported with philosophical realism.[5] As if to avoid the incendiary issue of textual politics, Hunter barely pauses over individual novels, which underscores how his "before" becomes everything in his analysis. This fact alone intimates that the easy assumptions of one age become the vexed questions to another. Yet as we have receded from genre criticism, intellectual history, and social philosophy, we have not managed to free ourselves from a diversely layered prehistory that somehow is supposed to unearth the mystery of origins.

The relevant prehistory Hunter draws upon emerges in a number of ways in early novels as internal methodologies, functional proclivities, characteristics, features, and the like. But the novel as a passive receptacle is not the genre Hunter describes; it is really more akin to a voracious consumer of the culture in whose waters it swims. Accordingly, "in seeking the origins of the novel we ought to cast our net widely, recognizing that the greedy maw of the novel takes what it wants where it can find it."[6] And, in a nod to the political capacity of the genre, he writes that the "novel's imperialism [is] its ability to take over features from other species and assimilate them into a new form."[7] While this back-and-forth maneuvering is necessary for the direction Hunter steers his argument, the methods, modes, and tendencies of the novel only reverse the process of formal definition, which is already implicit in those narratives he touches on or alludes to for the purpose of identifying shared features. From this semantics he reads backward into English culture to trace the generic sources that the novel ingests. The effect is at once paradoxical and ironic: predated materials justify the postdated novel, while the latter authorizes use of the former. Temporal sequencing accounts not only for this self-reflexivity but also a *novus ordo saeclorum*, through which time itself becomes divided and ordered, with the novel posing as a cultural savior.

An alternative to this approach is the "long ago" and paradoxical approach that Arthur Heiserman employs in *The Novel Before the Novel* (1977) to push back the date of the novel into the distant recesses of time. In one respect, Heiserman simply removes the "before" to a much earlier period in the Western tradition, without questioning the classifications and definitions that sustain literary history itself. But even if we are permanently attached to these forms of prejudice, Heiserman ought to give eighteenth-century scholars pause about their fascination with *termini a quo*. Well before the most recent outpouring of theories of the novel, he wrote that "the Greek romances work with 'novel'—that is, untraditional—stories drawn from the realities of ordinary life, while some of them also deal with the idealizations of love, adventure, and heroism we associate with romance."[8] Complementary problems surface from his analysis for students of the eighteenth-century novel: he goes on, for instance, to make a strong case for the earlier dating of the novel, leaving us to reflect on the habitual trafficking in pirated goods— love, adventure, and heroism—that enriches the realistic novel of the period. Heiserman, no doubt, makes some of us all the more determined to defend our proprietary ground, perhaps even hell-bent to particularize Bakhtin's creed that novels form the only genre "younger than writing and the book."[9] Thus, *Chaereas and Callirrhoë* may have appeared every bit a novel in the first century A.D. that *Clarissa*, with its gift of tongues, was in the eighteenth, but a very large world separates them.

There are, nevertheless, advantages in thinking of the novel as a variety of storytelling at least as old as prose fiction itself. But the burdens of history, including our own, labor against this notion. Instead, we might settle on a compromise position, one that defines the novel as a form of prose fiction in its printed form; this way it continues as an amalgam of features, a way of telling a story, while also maturing into a writing practice that is authored, time-bound, and proprietary, if not in fact, then in principle. Foucault tells part of this story when, with his characteristically bold insight, he observes that during the seventeenth and eighteenth centuries a remarkable reversal took place in the conceptualization of authorship, through which "literary discourses came to be accepted only when endowed with the author-function" and scientific writings, previously endowed, lost that status.[10] Originality, under these terms, becomes localized in the writer's imagination. Susan Stewart adds that the second way of construing this "original" is to trace its history in the "relation between authority and writing practices . . . [that emerged] in the decline of the absolutist state."[11] The relevance of the second model is limited in the eighteenth-century novel; we see it most clearly in *Joseph Andrews* (1742), for example, in which Fielding goes out of his way to establish the authority and hence originality of his novel. Richardson's practice in *Pamela* (1741/40) could not be further removed, as it makes no claims to authority, only authenticity. The originality of the novel, in this sense, linked property with the textual process—or, as William Warburton stipulates in 1762: "Literary Property . . . is the genuine Offspring of the Mind." He goes on to trace the origin of literary property back to ancient bards, to Roman patrons, and eventually to the book itself, a process that utterly transforms the nature of property in literary productions by subjecting any such proprietary claims to legal tribunals.[12]

Of significance too is that for several hundred years now we have been disinclined to trust anything amorphous, because so much of modern culture has invested heavily in the divisions of knowledge and classification systems within those divisions to help organize and arrange what we know. For better or worse, we have habituated ourselves to believe that the novel, unlike poetry or drama, is in fact historically new, with a history that, for the most part, only authority in competition with writing practices adequately defines. Also contributing to this disposition has been the institutional study of vernacular literatures—itself a form of cultural imperialism—and the models of literary history it relies upon to foster understanding of literary knowledge.[13] Although institutions and "discourse communities" place demands upon us, I intend to sidestep those demands as much as I can by holding the novel up to a nonliterary model. And because of my view of the novel as a textual property, I cannot accept that, come 1719 or 1740, it is a new genre with a distinctive prehistory and traceable origin. It is, quite simply, a different kind of property, but one no more real than what had preceded it.

The justification I offer for this view in part depends on the fact that we have come to recognize over the past fifteen or so years what has remained true: that the recognized property holdings of seventeenth- and eighteenth-century novelists go well beyond Defoe, Richardson, and Fielding; Burney, Radcliffe, and Inchbald wrote novels too; but so did Behn, Manley, and Haywood. The mothers and fathers of the novel have come together in such a way that only the most determined among us would hold that parthenogenesis explains the birth of the novel. Under the weight of this evidence, the hierarchies that literary history and canons perpetuate have begun to erode—and erode quickly. Because of this change, the interests in turning from the literary-history model in order to propose another that eschews hierarchies, as much as is possible, is compelling. I call the latter a history-based needs/wants model. As Mary Douglas has observed, the needs and wants of individuals have a long, transcultural history in social anthropology, as they serve both "spiritual and physical" life. Consistent with that purpose, they create and sustain social rituals that organize the meaning of society, by constructing "an intelligible universe [from] goods."[14] According to Douglas, however, neither the utility theory of the economists nor rational selection process has even begun to account for the breadth of this signifying system. The value of the needs/wants model is that it does not inherently discriminate and can encompass Behn to Burney, with stops in-between and after, in a way that accords with the decline of the hierarchical (not the absolutist) state, the advancement of civil liberty commentators routinely attributed to English commerce, and the acute sense of property, including moveable and literary property, that developed as well.

What is evident about the range of "novels" over the period is not the sudden emergence of a new form, but the differences that exist between the older so-called "romances" and "hitherto unattempted" novels, especially in the area of character representation. Not even Fielding's proud boast in *Joseph Andrews* about his "hitherto unattempted" writing can carry more than a stylistic or technical weight for a novel whose title page declares its narrative debt (*"Written in Imitation of The Manner of Cervantes, Author of Don Quixote"*) to a preexisting genre and goes on to renew ties with the ancient comic epic, the *Margites*. Pouring new wine into old bottles simply does not reveal the chemical mysteries of grape fermentation.

The novelists I study subsequently are those whose work is well known — perhaps too well known in the current climate of opinion. But it is these same writers — Defoe, Richardson, and Fielding, as well as Sterne, though he has been the anomaly — who have figured prominently in our conceptualizations of the novel's origins ever since *The Rise of the Novel*. It is important, I believe, to look at them yet again. My intention, however, is not to treat these standard figures as practitioners of a new form, but a different form, which amounts to the old form expanded and updated: that the origins they evoke are limited to the originality of individual novels; that they engage not prehistory but only history; and that the mindfulness they express is, as Richardson declared, to the moment, even when the subject matter has nothing especially to do with the here-and-now or even with what may be construed as realism. In practical terms, and in the short run, Robert Paltock's *Peter Wilkins* (1750) is no more or less a novel than Behn's *The Fair Jilt* (1688) or Lewis's *The Monk* (1796), since all three indulge from time to time in romance-like improbabilities or variations on the fantastic, while making necessary didactic stops along the way. What accounts for the differences in these novels depends on needs and wants as they were understood and represented in English economic history, a history written overwhelmingly by men. Yet it is equally clear that, while no two individuals have exactly the same needs and wants, the two genders did not share equal access to discourses, economic opportunities, or empowering professions during the eighteenth century—nor, for that matter, did most of the population.

The Ideology of Origins

It is one thing to decry inequality, to flush out insidious forms of ideology, or to label injustice and oppression accurately; it is another thing to assume that the methods of understanding we currently employ in our interpretive work manage somehow to force these otherwise buried truths of earlier periods to the surface. Complicating this discovery process even more is the fact that evidentiary problems inhere within historical periods themselves. By its very nature and for a simple reason, historical evidence remains skewed because, almost invariably, it is the product of few hands, not many. The further back we go in history, moreover, the greater this productive disproportion becomes. Yet, no matter how flawed any period evidence must remain, it seems only reasonable not to overlook what it communicates to us about the makeup of a given culture. Obviously, evidence can never stand by itself, but it ought to be judged on its own merits and figure prominently in those determinations we make about any subject, including the "origins" of the novel.

As students of the early modern novel are aware, so many of the most stimulating and rewarding studies that have appeared over the past fifteen years have argued for a highly politicized, often materialist/historicist approach to the genre. It is the latter especially, and none more so than those studies bearing the imprint of Marx, that explains the revision of economic and commercial matters that this study undertakes and that occasions my dispute with those who would propose the "origins" of the novel. Nor is it a coincidence that Marxist analysis has done much to impart a fine political edge to the idea of the prehistory and origins of the novel. But the weakness of the Marxist reading of origins is that it is too apt to pattern history to fit into a series of Chinese boxes that are indistinguishable other than by size. Thus, for example, nothing differentiates one national economy from another; the bourgeoisie must exist even when it may not; "class" should always signify conflict; ideology can only mean oppression; and so forth. Obviously, the needs/wants model I have identified overlaps with the kinds of concerns that invest the Marxist critique, including the development of political economy (with its implications for domestic and international capitalism); the divisions among social groupings; and the consumer revolution in general. If, however, we can find cause to suspect the utility or accuracy of an ideology-based criticism for a particular set of historical circumstances, then we may be in a stronger position to appreciate how, in occupying a central place in their cultural anthropology, needs and wants elevated the here and now to an unprecedented importance and simultaneously reduced "before" to the stuff of nostalgia.

As I have already indicated, the tendency of much literary commentary has been in practice to politicize the novel and, among the Marxists, to elevate it as a political instrument in the bourgeois dialectic. In his eleventh thesis on Feuerbach, Marx writes that "the philosophers have only *interpreted* the world, in various ways; the point, however, is to *change* it."[15] There is both paradox and irony to be gathered from this statement. By interpreting the novel and its origins, we have effectively changed both. But to do so has made us impose an ideology that may not be appropriate for the material examined, as we perpetuate the very thing (ideology) that is supposed to dissolve once we recognize the falseness of separating idealism — free-floating theory — from materialism.[16]

The first major study of recent memory to take up some of these issues is Lennard Davis's *Factual Fictions* (1983), a work that also renews debate with Watt's *The Rise of the Novel*. There is no disputing that Davis's study carries out an important function by identifying the mixed state of the period novel as a factual fiction. In the course of his argument, Davis also finds it necessary to segregate French romance, *vraisemblance*, and the nouvelle from the English novel. But he compromises this potentially useful division when, in an about-face, he turns it against the traditions of English narrative writing. The novel, we learn, differs fundamentally from the romance so that we are obligated to keep these two forms of narrative expression separate from each other. Without this procedural step, the history of the novel would reach so far back in time as to render origins irrelevant. Accordingly, Davis's own efforts at tracing them through the history of early journalism and the libel laws would also be rendered moot. Because he views the novel essentially as a vehicle struggling against oppression and ideology, he must preserve its origins; for it is only through them that oppression and ideology make sense.

This kind of tension goes to the heart of Davis's dialectic. At one point he asks the rhetorical question: "did the novel merely spring from the head of its earliest practitioners?"[17] He expects us to reply, "no, it did not," because the contrary affirmative, "yes, it did," would threaten the prehistory that supports his argument. Yet to ask the question another way — or, even worse, to personalize it — casts a wholly different light on the question itself. Did *Sir Charles Grandison* spring from the head of Richardson? did *Roxana* spring from the head of Defoe? did *Oroonoko* spring from the head of Behn? Few of us would care to defend the notion that writers write in a vacuum, though, in our embrace of Marxism, we seem perfectly content to dismiss the obvious. This pattern of subtle maneuvering follows Davis to the end, where he concludes his study with a chapter entitled, "Ideology and the Novel." For it is here we learn that although novels and ideology are not *identical*, they are *similar*. If they were identical, then the ideology of novels would constitute bad faith or false consciousness, since "ideology . . . serves to eliminate contradictions . . . [and] functions as a counterforce to criticism, rebellion, analysis, and knowledge." Novels, on the other hand, "require the existence of the shared signifying system of ideology to 'make sense' to readers, but they oppose that system in order to reveal sense."[18] In its "double function" as a factual fiction, the novel plays out that function in good faith. The point is clever: it fastens together all the sides of materialist culture, as Davis has established them, so that they perfectly frame the novels discussed. Yet while we all concede that works of fiction are replete with contradictions, do we go the next step to urge that the ideology of the critic ought to be spared the same fate as the novel? Is the critical conclusion or summary judgment any different or any less "double" than the happy marriage or the inherited estate?

If what we search for in the origin(s) of the novel is a Grand Unification Theory, we should probably expect its discovery for the universe before we are settled about it for the novel. We have arguably grown too guarded and suspicious about such efforts or, at least, have been inclined to refigure the matter of origins as an institutional concern about the institutions of criticism themselves—a shift that unavoidably ties the product to the place of its production.[19] In that spirit, Michael McKeon's *The Origins of the English Novel* (1987) stands as a masterwork of institutional criticism, which has, for better or worse, wedded the novel to prehistory for a new generation of students. Even though *The Origins of the English Novel* bears a strong but not identical resemblance to *Factual Fictions* in method, approach, and import, it has won greater accolades. It is a big book not just because of its heft, rather more so because of its breadth of learning and interpretive machinery. I want to look at this work, however, at its most functional level: the ideology that powers its interpretive machinery.

When McKeon defines the novel as a genre consistent with "what Marx calls a 'simple abstraction,' a deceptively monolithic category that encloses a complex historical process," he also obligates us to this definition—it "must be understood" this way, he says. From this correspondence he derives his foundational categories for examining the novel,

questions of truth and virtue. The first question, of truth, silently elabo-
rates Davis's concept of factual fictions in order to demonstrate how, in
essence, "one dominant prose form 'became' another, [which] is really
to ask how romance responded to the early modern historicist revolution."[20] The net result of this process entails the eventual dominance of
verisimilitude but, in and of itself, this displacement does not fully explain the institutionalization of the novel under Richardson and Fielding. The second question, of virtue, explores the shifting constitution
and instability of "social" life during the seventeenth and eighteenth
centuries in order to underscore the problems associated with ethical
self-regulation and the projection of virtue.[21] While these two questions
are distinct, they are also analogous; both, moreover, achieve their resolutions in the middle class: "like 'the novel,' 'the middle class' is one of
those simple abstractions whose early modern origins mask a considerable preexistence. And like 'the novel,' 'the middle class' . . . filled an
explanatory need for which there had been no satisfactory alternative."[22]

The history that McKeon stages for these questions involves a complex dialectical process, shifting between naive and skeptical extremes,
progressive and conservative ideologies, with associated countercri-
tiques for each, such that it is impossible for us not to recognize the
power of his explanatory mechanism. Although Richardson and Fielding seem muted, almost anticlimactic, by the end, both succeed through
their efforts in fulfilling the existential role McKeon has assigned the
novel—as a vehicle conditioned to mediate truth and virtue. For what
we learn is that their capacity "to reconcile, within the movement of
their respective careers, naive empiricism and extreme skepticism, progressive and conservative ideologies, attests not only to their supreme
virtuosity but also to the fact that these oppositions are losing their intellectual and social significance."[23]

I do not want to deny the value of McKeon's comprehensive model
or the mechanisms that render it operational; indeed, his model makes
a good deal of sense according to its terms. Of concern to me, however,
is the obligation he holds us to that we "must" see the novel as a simple
abstraction. In binding us to the simple abstraction this way, he casts
his lot with Marx and wants us to do the same. Essential to the prescrip-
tions of this allegiance is the idea of class or class struggle, which is
critical for McKeon because of the stress he places upon the shifting
social relations between the aristocracy and middle class in the general
passage from status to class.[24] Marx's own argument about matters of
class cites the bourgeois capitalist's uncontrolled need for surplus-value,
whose principal agent is the machine, as the tool which dehumanizes
and alienates the worker by rendering this individual "a *thing*," a cog in

the wheel. "Machinery does not just act as a superior competitor to the worker, always on the point of making him superfluous. It is a power inimical to him." And in large-scale operations the worker is converted "into a living appendage of the machine."[25] Obviously, the automaton worker, the laborer as Frankenstein's creature, makes much more sense if situated in the nineteenth century, not the eighteenth, but McKeon is satisfied with his determinations since scholars have found a dual usage of "class" in Marxist thought that extends, in one of its senses, to "a kind of socioeconomic relation and conflict that is generally characteristic of all human societies."[26] Such a position is not without attendant difficulties, however, because Marx's design in *Capital* is to lay bare the processes in history that gave rise to capital ("the circulation of commodities is the starting-point of capital," the ascendancy of industrial capitalism, and the demise of this form of economic organization).[27] Which is to say that not all forms of capital are alike, that the processes about which Marx writes expand over time, and that the whole is bound by history. Although the argument for a history-defying class promotes an institutional Marxist critique, it does so at the expense of the historical sense which lies at the heart of Marxism itself.

The other difficulty with this looser definition of class is its application to "all human societies." Even if we agree that Marx accurately predicted the course of capitalism, that should not mean that all capitalist nations collapse into one amorphous abstraction. The simple fact is that during the seventeenth and eighteenth centuries European nations moved at different paces in their capitalist development, which is a point that the emergence of political science during the middle decades of the eighteenth century makes clear. Whereas in the seventeenth century it was much more common for a political thinker to propose a model of government—a commonwealth or a republic, for example—this tendency gave way in the eighteenth century to more exacting examinations of individual nations—their histories, rise, and progress—relative to other European nations. The methodology for this kind of scrutiny was laid out in works such as *The Present State of Europe* (1750).[28] But even in the seventeenth century the English were already acutely aware of capital formation and the uses of commercial wealth among other nations: the Netherlands, France, and Italy, especially, as well as the unexemplary case of Spain, which had plundered vast capital deposits of gold with which it did nothing but impoverish itself. Under these circumstances, we must ask ourselves whether a universal class has any real meaning when applied to a range of national capitalisms and whether it should in turn serve as a modeling device for examining the "origins" of a particular novel.

Ellen Meiksins Wood, a Marxist historian, shows in her *The Pristine*

Culture of Capitalism (1991) that inflexibility is not a requirement for critique and that the habit of reading histories in the singular creates real dangers. At the outset she identifies the source of rigidity, the typical bipolarisms of the bourgeois paradigm — "rural vs urban, . . . status vs contract, coercion vs freedom and, above all, aristocracy vs bourgeoisie" — in order to expose their historical limitations.[29] She goes on to cite other grievances, in particular her disagreement with the Nairn-Anderson thesis, which holds that "the inadequacies of the British state [were/] are due to its incomplete modernization by a bourgeois revolution and a series of aftermaths."[30] Wood's contention is that rigid Marxist analysis misses the mark in its examination of early modern British political economy because it conflates England with France. "In England," she writes, "there was capitalism, but it was not called into being by the bourgeoisie. In France, there was a (more or less) triumphant bourgeoisie, but its revolutionary project had little to do with capitalism. Nowhere was capitalism the simple outcome of a contest between a (falling) aristocracy and a (rising) bourgeoisie, and nowhere was it the natural product of a fatal encounter between urban dynamism and rural idiocy."[31]

She proposes, instead, that this "model is, rather, a composite picture formed largely by a retrospective superimposition of the French Revolutionary experience upon the example of English capitalism and, conversely, an interpretation of the French political experience in the light of English economic development. Through the prism of . . . bourgeois ideology, relations not only between classes but between town and country, agriculture and commerce, and all related dichotomies, took on a new colour."[32] She further maintains that there was nothing inadequate or incomplete about English capitalism; in fact, it was "the world's first capitalist society," which emerged "as it were, spontaneously and not in response to external competitive pressures from more 'modern' states."[33] Although it is true that capitalist development in England "left archaic forms in place," "it may also be true, and for the same reason, that capitalism was more deeply rooted and its laws of motion more firmly established [t]here while preserving old forms."[34]

In establishing her position, Wood also makes the case that English political culture was never dominated by the "state" or a revolutionary bourgeoisie of professionals and office holders in the way other European nations had been.[35] This avoidance in turn evinces the "conceptual and ideological weakness of the 'state' in English culture," which was "determined by its early and more complete evolution of a 'modern' relation between state and civil society associated with the rise of capitalism."[36] It was in fact the residue of precapitalist forms in other European governments that gummed up political economy and, hence, politicized class relations. The absence of this "dynamic tension" in England, where both the aristocracy and bourgeoisie were capitalist, sets its capitalism apart from France, where the "bourgeoisie was on the whole no more capitalist than the aristocracy."[37]

Under the terms of the distinctive type of English capitalism she sketches, Wood asks us to rethink class and all for which we have made it stand. McKeon, by contrast, tells us again that "'class' takes on the character of what Marx calls a 'simple abstraction,' a conceptualization whose experiential referent has a prehistory that is rich enough both to permit, and to require, the abstraction and the dominance of the general category itself."[38] Hence, the use of this word prior to the middle of the eighteenth century means but one thing: "'class,' like 'the novel,' marks not the tentative inception, but the active dominance, of the category."[39] "Tentative inception" presumably predates the use of the word; once the word is used, however, it links itself inevitably to the Marxist definition of the next century. But this is a paradox: situate the word in history and its definition becomes timeless and universal. What do we do with the word "rank," then, since its use prior to midcentury occurred with much greater frequency than "class"? Only after the majority of the population began working in the nonagricultural sector does "class" become more common.

Thus, with the publication of Robert Acklom Ingram's *An Enquiry into the Present Condition of the Lower Classes* (1797), William Wilberforce's *A Practical View of the Prevailing Religious System of Professed Christians, in the Higher and Middle Classes in this Country* (1797), Arthur Young's *An Enquiry into the State of the Public Mind amongst the lower classes . . . In a letter to William Wilberforce* (1798), or Thomas Belsham's *A Review of Mr. Wilberforce's Treatise* (1798), there could be no mistaking the politicization of class in these or other like works. Were circumstances otherwise, one might be forced to defend the writings of The London Association for Preserving Liberty and Property as apolitical and without class consciousness, or to claim that one of its instruments, *An Address to Britons of all Ranks* (1792), speaks a neutral truth upon insisting that "when all were equalized, there would no longer be a superfluity to pay the hire of servants, or purchase the productions of art or manufacture; no commerce, no credit, no resource for the active, but in robbery, and in all those public disorders which make life miserable."[40] McKeon is aware of these literal developments, when he remarks that "although [class] does not appear to provide a truly secure basis for the comprehensive classification of people until the beginning of the nineteenth century, the socioeconomic terminology of 'class' begins to be used before the middle of the eighteenth."[41] But the independent clause offers a distinction without a difference. How else, under Marxism, does one specify classification?

The Institution of Origins

The issues I have been dealing with can, at this point, be collapsed into a question: is an institutionally sanctioned critical ideology sufficient as an explanatory mechanism for the origins of the novel, particularly if that ideology has a dubious historical grounding in the matter that it treats? There is, unfortunately, no easy answer to the question, for, among other things, we have been so conditioned to think in terms of the literary-production model, with its elaborate prehistories and dialectical processes, that we find it difficult to think outside the paradigm and tend as a result to universalize its applications. Hence, Frederic Jameson observes that "ideology is not something which informs or invests symbolic production; rather the aesthetic act is itself ideological, and the production of aesthetic or narrative forms is to be seen as an ideological act in its own right, with the function of inventing imaginary or formal 'solutions' to unresolvable social contradictions."[42] Even if we agree in principle with Jameson's imperative, that the production of narrative form "is to be seen as an ideological act," do we go the next step and decree that only Marxism—the truly genuine interpretation of history—"can give us an adequate account of the essential *mystery* of the cultural past"?[43]

John Tomlinson, by contrast, has maintained that "Marxism has difficulties with the notion of 'culture' itself. The problem usually presents itself at a surface level in what is often called the 'economic reductionism' of Marxist analysis[, which] refers to the tendency for (some) Marxists to represent everything . . . in terms of a supposed underlying and, in some sense, *causal*, political-economic process." No doubt, this process is detectable in such things as a global economy, mass consumerism, worldwide media outlets, and a "drift towards cultural convergence," but these same conditions can scarcely apply to eighteenth-century England.[44]

If we return briefly again to McKeon, we can see that his questions of truth and virtue elaborate the "*causal*, political-economic process" Tomlinson refers to, but only as they probe the "essential mystery" of the novel, its origins hidden in a "cultural past." *The Origins of the English Novel* in effect epitomizes an institutional Marxism that, with its postindustrial sensibility, creates conditions that appear simply not to be borne out by history itself. So far as Homer Obed Brown (see endnote 19) is concerned, McKeon is overhasty and premature even in bestowing "institutional" status to the novels of Richardson and Fielding. Nancy Armstrong, by contrast, is not and thus earns higher marks from Brown for her *Desire and Domestic Fiction* (1987). In it, as he notes, she stresses the processes by which " 'gendered forms of identity determined more and more how people learned to think of themselves as well as of others, [and] that self became the dominant social reality.' "[45] That is to say, she deals with the politics of the domestic sphere in a way that explains the rise of female subjectivity and the subtle empowerment of women. Perhaps because of his own interests in when the institutionalization of the novel occurred and the nature of its import, Brown lets stand a series of paradoxes that propel Armstrong's argument, with the most significant one only indirectly alluded to. For whatever reason, *Pamela* is the only eighteenth-century novel Armstrong treats, as Richardson's heroine emerges from a context that reworks the social and sexual contracts and defines the rank-bound duties of a woman, who, with few other choices, engages in labor that is not labor and an economy that is not money. Gender conflict and its uneasy resolution run throughout Armstrong's analysis, but, as with others before her, she wants to elevate a particular type of narrative telling in order to explain the rise of the novel and the emergence of the middle class—or, at least, "a middle class that was not actually there."[46] Even with its contextualizing of conduct literature, *Desire and Domestic Fiction* is intent upon "domesticating" the English economy, which, though clearly one of the arms of economic development by 1740, did not comprehend the range of theoretical and practical concerns of economic life.

Let us assume for the moment that Armstrong would agree to the final paradox, that the novel is not actually an (institutionalized) novel. Her examination of it, nonetheless, performs a powerful institutional service, as Brown rightly observes—and so does McKeon's. "These significant studies by McKeon and Armstrong are themselves powerfully institutional acts. We must learn how to figure into these histories," Brown counsels, "a complicated institutional narrative of entitlement, one full of conflicting stories and contested claims for the power over narrative and narration."[47] Institution of course means more than just the cultural institution of the novel; it also signifies the channels of scholarly productivity that legitimize a certain type of response or sanction a particular kind of critical methodology. It would be wrong, however, either to expect or to want uniformity under this "capitalist" system of production, but the process of generating novelty can create a confusing array of choices if examined collectively. Robert Folkenflik (see endnote 19) implies as much in an essay that evaluates the work of American-based scholars who, in the wake of Ian Watt, have contributed to the "origins . . . and genealogies" we associate with the early modern novel.[48] Throughout his critical survey, Folkenflik raises large issues about each of their studies, especially regarding matters of theoretical affiliation and consistency. But what is most striking about his effort is that he assembles Watt, McKeon, Armstrong, Bender, and others under one umbrella so that we lack the luxury of contemplating the single work of criticism and must wrestle with the sometimes contradictory and mutually negating significance that this incorporated body of scholarship holds.

Like Brown, Folkenflik also offers a strong endorsement of Armstrong's *Desire and Domestic Fiction*, yet in a subsequent work that she co-authored with Leonard Tennenhouse, *The Imaginary Puritan* (1992), which deals with origins and genealogies, Armstrong registers disagreement with her earlier work. Again, as in *Desire and Domestic Fiction*, *Pamela* serves as the Ur-novel—here, because it is a novel about captivity and because the real origins of the English novel have a transatlantic, not a domestic, source in the captivity narratives penned by Mary Rowlandson and others. For it was these narratives that "required readers to change the way they imagined being English, because they had to imagine being English in America"; and Rowlandson herself who demonstrated "how an individual could acquire value quite apart from wealth and station simply because she was the source of writing."[49]

While it is refreshing to see a scholar rethink an established position, the sheer novelty of Armstrong's deed bears comparison with the epic-novel debate from earlier in the century. Her analysis in fact stems from a reading of *Paradise Lost*, not for the sake of probing the generic devolution from epic to novel, but for the purpose of arguing that Milton's work inaugurated a "brand-new category, which might be called 'personal life,'" as well as signaled the demise of aristocratic culture and "the sudden visibility of labor and an economic definition of the nation as part of a larger revolution in consciousness."[50] Following the English Revolution, the net effect of this visibility was the sudden invisibility of the intellectual and the aristocratic foundations of knowledge. This change occurred under the auspices of "writing," which elevated "the modern middle class not as a class of owners and merchants so much as a class of people whose power derives from a monopoly on information, knowledge, or truth."[51]

Yet, in crafting their striking argument, Armstrong and Tennenhouse seem needlessly guarded about the evidence they cite, as if any novelist, other than Richardson, would bankrupt their investment or raze their precisely built edifice. After English social history has been pared back to its middle-class core, Milton effectively prefigures Richardson, the epic shadows forth domestic fiction. Thus, we are not surprised to learn that Defoe is excluded from the middle-class mix because, even when he "used female narrators, they were always entrepreneurs, excellent businesswomen who actually made a go of it in the colonies."[52] But when does Roxana visit the colonies? Should Behn's Oroonoko suffer a similar fate because he is of royal blood? Or Gulliver, since, after his departure from Leyden and nearly a decade of struggle following it, he finds himself literally a captive when he awakens on the shores of Lilliput? Captivity is neither the only nor the exclusive fate that befalls Pamela—she must also ward off seduction attempts and, in due course, marry her would-be seducer, which, one would think, are matters that fall more directly under the auspices of domesticity. Not even Joseph Andrews is prey to the last of these, though he too suffers captivity when he and Parson Adams are tied back-to-back in a public house, during the abduction of Fanny, Joseph's wife-to-be. These few examples, along with others that will pass unmentioned, apparently do not conform to the model of origins proposed—but should they? Is the model itself too restrictive? We are left entertaining at least the possibility that Armstrong and Tennenhouse tailor origins to a single novel that in turn reflects the structure of an English middle class conditioned by a sensibility of nationalism.

If we were so inclined, we could plot the increased attention paid to domestic and family matters relative to growing nationalist concerns during the eighteenth century. But we would be hard pressed to uncover any direct evidence in *Pamela* that links domesticity to what was going on in the colonies. I am not implying that *Pamela* is devoid of nationalistic concerns or avoids any mention of what might be construed as colonial venturing. After all, Sally Godfrey, in her escape from B., travels as far as Jamaica, where she takes up residence and marries; she even sends a "Negro Boy" to her daughter, the now renamed Miss Goodwin, but he dies from smallpox within a month of his landing. However, the most explicit references to a nationalistic consciousness occur in the introductory letters that precede the first edition: there, the anti-Gallic sentiment is unmistakable. In light of this evidence, it is possible to downplay both nationalism and colonialism as informing structures in *Pamela*.

In so many ways our desire to impose postdated ideologies on the eighteenth century has in practice taxed our credibility, as we try to construct baroque systems of origins and prehistories that have their grounding in post-eighteenth-century historicist inquiry and subscribe to prevailing institutional discourses. In this study I propose that we stop and at least entertain the idea that the origins of the novel are nearly as old as the origins of poetry and drama, and beyond that, they do not signify much for the period in question. I will propose in the next two chapters that we can gauge the changes that occurred to the novel during the eighteenth century by studying the culture of material needs and wants, which, as period documentation attests, developed in ways that render obligation to the past or the informing structures of an English "prehistory" of little immediate value. Instead, suspense—living in a semantically confused present—takes root as a direct consequence of commercial capitalism, as does a particularly complex form of character that appears in the realistic novel.[53] Whatever "originality" the novel enjoys as a consequence is hardly worth worrying over. Still, I do not wish to deny the existence of ideology in the period novel, but I see no compelling reason to look after the eighteenth century to find it. The tendency to do just the opposite, even though I find its application questionable, has certainly fostered shrewd and striking analysis; and clearly no body of scholarship has done more to illuminate the eighteenth-century novel as a complex form of cultural expression. For better or worse, my study "goes against the grain" of received opinion and institutional practice to advance a history-based theory of the "unoriginal" eighteenth-century novel, which I attempt for one very simple reason: the evidence, as I understand it, leads in that direction.[54]

Chapter 2 will continue to question this institution. I will do so by laying out the next stage of an alternative model to "origins," with needs and wants occupying a central place in it. This privilege of place is not attributable to critical caprice or theoretical affiliation; rather, needs and wants were themselves central to the period economy, as again the evidence confirms, and foundational to what was then labeled civilized life. Once needs and wants have been identified and established in this way, I will direct them to character (chapter 3) and the demands that the economy placed upon its formation. In subsequent chapters, needs and wants and character will form the basis of my examination of novels by Defoe, Richardson, Fielding, and Sterne. Their contribution, as I propose, depended on not just the preexistence of the novel form but also their own ability to capitalize on the unrealized promise of the genre. Although this quadrivirate may have generally enjoyed greater access to the marketplace, none of this grouping managed to squeeze out the competition, the majority of whom—before, during, and after—were women. Whether any one of these four writers was capable of such discrimination is a matter for debate, though the point itself is moot. For it was the market alone that rewarded the successful novelist; Defoe, Richardson, Fielding, and Sterne merely penned a new episode and pushed the genre in a new direction—one, in fact, that many chose to follow.

2

From Anthropology to Economy: Needs and Wants and the Narrative of Commerce

BEHIND EVERY MANIFESTATION OF CULTURE LIES A NEED OR A WANT; in cultures organized around capitalism those needs and wants not only multiply and divide but also seem to take on a life of their own. Under most circumstances we pay little heed to this dimension of the material culture or acknowledge needs and wants only in passing, often in name alone. If, on the other hand, we try to pin down needs and wants, we quickly discover their resistance to definition, as they compel us to talk about something—a force, a drive, a power—that appears everywhere and nowhere at the same time. However troubling these forms of resistance may be, I would propose that our *inability* to define needs and wants once and for all makes them an essential tool in the reproduction of culture. The fact is we do not see needs and wants; we see only what they target. If, in this light, we can assume that the most basic design of culture is to ensure its own survival, then those who direct their aim at the objects, activities, and goods that a culture values have already signaled their belief in the values of that culture. Accordingly, by realizing the promised rewards of their participation, those same individuals in turn advance the survival of culture through its self-replicating and sustaining properties.

Nevertheless, all individuals do not participate alike in cultural settings, nor are they expected to. Political systems intercede and received notions of authority can and often do limit access to objects, activities, and goods. In 1656 Marchamont Nedham, in a work rightly or wrongly entitled *The Excellencie of a Free State*, declares that "People must needs to be less luxurious than Kings or the Great ones, because they are bounded within a more lowly pitch of Desire and Imagination," this in a book that describes the just power seated in the people as a clear departure from "the primitive or first Governments of the World."[1] For some, in fact, needs and wants appear either to fall short of or exceed their objectification. In either instance these individuals challenge the self-policing features of culture, and risk either marginalization or dismissal by those more firmly entrenched in its ideological values.

Frances Burney, for one, experiments with just this idea in *Evelina* (1778), a novel so thoroughly immersed in a culture of material goods that we actually follow its heroine into the shops. On the outskirts of the consumer bustle represented in this novel lurks Burney's brooding Scots poet Macartney, who endures the hardship of lodging in the shop and home of the Branghtons, kin whom Evelina would prefer not to acknowledge. Initially, at least, Macartney seems to exist for the single-minded purpose of offsetting Evelina's upstart relations. According to Branghton siblings, this enigmatic visitor from the North lives on either nothing at all or, what is worse, learning, which befits his labor as a poet. In either case, their assessment is telling in light of the values they stand for. We learn, nonetheless, that their judgment does not miss the mark by much—guilt and love sustain this poet, little else. And, as events unfold, not even the man Jesus, Lord Orville himself, trusts Macartney. At Mrs. Beaumont's otherwise leisurely retreat at Clifton, he rebukes Evelina for encouraging and indulging such a figure and, in his oblique manner, warns her to steer clear of him.[2]

What is true of Burney's novel is true of other social and cultural formations as well: a hierarchy of needs and wants organizes behavior, and, for those with access, privilege ensues. This same pattern obtains, according to Mary Douglas, even in apparently egalitarian cultures, because "consumption is about power." Thus, it is not surprising that those excluded from power have two strategies at their disposal: either "to withdraw and consolidate around remaining opportunities," such as Macartney does, "or to seek to infiltrate monopolistic barriers," the course the Branghtons pursue.[3] In either case, goods themselves become the defining agents of culture, which, as Douglas advances in *The World of Goods* (1979), form a reciprocal bond with needs and wants. I intend to return to this point shortly, but first want to underscore the issue she raises at the outset of her study concerning the inability of economists to explain why people want goods. The fault, she argues, lies with the utility theory of economics, a theory that forgets social reality. Thus, it becomes the job of the anthropologist to explain what "is at the very center, even at the origin of economics as a discipline": demand theory.[4] But to speak as an economist is not to be an anthropologist. Economists, in fact, speak about needs and wants all the time; it is just that these matters become so buried in technical jargon or lost in tables, graphs, and equations that the language of economics takes on a reality all its own. All of us can, I believe, acknowledge the primal urgency in needing or wanting something, if not in ourselves, then in our children. The point is that where complex systems of delivery exist, of the sort that economists can order, markets have already come between consumer and product to influence exchange—that is, one discourse impinges upon the other to effect what Douglas herself calls the "spirit of the age."[5]

The model of culture which can govern and police itself through *un-self-conscious* channels forms the basis of a needs/wants anthropology, which, presumably, every "simple" culture evidences. With the introduction of other factors and variables that alter or transform the range of needs and wants, their governance and regulation undergo a much more tortured, self-conscious, and politically disputatious form of enactment. Under these conditions, the distinctions between needs and wants that formerly held no longer do. Neil McKendrick's research on consumption habits in the eighteenth century leads us in this direction when he notes the fifteenfold increase in tea consumption per capita over the period. In the same breath he also cites Jonas Hanway, who, in 1756, was mortified to learn that simple laborers demanded—and apparently were able to pay for—their daily cup.[6] After a point, anthropologies cease to be naked.

That we instinctively gravitate to particular items—who drank what, wore what, ate what, smoked what, attended what, was transported in what—tells us a lot about the ways in which a needs/wants culture has influenced our own cognitive requirements for the acquisition of knowledge. By contrast—and of course I simplify—scholastic philosophers living in a different culture produced a different sort of knowledge. The difficulty in pining down needs and wants is that, after a certain stage of development, cultures produce secrets. In writing about ancient Egyptian civilization in *The Divine Legation of Moses* (1737–41), Bishop Warburton calls attention to this tendency, as he disputes the commonly held view, expressed by Thomas Sprat and others, that the Egyptians employed hieroglyphics, a secret language, to preserve the hieratic class. He contends that "it was the *first literary writing*, not the *first hieroglyphical*, which was invented for *secrecy*. In the course of time, indeed, they naturally changed their use; *letters* became common, and *hieroglyphics* hidden and mysterious."[7] In our attentiveness to the mysteries of material culture, we come to see that single commodities, while compelling for their solidity, do not stand alone because as we attempt to penetrate their mystery, they invariably recur to the forces that propel their acquisition.

This pattern is true even in critical studies that spotlight the "single artifact." Let me illustrate by turning to Simon Varey's *Space and the Eighteenth-Century English Novel* (1990), which, in effect, disassembles Bath stone-by-stone, only to reerect it with all of its representational nuances intact. Quite clearly Bath was not the only town with buildings

in the eighteenth century, nor was it the only urban locale that undertook new construction. This understanding cues us to see all of the specific architectural features of Bath, not in isolation or as a self-contained
entity, but as an example of how one closely examined part of British
spatial ordering exceeded itself, while still managing to participate in
the cultural organization of space. Bath, in this sense, serves as a type
that simultaneously pre- and postfigures an ideology of control.[8]

At the heart of Varey's depiction of Bath lies an even more basic truth
about the culture of goods. Of Bath's principal modern architect, John
Wood, he offers this appraisal of his enterprise: his "new buildings . . .
catered to the territorial instincts, needs, or desires of the leisured
classes."[9] We do not imagine that, at the planning stages of his construction, Wood engaged visitors to Bath in open forums to discuss his proposed methods for ensuring that buildings communicated the right
ideological messages, yet the complicated supply/demand mechanism
between leisured need and architectural catering might suggest otherwise. The larger lesson Varey subtly impresses upon us is that, at some
point, the distinctions between demand and supply, want and its satisfaction, grow too complex to unravel, particularly after they are entwined and knotted by desire. Mr. Simkin B——n——r——d, a
character in Christopher Anstey's *New Bath Guide* (1766), certainly
would have itched to leave Wood's imaginary lectures on buildings and
ideology, yet in his own way he appreciates the part desire plays in the
grand displays of need and want.

It is fair to say of him that his powers of penetration are not good; he
is, if anything, a vast consumer of undigested facts and digestible foods.
At a public breakfast he can only report on the deeds of Lord Ragga-
muffenn and Lady Bunbutter without appreciating the delicious folly
they enact. Despite their promising names as breakfast dishes, neither
the lord nor the lady is edible, so the pleasure Simkin B. derives from
this public occasion comes from the parting memory of the food he has
consumed at the lord's expense. Yet, at the beginning of the letter thirteen, which he addresses to his mother, he succeeds in staking out the
boundaries of needs and wants without defining their properties once
and for all: "What Blessings attend, my dear Mother, all those, / Who
to Crowds of Admirers their Persons expose? / Do the Gods such a
noble Ambition inspire; / Or Gods do we make of each ardent Desire?"[10]

Mary Douglas would explain Simkin B.'s uncertainty over the "origins" of what attracts him this way: "consumption goods are most defi-
nitely not mere messages," tidbits of data of use only to economic
analysts, rather "they constitute the very system itself . . . [that] dis-

solves the Cartesian dichotomy between physical and psychic experience."[11] We can expand Douglas's claim about the self-sustaining properties of goods and culture a bit further by proposing that this undifferentiated state of goods and desires defines "origins" as an undifferentiable cultural mass, subject not to transcultural similarities, but to a particular set of historical circumstances that made origins a compelling national concern in the first place—in short, to a place and time in English history when commodities became their own "origins," without anyone knowing exactly how, why, or what this development augured. As students of the period are aware, inquiries into origins flood the print world during the seventeenth and eighteenth centuries. Yet, in reading these works, we often sense that what passes as "origins" has little to do with a discrete alpha; rather, they strike us as an inseparable feature of the "progress" of an idea and its place in contemporary history and culture.

Reading backward in time to find the present is akin to our manner of dealing with the early modern novel and the interest we have staked in its origins. Lost in this orthodoxy is the anthropology of consumption, as tailored by economic theory, to fit the commercial proportions of the nation itself. The "progress" of needs and wants, however, was not seamless. From start to finish, partisanship wove its threads into the commercial fabric. To be sure, gainsayers and skeptics reacted to progressivist claims, and thus the more vocal, traditionally inclined, or vested participants in the debate sought to restrain commercialization by invoking a range of "original" states so ordered to caution against those material developments and changes that made England's future unpredictable—less like the past. In this regard, to speak at all about the progress of needs and wants is to speak in equal portions about those who welcomed the dissolution of origins into things and those who imagined origins as discrete and recoverable.

From the tension of these divergent interests emerged a surprising form of coherence that in provoking discord and division also rerouted their potential destructiveness into productive channels. What becomes evident is that as the story of mercantile capitalism grew larger and more varied a plot of sorts began to unfold. As a complex metanarrative, which I call the "narrative of commerce," this plot ordered and adjudicated the needs/wants economy and assured that competing interests, divisions, and the state of "suspense" that marked these phenomena could not extend beyond the pale of governance. In this chapter and the next, I attempt to detail these processes and their consequences in ways that lay the foundation for my discussion of the novel in the final three chapters.

Origins and Progress

In contemporary critical discourse on the novel we prefer to shun "progress," for its political insensitivities, and seize "origins," for their political assurances. During the eighteenth century, "origins and progress" were the twins of discourse: to get the one, so often, was to get the other. As the provenance of progress, origins characterized a body of thought, especially certain kinds of political writings, that mined nostalgia in search of a treasured past. Susan Stewart's *On Longing* (1993) helps to orient us to the paradoxes of this collective impulse. "Hostile to history and its invisible origins, and yet longing for an impossibly pure context of lived experience at a place of origin," she writes, "nostalgia wears a distinctly utopian face, a face that turns toward a future-past, a past which has only ideological reality."[12] Given the culturally unsettling dimensions of material change, particularly during the eighteenth century, when, for example, aping one's betters inspired petulant criticism, we can sense why some retreated into nostalgia.[13]

Emulation was, to be sure, a symptom of a much larger change. Already in the seventeenth century it was possible to imagine not just a material-based culture, as John Wheeler did in 1601: "the Gouernment of things conuenient and fit for the maintenance of Humane Societie: wherevnto mens actions and affections are chieflie directed, . . . so they may drawe from thence either commoditie or pleasure, or at leastwise therby supplie, & furnish their seuerall wantes, and necessities"; but also civilization itself predicated on systems of available goods and services, which Nicholas Barbon claimed in 1685: "When Mankind is civilized, instructed with Arts, and under good Government, every man doth not dress his own *meat*, make his own *Clothes*, nor *build his own House*."[14] C. John Sommerville, in *The Secularization of Early Modern England* (1992), supplies the necessary historical overview these citations call for when he notes that seventeenth-century "scholars were beginning to imagine a society held together not by divine sanction or a common piety or even political force, but by something as natural as prudent self-interest."[15] But "beginning to imagine" means that not everyone did, leaving the work of reorientation far from finished. What I want to suggest is that between start and finish, origins and progress, then and now lies suspense. To my knowledge, however, no period treatises exist on the origins and progress of suspense. Suspense, in this regard, is not a discourse unto itself, but a by-product of discourse—the unspeakable consequence of the historical disruption and change that needs and wants had effected.

We can approach this problem indirectly but, I think, fruitfully, by turning to a fairly recent work on progress, David Spadafora's *The Idea of Progress in Eighteenth-Century Britain* (1990). Origins, as we notice, have no topical play in Spadafora's argument, in part because he takes a defiant attitude toward those who would gainsay the importance of progress in the annals of eighteenth-century thought. *The Idea of Progress* attempts, in short, to reassert the legitimacy of the history-of-ideas approach to progress. Accordingly, Spadafora defines progress as improvement: "the movement over time of some aspect or aspects of human existence, within a social setting, toward a better condition"; and is particularly keen about extending the discursive reach of progress, what he calls its "doctrines," to include virtually every major intellectual component of the age: religion, history, the arts and sciences, social theory, language, and so forth. His design in doing so is to paint a large canvas of progress but, even more than that, to dispute Bury's notion that progress has a largely French provenance and is exclusively a secular dynamic, one that could not depend upon providentialism—or anything associated with it—if it were to have anything like the staying power it needed for cultural survival.[16]

But so often in Spadafora's analysis we sense the want of origins. This omission avoids a source of internal friction that occurred within origins/progress discourse, between "once upon a time," when life was good, and "now," the time rife with corruption. These polarities were not new to the eighteenth century. During the first-quarter of the seventeenth century, for instance, the controversy between Godfrey Goodman (*The Fall of Man* [1616]) and George Hakewill (*An Apologie of the Power and Providence of God in the Government of the World* [1627]) played out much the same sort of debate, though in an idiom generally different from later renderings.[17] Even in his discussion of this early controversy Spadafora is quick to neutralize any and all forms of antagonism toward the progressivist view, as if progress itself could only exist "without contraries."[18] And the pattern haunts him. The Lord Monboddo who, in *Of the Origin and Progress of Language* (1774), repeatedly "discoursed on the constant decline of civilized man" becomes the same Lord Monboddo who "merely supported the old saying that the corruption of the best things is the worst."[19] Similarly, "Estimate" Brown's scathing denunciation of a profligate England—and one might add his high praise of the French political state—in his *Estimate of the Manners and Principles of the Times* (1757) asserts a "core of ultimate optimism" simply because Brown may intimate as much: "'*Permanency* or *Duration* of the State, is the main Object' of the *Estimate*."[20] These sudden and, after a while, predictable assertions weaken Spadafora's argument, instead of doing what they are supposed to do. We are left to assume that British culture of the "high eighteenth century" managed

somehow to twist the diverse strands of "doctrine" into a rope of progress pulled taut — I am not convinced that this was the case.

Progress is probably better likened to a frayed and knotted rope gone
slack — or to the graphs that Tristram Shandy uses to map his progress
through the first five volumes of *Tristram Shandy*. If progress is to mean
anything at all in the eighteenth century, it derives its significance from
systems of exchange: that is, to get something — namely, progress —
something had to be given up. It was in short a need/want driven system, not perfect or continuous, certainly infused with politics, but
essentially a system that underscored the differences and changes
wrought over an imagined span of time. Let me illustrate by returning
to the examples of Lord Monboddo and "Estimate" Brown that Spadafora cites to suggest some of the contradictions that emerge from the
ways in which each engages origins *and* progress.

There is nothing sly or oblique about the methods and approach
Monboddo uses in *Of the Origin and Progress of Language* to substantiate
Spadafora's claim that the "best is worst" or the progressivist/improve-
ment model it is suppose to endorse. Nearly from the beginning Monboddo draws a sharp line between the "natural" and "acquired" powers
of mankind, roughly those that segregate the needs of existence from its
wants. His list includes the sciences, liberal and mechanical arts, commodities and pleasures, as well as civil society itself.[21] The evidence he
draws upon to make this distinction is complex, but most of it pertains
to the biological, developmental, anthropological, or ethnographic
("original") features of the species. For example, he notes of human in-
testines that their length supports either a frugivorous or carnivorous
diet, while the latter, he argues, signifies a late change wrought by "acquired habit" (230), a class of cultural practices often mistaken for "natural operations" (197). Monboddo cautions that the mere capacity for
doing something does not qualify it as natural, original, or innate, the
best example of which is the human ability to speak. Of this capacity
he observes: "it is an art that is not to be taught without the greatest
labor and difficulty . . . nor to be learned by imitation, without continual
practice, from our infancy upwards" (197). His most memorable evidence draws from anthropological and ethnographical findings about
the speechlessness of primitive peoples, including savages captured in
Europe. Within this context, he challenges the classification Buffon and
Linnaeus accord the orangutan, proposing that this "man of nature" is
without virtue of speech (contra Buffon) but of the species of man (contra Linnaeus) (292–306). Language, in other words, is "the fruit of
human art," which is an indictment so severe that Monboddo adjudges
the capacity to speak as inconsistent with the divine plan: "if we hold

language to be revealed, we cannot stop there, but must maintain that all the other arts of social life were likewise revealed" (207, 380).

All that Monboddo adduces points to the primitive ideal, yet the most unencumbered incarnation of this figure in *Of the Origin* leads a life determined by environmental luck: an equable climate and the absence of savage beasts. In these circumstances the language-free primitive would have no need for civil society. Only under conditions less favorable do social formations emerge, organized around the need for and want of defense, "men, at first, . . . used inarticulate cries, to communicate their wants and desires, and to give signals necessary for carrying on the business in which they were engaged" (495). Over time, the progress toward more civilized forms of existence moved apace with articulable and imitative language, so that, under the jurisdiction of "acquired habits," reason, ideas, and systems coalesced into the creation of civil societies: "the same cause that first produced ideas, and made men rational creatures, did also make them social and political, and . . . produced all the arts of life; and this cause is no other than the necessities of human life." Once these needs were satisfied, others followed: "the want of occupation, of pleasure, and amusement, which gave birth to the pleasurable arts; and, when the mind came to be cultivated, there arose a curiosity, and desire of knowledge, which produced the sciences" (382).

All of these progressive developments would have been impossible without language, the agent of needs and wants in civil society, according to Monboddo's system. But because of the instrumentality of language in advanced forms of social organization, this medium can only be classed an adventitious tool, an "acquired habit," among civilized creatures. Beneath these layers of the superfluous and acquired lies a core, albeit a borrowed core, even more original than primitivism; for Monboddo's true longings and abiding nostalgia, as we discover, are Platonic, as mediated through primitive settings. Large portions of his study engage in philosophical quarreling, with Locke especially, whose materialism creates "civilized" distortions and avoids the higher truth of forms: "That therefore there are *ideas* of a much higher order than those which we abstract from matter, being the *models* or *archetypes* of all *material forms*: That of such ideas the *intellectual world* is composed; of which *the material* is no more than a copy" (88). Perhaps Monboddo anticipates the more formal lucubrations of Heidegger and his theory of Dasein, but he also summons images of Socrates hectoring a hapless Glaucon. The real unanswered questions in *Of the Origin and Progress of Language* ask how the flawed instrument of language is supposed to recover the Platonic forms, intelligence unclouded by materialism, the glimmerings of life before the Fall, the primitive ideal, or any of the other multiple origins that he invokes. Later he even concedes that "if language was at all invented, there is no reason to believe that it was invented only in one nation, and that all the languages of the earth are but dialects of that one original language" (677–78). Through it all, the progress he attributes to civil society exists by default and yields no discernible improvement: "there is progress in civil society, at least, such as is not to be found in natural things, but only in things of human institution" (361). But progress built upon the shifting plates of historically distant and discrete origins has little chance of remaining stable in an advanced consumer culture. The fault lines that cut through Monboddo's language result from his attempt to govern needs and wants, those steady and unchanging forces that link "inarticulate cries" to the "desire of knowledge"—and, as is evident, the *forms* themselves of civil society, which, through their phenomenal displays, render present and past discontinuous, unbridged by language, to endure in a state of suspense.

In many ways, *Of the Origin and Progress of Language* has all of the tracings of civic-republican discourse but without the trappings of its language. Brown's *Estimate*, by contrast, is truer to this ideological affiliation in both language and idiom—J. G. A. Pocock, for instance, positions Brown in the republican line of descent running from Machiavelli to Montesquieu.[22] Less certain is its "core of ultimate optimism," unless it can be likened to the disease-ravaged sufferer who welcomes death as the promise of a better life. The central contradiction in Brown's curious work emanates from the friction between the moral idealism it pleads and the political solution it proposes. The source of that friction was the nation's commercial engine, which ran hot and caused potentially destructive levels of indulgence among the citizenry. Although the *Estimate* was not primarily a vehicle of commercial analysis, Brown's world still turned on the poles of needs and wants, a concession, no doubt, to the ruling passion and manners of his time.[23] In the wake of its publication, Brown's critique elicited public reaction just as Mandeville's *Fable of the Bees* (1724) had done some three decades earlier. But there all comparisons stop. Those who responded to Mandeville were mostly outraged detractors, shocked by his parted curtain and the secrets it revealed. If anything, the *Estimate*, with its backward glance and abiding nostalgia, made the bulk of Brown's responders dubious about the legitimacy of his lofty moral appeals.

Like so many other writers, including Monboddo later in the century, Brown's notion of progress is defined by historical stages or discrete and definable periods of development, with the "original" ones modeling amelioration. During the first and middle stages, as Brown notes, commerce plays a pivotal role in securing improvement by satisfying need/want based demand: in the first stage "it supplies mutual

Necessities, prevents mutual Wants, extends mutual Knowledge, eradicates mutual Prejudice, and spreads mutual Humanity." Additional refinements follow in the second stage: "it provides Conveniencies, increaseth Numbers, coins Money, gives Birth to Arts and Science, creates equal Laws, diffuses general Plenty and general Happiness." During the third stage, however, iniquity roots itself amid the very things that formerly provided amelioration. Thus, "Avarice," "Luxury," "effeminate Refinement," and a "general Loss of Principle" manifest themselves as the habitual tendencies of a culture on the skids.[24] Yet in the progress of stages the third becomes suspended from and discontinuous with the first two stages—hence, the awkwardness Brown evinces in his proposed remedy.

His solution, which even Pocock describes as "unexpected," sacrifices moral suasion to the political example "of SOME GREAT MINISTER" whose "Wisdom," "Integrity," and "unshaken Courage," like Bolingbroke's Patriot King, will single-handedly steer the ship of state back on its civic-republican course (221).[25] The most telling moment of suspense in his work, however, precedes its near-desperate valedictory. Despite the *Estimate*'s appeal to an earlier history and its ideal republic, Brown, at a critical juncture, could have assembled classical and Christian authorities to add moral and historical weight to his argument, but records instead the futility of even attempting "to enlarge on these Subjects in that vague and undistinguishing Manner, which most Writers have pursued in treating them, tho' it might carry the *Appearance* of Reasoning, would in Truth be no more than *Declamation* in Disguise" (212). Again, we can observe how the difference between origins and progress breaches historical continuity, forcing Brown to come up with an "unexpected" or even "absolutist" solution, given his preference for the French political state, to the moral nosedive he thought his nation taking.

As I hope the illustrations of Monboddo and Brown make clear, progress cannot simply be equated with improvement, or as the determined opponent of origins. The fact is that not everything written in an age of ubiquitous "origins and progress" fits neatly into one container or the other, even if one persists in believing in either a "core of ultimate optimism" or an oppressive hegemony. Even though needs and wants were the catalysts of progress, they complicated it, in the same way that they redefined "origins." What we cannot lose sight of, however, is that these same needs and wants enacted change and produced an awkward tension between what Pocock himself calls "continuous" and "contingent" history.[26]

Civilizing Wants and Original Needs

No political discourse of the period underscored this tension more than the civic republicanism Pocock has championed through his extensive scholarship. By the same token, no discourse was more nostalgic or more committed to an "original" past—an ideological "future-past"—in its confrontation with commercial modernity. For Charles Davenant it was Lycurgus who provided "the most perfect Model of Government that was ever fram'd."[27] With a template like this virtue neutralizes vice, and love of country conquers private seeking. What follows is "Temper in Prosperity, Obedience to Discipline and the Laws, Foresight in Business, Secrecy and Firmness in Councils, Vigour in Action, Courage, Military Skill, Thrift of Honour, Magnanimity; [in short] . . . the Virtues upon which Dominion is founded."[28] Realizing these virtues in political practice, however, is the hard nut, as commercial "virtues" have swallowed republican ideology shell and kernel: "how have these Errors, Publick and Private, taken their Rise? In all appearance it is from hence, that ever since the Corruption of Nature, which is very ancient, we have given wrong Names to Things, and have allotted to Vice the Stamps and Attributes of Vertue. We term Avarice, Prudence and Oeconomy; We think none Wise, but who abound in Wealth; and none Honest, but whom Fortune favours" (Davenant, "Universal Monarchy," in *Essays*, 236). But it clear from this allusive passage that Davenant struggles to look before a Babel of confusion and misallocation to some kind of antediluvian original in order to posit a "future-past" as an ideal worth seeking.

Even Pocock has conceded, "we cannot understand the vindication of commercial society unless we understand the grounds on which it was assailed and acknowledge the attack's continuous vitality."[29] The only difficulty with this statement is that it accords privilege of place to a minority point of view, as if the success or failure of commercial society depended upon civic republicanism, a position that extant documentation fails to support. Those brave "Generals [who] came from the Plough" in ancient times to serve their nations had a vested interest in doing so; their numbers in eighteenth-century England probably had little statistical relevance, as the population rose and commercial/industrial expansion proceeded.[30] John Robertson provides what I think is the necessary codicil to civic republicanism when he states: "participatory virtue . . . depends on a material condition."[31]

Virtue, needless to say, was not a neutral term during the period. By any standard it was suffused with ideology, especially among those who feared the balance of power shifting against them and the inadequacy of moral imperatives to counter tipping scales. "[T]he right Strength of this Kingdom," cried Davenant, "depends upon the Land, which is infinitely Superior and ought much more to be regarded than our Concerns in Trade."[32] But even though the annals of past history were filled with examples of political corruption, as Davenant himself recited chapter and verse of these tales, the present was the great obstacle in republican thought: "Trade, without doubt, is in its nature a pernicious thing; it brings in that Wealth which introduces Luxury; it gives rise to Fraud and Avarice, and extinguishes Virtue and Simplicity. . . . But, . . . 'tis become a necessary Evil."[33]

Republican discourse has much to teach, however, for it underscores not only the imperatives of governance that attended commercial civilization but also the process by which cultural participation was redefined under the auspices of a needs/wants economy. With its strong historicist outlook and fear of the capitalist maw, the republican critique isolated some of the manifestations of suspense, matters such as divorce and estrangement, for example, which were still apparent in the next century as *Entfremdung*. Adam Ferguson depicts these aspects early in his *An Essay on the History of Civil Society* (1767), a work Pocock has characterized as "perhaps the most Machiavellian of the Scottish disquisitions on [the republican] theme."[34] There, in a passage that celebrates the spirit of irrational attachment, Ferguson contrasts this quality of citizenship "with the spirit which reigns in a commercial state." "It is here indeed, if ever," he writes, "that man is sometimes found a detached and a solitary being: he has found an object which sets him in competition with his fellow-creatures, and he deals with them as he does with his cattle and his soil. . . . The mighty engine which we suppose to have formed society, only tends to set its members at variance, or to continue their intercourse after the bands of affection are broken."[35]

The picture is not flattering, nor is it meant to be. The threat it implies is that capitalism redefines cultural participation in ways that are immune to the recalled virtues, nostalgic attachments, or imposed principles of the republican's public-spirited citizen. Accordingly, this mode of economy "suspends" individuals from informing structures of meaning.[36] As Michael Ignatieff has observed, "in all the moral traditions that confronted the coming of capitalist modernity, the man of virtue was the man of few needs."[37] In this light, we can trace the "origin" of republican discontent to the substitution of the man of needs for the man of virtue; as well as to the valuing of a culture organized around moveable property in which aspiration and emulation defined the semantics of its power.

For civic republicans, difficulties with sociopolitical change arose because of their belief in a preexisting morality, which they then imposed as a typology upon the polity only to find the latter wanting. The more flexible "commercial"-based solution to this problem simply tailored morality to fit the polity. In the second half of the eighteenth century John Trusler offered the most complete expression of this adaptive measure when he assigned the material and spiritual their separate spheres. "Speculative morality," this cleric announced, "tends to guide us by a pure and disinterested love of rectitude; or to detach us from temporal things, by directing our views to those which are eternal. Considering actions in themselves, independent of all relation to society, and connected only with the rules of perfection, it will not admit of any deviation. What I call civil morality, which has no object but to sweeten and secure the commerce of men among themselves, and to maintain good public order, requires not a strict observation of all its precepts, but admits of every relaxation consistent with the peace and prosperity of society."[38] That he can accept that goods and their pursuit yield their own morality—a Cartesian dissolution—allows Trusler to advance a model of civil functioning in which the signs of suspense, estrangement and divorce, take on the qualities of everyday reality.

One did not have to subscribe to ideological pure forms of civic republicanism to be taxed by the contradictions that developed from belief in discrete and separable original states. Other variations on this theme followed, particularly in cases when commentators worked within the differences between advanced forms of civilization and their more "primitive" counterparts. In his *An Essay Towards Preventing the Ruine of Great Britain* (1721), for instance, George Berkeley borrows heavily from the known and familiar republican tradition in order to challenge the creed that encourages the citizenry "to measure national Prosperity by Riches; [whereas] it would be righter to measure it by the Use that is made of them." "So just," he continues, "is that Remark of *Machiavel*'s, that there is no truth in the common Saying, *Mony is the Nerves of War*. And tho' we may subsist tolerably for a time among corrupt Neighbours, yet if ever we have to do with a hardy, temperate, religious sort of Men, we shall find, to our cost, that all our Riches are but a poor exchange for the Simplicity of Manners which we despise in our Ancestors. This sole advantage hath been the main support of all those Republics that have made a figure in the World."[39] In other words, it is the ethical character of the citizenry, in harmony with past precedents, that determines national integrity, not the plumpness of one's purse. To help secure this desired end, Berkeley recommends that a number of steps be taken to rid the nation of venality: the renewal of sumptuary laws, the regulation of public diversions—some through absolute prohibition—the reformation of drama, and the complete banishment of masquerades, the continuance of which "is sufficient to inflame and satisfy the several Appetites for Gaming, Dressing, Intriguing, luxurious Eating and Drinking" (15).

This litany proceeds against the backdrop of the South Sea Bubble, the only contemporary "political" event Berkeley refers to in *An Essay*. From this popular nightmare he exploits a common theme among republican thinkers, who, in following Polybius, plotted history in terms of a cyclic revolution—from virtuous government to corrupt and back again through all its intermediate stages. So far as Berkeley is concerned, the sad end of one phase was drawing nigh, though the longevity of Walpole in fact would dispute a hasty closure. Although *An Essay* may not hold our attention for long, given its standard republican themes, it is important to remember that Berkeley directs his criticism at England. With the publication of *The Querist* (1735–37), however, *An Essay* totters under its republican weight, as the juxtaposition of these two works gives rise to matters of contradiction and suspense. Through a series of almost six hundred questions, Berkeley interrogates his native Ireland in order to speculate on its backwardness and the possibilities of its improvement. All of his questions, it seems, call for answers in the affirmative. In this light, some stand out as especially curious. Number twenty, for instance, has him ask "whether the creating of wants be not the likeliest way to produce industry in a people? And whether, if our peasants were accustomed to eat beef and wear shoes, they would not be more industrious?"[40] One might as well ask whether they would be better served attending masquerades or plays. The untroubled answer is that improvement must move apace but cannot go too far. Even so, a common thread joins the London of ruin and the Ireland of devastation and languor, as the distinctions between barbarous and civilized become differences of degree only. And, it would seem, to introduce the needs and wants of a people less materially privileged is to suspend the moral censure that requires those more privileged to wear shoes and eat beef only.

Like Berkeley, William Paley also recognized the centrality of needs and wants but goes beyond him to acknowledge how they melt into each other. He remarks in *Moral and Political Philosophy* (1785) that "it is not enough that men's *natural* wants be supplied; that a provision adequate to the real exigencies of human life be attainable: habitual superfluities become actual wants; opinion and fashion convert articles of ornament and luxury into necessaries of life."[41] In this context Paley also recalls the Berkeley who claimed for his native Ireland a national economy perfectly capable of sustaining itself, given the incentives for doing so. Paley writes: "I believe it may be affirmed of Great Britain, what Bishop Berkeley said of a neighbouring island, that, if it were encompassed with a wall of brass fifty cubits high, the country might maintain the same number of inhabitants that find subsistence in it at present; and that every necessary, and even every real comfort and accommodation of human life, might be supplied in as great abundance as they now are" (2:66–67). While Paley's proud boast about the insular self-sufficiency of England is, no doubt, genuine, bluster itself is cheap, often having no discernible impact on either the battle or its outcome. In the absence of brass walls, national autonomy and self-sufficiency can endure, according to Paley, but only as long as "trade conduces to the production of [agricultural] provision" (2:70). Beyond that, trade imperils the wealth vested in land ownership and the distribution of power that ensues from that disproportion.

In a liberal gesture that discloses his conservative politics, he approves of the "peasant," who, in itching to own a watch, "will till the ground in order to obtain" one; for it is under the jurisdiction of one of capitalism's indirect relations that the watchmaker contributes "to the production of corn as effectually, though not so directly, as if he handled the spade, or held the plough" (2:68). As Paley's examples expand, however, the rigor of his model begins to collapse. He next refers to that "acknowledged superfluity," tobacco—a product, to my knowledge, neither indigenous to England nor cultivated in it during the eighteenth century—only to make tobacco the *desideratum* of a seaman on a global odyssey, "the mariner [who] fetch[es] rice from foreign countries, in order to procure to himself this indulgence, . . . a merchandise which has no other apparent use than the gratification of a vitiated palate" (2:68–69). Somewhere between Cheshire and China, we suspect, the idea of insularity dwindles to a farce, and brass walls serve as metaphors for something else.

Had Paley been more attentive to the comment he made about needs and wants, he would have discovered the reason why not even he could sustain the illusion of England as a kind of commercial utopia. The reason did not lie merely in the availability of imports such as rice and tobacco, for surely no one needed either to satisfy "the real exigencies of human life." But as these articles of consumption shifted from wants to needs, they assumed levels of cultural meaning and significance that were indivisible from the articles themselves. Those same workers who set Jonas Hanway on edge when they called for their teacups duplicated the same cultural pattern: they suspended and frustrated the ideology of moral governance.

Although Dr. Johnson is supposed to have refuted Berkeley by kicking a stone, he at least shared the same outlook as the bishop when, according to Boswell, he boasted prior to services at St. Clement's that, in the absence of any "commerce at all," the English "could live very well on the produce of [their] own country."[42] Boswell next reports that at Johnson's home that evening they drank tea, which had and contin- ues to have the same status as the tobacco of Paley's seaman. And, as we all know, it was Johnson's consumption of this beverage that dem- onstrated little governability. It goes without saying that the availability and distribution of goods mattered significantly in the development of a needs/wants culture. It was precisely this consciousness that Johnson, citizen of London, carried with him to Skye. In the great metropolis, where the consumer "is tempted to contrive wants for the pleasure of supplying them, a shop affords no image worthy of attention." Whereas on an island, such as Skye, one must await the "wandering pedlar." The want of a shop on an island, says Johnson, "turns the balance of exis- tence between good and evil."[43] No doubt, but so does the proliferation of shops, as Evelina reminds us and as Johnson, the great student of his age, should have reminded himself. But Johnson profoundly forgets his point of "origin," the larger island of England, in his journey to the Hebrides and, by doing so, suspends moral judgment about the "civi- lized" world from which he has come. He is, in this way, Berkeley-like, the man at odds with his own assumptions and perceptions. The same is true of Paley who censures the tobacco-hungry seaman who travels the globe. However indulgent this act may appear to him, the context that occasions the charge fails to sustain its own premises because needs and wants suspended both hortatory governance and imposed moral imperatives.

The Narrative of Commerce

Perhaps it is that when watchmakers and tobacconists have shops the next street over, consumers are apt to forget or disregard everything else about the goods they desire or simply cannot fathom the import of wanting these things. But in a world of preferences and acquired habits the difference between a watch and a pipe is enough to fashion a moral universe, albeit a precarious one. The certain truth is that William Paley did not smoke a pipe, nor did Adam Ferguson raise herds for a living. The intercourse that goods demanded with "strangers" had its toll.[44] Yet these same goods had other "estranging" and divisive effects, and not just for those who wanted to reassert "original" states. As John Barrell has remarked, commerce did not discriminate in terms of what it di- vided: "the real history of society [hinged on] the unchanging coher- ence of continuously subdivided activities and interests."[45] But the question is what supplied that coherence, and how was it managed? Barrell takes us part of the way in our search for answers with his dis- cussion of the division of labor, which he associates "with the institution of political economy: with the celebration of economic expansion and industrial improvement, and with the attempt to vindicate the structure of modern commercial societies as, precisely, a structure. . . . [F]or the political economists," he concludes, "it was a discourse which had . . . a good story to tell." We might dismiss "a good story to tell" were it not for the fact that he details how the plates in William Pyne's *Microcosm* (1806–8) tell "a coherent story."[46] Jean-Christophe Agnew makes the same sort of claim in *Worlds Apart* (1986) when he discusses "outward" and "inward" responses to market change, a division patterned after the "historical shift in the market's meaning—from a place to a process to a principle to a power." It is from this pattern that he traces historical reconceptualization in terms of the "literary" model, the *theatrum mundi*—the world as theatrical spectacle—under the auspices of market change.[47]

Those habituated to the ways of the highly specialized postindustrial world are likely to be skeptical of associations linking commerce with the story or theater, but the fact is that the forgotten power of the story as an informing structure had a central role to play in preindustrial cultures.[48] While it is a pretty straightforward business to measure the impact of commercialization on recognized literary forms and other modes of cultural storytelling, what I propose is that we try to think of commerce as a narrative unto itself—a *new* story akin to a master narrative, if only one were possible in a commercial culture—that influenced everything, including its less wealthy, though more ancient, cousins: poetry and drama, history and philosophy, essays and narratives—all of them genres and modes that had traditionally benefited from their more noble lineages.[49] Let me illustrate with a period example. In 1701 Charles Povey wrote a substantial piece entitled *The Unhappiness of England as to its Trade by Sea and Land*. Already far along in his argument, he draws what appears to be a comparison between the irregularities of commercial practice with a stage full of characters. In this theater "all manner of Vices are strenuously maintained, and set out to the best Advantage: There the Atheist may be confirmed in his loose Principles; and the Prodigal encouraged in Luxury, till he consume his Substance on a Crowd of Strumpets . . . : There you may see a Buffoon dress'd in the Habit of a Grave Divine, on the purpose to be made the Game of the Play, and expos'd to the publick Contempt: There you are told, that all Religion is nothing else but State-Policy, or a piece of vile Hypocrisie."[50] Why reflections such as these occur in a book about the decay of trade raises important questions about the *theatrum mundi*. But it is clear that Povey regarded social life as a prism, a single glass that divides light into its constituent bands. His solution, however, is really quite simple and as applicable to the theater as it was to trade: reform the latter and the former would follow. With the rise of the commercial narrative, fictional facts—a "literary" reality, so to speak, or social constructivism—mattered in profound ways for the exchange of ideas because, in the absence of a single master narrative or some other uncontested paradigm of cultural reality, only partisanship and self-interest made sense among competitive camps determined to govern reality. Or, as the author of *The Character of the True Publick Spirit* remarked in 1702: the pursuit of "*privat profit* [erases] all *Power* and *Authority*," including the authority of God himself, so that "there is no real truth, no falsehood, no good, no evil, but all things are as men take them, and Consequently there is no *Realities* at all, . . . only . . . *Figments* and *Chimeras*."[51]

As the productive repository of a new cultural semantics, the narrative of commerce estranged and held in suspense traditionally received meanings of place and purpose, while simultaneously fashioning a void in which luminous theatricality and new constellations of stories mapped the cultural firmament. Unto itself, however, the narrative of commerce told a story we scarcely recognize, one that was filled with bits and fragments of character, action, and plot, yet without the pleasure of coherence we derive from literary tales with discrete beginnings, middles, and ends. While its impact can only be gauged indirectly or through its elusive ubiquity, its power manifested itself not just in the other "cultural discourse" it gave vent to but also in the way it controlled and governed those other discourses. In the end, the narrative of commerce did not discriminate against proponents or opponents of commercialization but was quick to expose the *contradictions* of partisanship and competing interests, while fostering precisely these divisions. However paradoxical it was in the administration of coherence, the narrative of commerce, in eluding conscious recognition, assured the continued "progress" of material culture.

When we turn to works such as the widely popular *Spectator* essays (1711–12; 1714), it is often easy to see the visible hand of a needs/wants culture in its numbers but, if we look closely, we can also detect the more filmy narrative of commerce as well. Addison's number sixty-nine (19 May 1711), for instance, has Mr. Spectator reporting on his Saturday visit to the Royal Exchange. Business is brisk, he tells us, as he stands beaming amid a swirl of foreign agents and within earshot of the world's confusion of tongues. From his long experience of the Exchange, Mr. Spectator imagines himself as any number of foreign nationalities, trying one on and then another, with the ease of a man shopping for a new hat. He confesses to a secret joy in being there and, on more than one occasion, has shed tears of happiness "that have stoln down [his] Cheeks" for the privilege of standing, watching, and reflecting on all the good, as well as the goods, that this congeries of mankind represents.[52] This brotherhood of feeling is not without its tensions and awkward rivalries, however, as Mr. Spectator remarks that amid "this busie Multitude of People, I am known to nobody there but my Friend Sir Andrew [Freeport]," who smiles in passing but never stops—or an Egyptian merchant, "our Conferences go no further than a Bow and Grimace" (1:260–61).

At the end of the number he imagines one of the stone monarchs ornamenting the Exchange returned to life to witness this vast confluence of goods and people. "[H]ow would he be surprized," Mr. Spectator almost asks, "to hear all the Languages of *Europe* spoken in this little Spot of his former Dominions, and to see so many private Men, who in his Time would have been Vassals of some powerful Baron, Negotiating like Princes for greater Sums of Mony than were formerly to be met with in the Royal Treasury! Trade, without enlarging the *British* Territories, has given us a kind of additional Empire" (1:263). Although the *doux commerce* Mr. Spectator alludes to at the close of his number does not materialize by itself, the distant past did not, nor could it, anticipate such gentle refinements to the theory of exchange. The feudal king watching former vassals cut deals quite clearly would be shocked to witness a swarming mob busy about the business of upsetting the balance of power.[53]

Against the backdrop of the Royal Exchange—at once a place, process, principle, and power—and the historical progress it intimates as an entrepôt of the world's goods, Mr. Spectator also suggests an important lesson about the nature of participation in a needs/wants culture sized to the proportions of the nation. Because he only watches, observes, and records, his participation is as a matter of practice fanciful, imaginary, even fictional, as we judge from the incongruity between reported experience and derived lessons. There is, in short, a price to be paid for belonging, just as some portion of the commercial story escapes conscious realization. In many ways Mr. Spectator anticipates citizenship in Benedict Anderson's "nation," even the smallest of which, Anderson contends, is circumscribed by a sense of communal belonging or a fanciful communion that obtains despite the fact that the vast majority of a nation's citizenry remain disembodied abstractions to the individual citizen.[54] Pocock uses similar language when discussing the rise of the credit economy during the eighteenth century and its displacement of republican virtue as the foundation of civil society: "to observers of the new economics," he remarks, credit "symbolized and made actual the power of opinion, passion, and fantasy in human affairs."[55]

The same sort of pattern haunts the spectator/narrator in Goldsmith's *The Deserted Village* (1770), a poem hostile to commerce. In his prefatory letter to Sir Joshua Reynolds, Goldsmith decries the luxury of the age and its impact upon traditional farming communities experiencing depopulation. In the poem proper he sets forth these concerns under the rubric of historical change: "But times are altered; trade's unfeeling train / Usurp the land and dispossess the swain."[56] And it is this change—the irrecoverable origin or the literary pastoral—which serves as the narrator's source of lamentation; for in coming back to relive the scenes of his youth he discovers that the "Sweet Auburn" he once left no longer exists. But no matter how great the strength of sentiment in the poem, the accumulation of "sedges" at the "glassy brook" does not grow in proportion to the wealth of the property owner. Nor is the land itself any less fertile or any less productive, for how could riches spring from a barren soil? Yet this is the impression the narrator wishes to convey: "Around the world each needful product flies, / For all the luxuries the world supplies: / While thus the land, adorned for pleasure all, / In barren splendour feebly waits the fall" (lines 283–86). Yet he cannot have it both ways: an export trade that depends upon shipping "needful product[s]" in sufficient quantities for the importation of luxury items requires more than fallow fields and barren lands in order to prosper.[57]

The "facts" of later eighteenth-century agricultural development would dispute Goldsmith's contention; but facts do not matter, only fictionalizing counts.[58] While we can dispute the precise features of economy written into *The Deserted Village*, we cannot contest the fictional fact that the narrator who intones a jeremiad about the English rural diaspora left his place of origin many years before. Like his counterpart, Mr. Spectator, Goldsmith's narrator is free to imagine, even to provide, for that matter, a coherent account of loss that does not implicate himself, which he addresses not to the "swains" who will never hear him, but to "Ye friends to truth, ye statesmen."[59] Had James Anderson been asked his explanation of the rural diaspora, however, he would have said: "as the lower class of people, in these circumstances, find they can earn money by a kind of labor that is less severe than the operations of agriculture, they naturally desert that mode of living, and apply to the other; so that the farmer in a short time finds himself at a loss for servants to carry on his necessary operations."[60] Under the narrative of commerce, divided opinion compelled inescapable forms of productivity—for Goldsmith, a lost landscape is balanced by a poem gained—whereas the truth of any matter could only be ideological.

One of the more significant gauges of what the commercial narrative represented was in the way that political commentators and commercial advocates came to accuse their opponents of practicing fiction. One of "Estimate" Brown's most uninhibited critics, William Temple of Trowbridge, charges, for instance, that "when we hear of the reign of *Saturn*, the *golden* age, &c. to be sure, the writer never forgets to make his own the age of *iron*," particularly Brown, who "vomits out a great deal of *filth, froth*, and *venom*."[61] Another of Brown's critics, the more sober-minded Robert Wallace, exposed the fiction of civic republicanism another way, by appropriating all of its virtues for the commercial polity itself, in which citizens "want finer cloaths, finer furniture; and, besides corn, beef and beer of a better kind, they must have spiceries, fruits, and wines, and stand in need of more money to procure them."[62] Against Brown and his preference for the French state, Wallace repositions republican demands. "The attachment to the family, the person, or the glory of the prince cannot be so powerful under an absolute monarchy, as the *amor patriae* under a free constitution. . . . [I]n a free government, little depends on the character and genius either of any one man, or of a few men. Its wise institutions, customs, and laws must be supposed more steady and durable, and consequently more able to form the people to virtue" (244–45). That is to say, the state as an abstract dispenser of representational forms, not a leviathan of incorporated bodies—families, persons, and princes—ensures coherence. Several years later, Wallace actually proposed a new "fictional" model to accommodate a needs/wants based culture. Rather than measure the success or failure of government in terms of past historical precedents ("chiefly under the Roman Empire . . . Liberty was subdued in Europe"), he does so against More's *Utopia*; not to recover some ideal kingdom, since, as he admits, "no government can render mankind absolutely perfect," but to light upon just the right political "construction" that would facilitate progress and improvement, through which the "natural passions and appetites of mankind" may be realized, including the love of ease, sensual pleasure, and liberty.[63]

Although departing in striking ways from the political prizefighting that occupied Brown, Temple, and Wallace, Joseph Massie, in *A Representation Concerning the Knowledge of Commerce as a National Concern* (1760), not only called for a brave writer to distill all the necessary knowledge of commerce into a volume or two but also styled his own reflections on the subject of commerce "a representation," which, in the context he establishes, has a double meaning as "a case for" as well as a "fictional construct." Tired of the partisanship that had ransacked commercial knowledge and wearied by the confusions that had overrun it, Massie virtually wished into existence a new narrative, a systematic and coherent story that subscribed to the rules that guide the arts and sciences, which "are [not] at all affected by the Removal or Decay of those Things to which they give Being and Form."[64] To help right the course of commerce, Massie promoted "fixed Principles" in its conduct and, as an inducement to those "Men [who] will have to employ their Time in a Branch of Knowledge that hitherto hath generally been thought dry and mean," he encouraged them to "consider Trade nationally" (1, 9). Within a few years of Massie's request, James Steuart published his multivolume study, *An Inquiry into the Principles of Political Œconomy* (1767), which advanced a method of economic analysis that could only develop out of commerce conceived of as a series of abstractions and principles designed to serve national ends.[65]

Although Massie was an inveterate collector of books and pamphlets on commercial subjects, having amassed a library of over fifteen hundred such publications, he was dead-wrong on one score: since early in the seventeenth century the "nation" had been the principal character in the commercial narrative. Only its plot was in doubt. Neither as a petition nor as a self-contained representation did Massie's work break new ground. It simply underscored what had long been true about the narrative of commerce: that its story worked toward abstractions and that it governed best when no one could see it. The notion of "political economy," in this sense, was the final chapter in the period commercial narrative.[66]

But from overuse political economy has come to mean practically nothing. In defining a particular form of economic theorizing, its real significance was that it collapsed the narrative of commerce into a single inscrutable character, Adam Smith's invisible hand, an unattached rhetorical figure that managed somehow to steer the kind of economy that, in Richard E. Teichgraeber III's words, ensures a "common social destination will take care of itself" without regard for "positive moral value or purpose." Thus, as Teichgraeber points out, "capitalism can be seen as the realistic alternative to authoritative, but also chimerical, moral codes"—"realistic," however, only in the sense that illusions or representations can be realistic. This development in economic theory sealed estrangement: the commercial economy that supplied the needs and wants of the general population took on the proportions of a cultural secret accessible to only the very few.[67] The "mysteries" and "secrets" of the trading world that were commonly referred to during the middle of the seventeenth century—the old hieroglyphical writing, to fashion an analogy from Warburton—became, in effect, the "literary writing" of trade, a discursive repository that demanded probing analysis and expertise. In this way, the narrative of commerce had simply fulfilled a long-standing promise.[68] But if political economy functioned according to self-regulating principles, evincing no real need for either human or divine intercession, mercantilism, by contrast, was full of moral watchfulness and caution, as well as intercessions, both human and divine.

These interlardings enriched the commercial narrative and imparted to it the body that made it in its time and place an "original."

Competing Narratives and Displaced Origins

In 1756 a group of Cambridge undergraduates—dissertation writers—submitted essays to Lord Townshend's competition on the topic: "In what manner do Trade and Civil Liberty support and assist each other?" William Hazeland, who won the prize, wrote that the "wide experience of men and things which [a commercial society] affords, that active and enterprising spirit which it cherishes, those encouragements of genius and invention that are proposed by it, have changed ignorance, barbarity, and inhospitable distrust into mutual confidence, arts and humanity; have given rise to all that is useful and ornamental in human nature."[69] W. Weston, another contestant, urged that commerce "break[s] the fierceness of our manners, and soften[s] and humanize[s] the mind. This almost necessarily introduces on the one hand a certain lenity of government, and moderation . . . ; and on the other hand, a due restraint on those turbulent and unruly spirits."[70] Students of British military history between 1652 and 1783 might reasonably question whether these scholars had lost their footing somewhere between Jesus Green and Parkers Piece. The answer, I think, is that they did not. While it would be fairly easy to identify the connections between war and the pursuit of commercial advantage during the years marked off, this lapse into public history would fail to explain how, in the face of overwhelming evidence, Cambridge undergraduates could be rewarded for professing "fictions."

Over the seventeenth and eighteenth centuries "commerce" took on a variety of shapes and forms, including military conflict. But even before a century or so of warfare broke out, commercial discourse was already aggressive and opportunistic in its conduct—the remora to the shark—even better perhaps, the shark itself. Within the broad jurisdiction of the narrative of commerce, domestic campaigns were launched, partisanship was heated to the boil, and divisions of all sorts left sharp edges that were not to be blunted. Through it all, the ineffable coherence of this "metanarrative" governed the adaptive processes that political and social change called for. In this respect, the narrative of commerce was, like the needs and wants that mirrored it, knowable only through its effects.

The modern story of commerce, however, originated in the seventeenth century, when, through inscrutable channels of transmission, it mysteriously began to turn up in unexpected places. The effect of this interloping was that sacred origins were compromised—held in a state of suspense—so that commerce could, in a manner of speaking, declare its own origins. This process involved widespread historical revisionism, which accelerated after the Restoration when apologists were quick to distance legitimate government from the usurpation of legitimacy. That was the political trigger at any rate; philosophically, empiricism was another. But from the theological standpoint, the evangelical dispensation, which reached further back as a source, provided the structure for revision.[71]

This dispensation drew a strong line of demarcation between the capacity of Christians and Jews.[72] The latter, in a variety of writings, were often crucified for their native ignorance and tribal primitivism and routinely characterized as a people whose proclivities for idol worship were so great that only the fantastic stories and figurative language of Hebrew Scripture could nudge them in the direction of an ennobling religious sense. Ever since the Gospels, by contrast, rational appeal, not poetry, formed the foundation of spiritual enlightenment. Just a few years after the Restoration, John Spencer described this new era accordingly: "*the condition and temper of the Oeconomy we are now under admits not our expectation of any Signs from Heaven, either to witness against the practices or opinions of any party of men, to give notice of an approaching mercy or judgment.*"[73] Joseph Glanvill, in 1668, distinguished this historical passage in proprietary terms: "the *Prophetick Writings*, which are very little suted to the *ways* of our *Order*. And in consequence of *this*, I [affirm], *That God was pleased in those Inspirations to apply himself much to the Imagination of the Prophets*; which *Faculty* . . . was *desultory*, and did seldom *tie* itself to *strict coherence.*"[74] These are but two of many such examples.

But with their cultural and political identities determined by rational scrutiny, historical difference, and, less apparent, the impact of a needs/wants economy, commentators in large numbers discovered that the "biblical master narrative," to borrow Everett Zimmerman's language, was a text brimming with problems.[75] Because of the passage of history, as Robert Boyle noted, "we have also lost the means of acquainting our selves with a multitude of particulars relating to the Topography, History, Rites, Opinions, Factions, Customes, &c. of the Antient Jews and neighbouring Nations, without the knowledge of which we cannot in the perusing of Books of such Antiquity as those of the Old Testament . . . delight and relish with which we should read very many passages."[76] Deists of course had a field day with the historical continuity of the two Scriptures, what Anthony Collins would later recapitulate as "the New Testament . . . *but an unfolding of the Old.*"[77] Around the turn of the eighteenth century, John Toland, no impartial observer on these developments, drew from the annals of history a lesson that resonated in his own. In *Letters to Serena* (1704), he notes a curious division that arose from the tension between material progress and political governance in ancient times: "according to the degrees of Improvement any Nation made in Politeness, Literature, or Government, the less they were addicted to the impious Humor of God-making."[78]

But even clerical worthies of the Established Church, including figures as notable as Robert South, remained troubled by prophetic overreaching, in particular, Revelations, a text that was as distant and as far removed historically from Hebrew Scripture as is possible.[79] What is perhaps most interesting throughout this period of soul-searching and head-scratching over Scripture is that merely reading it and witnessing the truth it told were no longer good enough—in fact, could be dangerous if those without authority proclaimed the Word.[80] The focus had shifted in other words from exegesis to matters concerned with the production and consumption of Scripture: its historical setting and textual transmission, the formation of canon, methods of evaluation, and so forth—the domain, in short, of scholars and experts.[81] In practice, delivering the Word or its truth had taken on the features we associate with the commercial model.

During the seventeenth century the commercial model itself experienced similar convulsions, which, as Joyce Oldham Appleby has prompted, were organized around bullionists on one side and free-traders on the other. Although she rejects mercantilism as inappropriate, it is, I believe, a still useful term that simply redirects the tension of the economy in another way. As a paper discipline, mercantilism promoted a largely inelastic system because gain functioned within a fixed order. Merchants were deemed crucial players, but only as exporters—they carried English goods abroad and returned home with the gold and bullion that was to fill the national treasury, the only real measure of economic well-being. Importers and retailers, by contrast, were thought of as blights because they made the citizenry into consumers.[82] Whether the French wines that were so often targeted left the citizenry fuddled or their palates keen for a plate of ortolans did not matter; what did was that English gold had to be shipped across the channel. Mercantilism accordingly depended upon authority and hierarchies, especially as figured by the monarch and, by extension, the nation as a whole.[83]

If we exclude earlier writers such as Thomas Mun, Gerald de Malynes, and Edward Misselden, who fought their own wars, the first real explosion of commercial writing occurred during the 1640s, at a time of disquiet and revolution that tested the limits of political authority.[84] Interestingly, the common theme that so many commercial writers seized on was the injustice of government patents and monopolies, hallmarks of mercantilism. During this time, Scripture had a kind of lived reality, indeed scripted political action, so that the justification for these complaints almost invariably had some grounding in the divine fiat to trade. That is, Providence saw fit to divide the terrestrial globe into discrete land masses, configured by oceans and seas. Thus, as this dusted-off line of thinking went, the hand of God stamped its will into the face of the earth to encourage international commerce. After the Restoration the incidence of providential commerce waned without disappearing but, as I have already indicated, Scripture itself, while retaining its status as a cultural cynosure, no longer justified action as much as it had to be justified and authenticated unto itself. Now, though it is reasonable to assume that commercial works of a certain period will include some theological posturing, what we find is that other works seemingly unrelated to trading concerns, especially those of a theological character, have strong commercial subtexts. Often in fact this subtext figures as the point of departure between the continuities of the master narrative and the emergence of historical discontinuity and suspense.

Clavis Apocalyptica (1627) is a good starting point. This work, written by "old *Daemetas*," Milton's tutor at Cambridge, Joseph Mead, advanced a "scientific" method of deciphering the prophecies contained in Revelations. In time, *Clavis* became an important work among "Puritan" political visionaries. William Twisse translated it in 1643, with a second edition that followed in 1650, and it is he, not Mead, who is of note. In the preface to his translated edition he remarks about "the opening of the world by Trade and Commerce" and the "encrease of knowledge" it has brought.[85] Even so, Twisse does not make much of this fact, because, one suspects, Mead's synchronisms comprehended the whole of God's plot of which trade was only a part. Lest we have forgotten, Twisse reminds us that Daniel 12.4 prophesies that "encrease" so, by implication at least, the expansion of knowledge via trade should shock no one. Mead's work was typical of a vast range of writings that explored millennial and millenary themes; of each it is fair to say that sacred origins remained intact because the narrative of God's will and purpose, as expressed through Scripture, was both complete and self-sufficient.

One purpose in pausing over Mead/Twisse is that *Clavis/Key* frames Antony Ascham's often overlooked *Of the Confusions and Revolutions of Governments* (1649), which can be viewed as its secular counterpart. Although Ascham pays uncompromising respect to divine covenants and the biblical master narrative, he is equally keen to attack the perceived premise of the Puritan Revolution, the "leveling" of property, though in truth this platform belonged only to certain factions within the revolutionary corps. Still, even before Hobbes equated the state of nature with the state of war, Ascham had already done so.[86] But between the "original" ideal of civilization and its advanced forms, he argues, comes human intercession: the practices and institutions of civil society. Ascham goes on to contend that in contemporary society fewer men work necessary employments, only two out of five; whereas the other three work in luxury employments. He comments, "Out of this we may easily discover the occasion of mens receding from their originall community, both in moveable and unmoveable goods" (9). To counter the Puritan concept of polity, he explains why people should be content with their existing rulers because of the critical difference between mankind and God: "Gods language is always the same: But man is imperfect both in his understanding and will . . . : His habit, manners, Lawes and Words derive his Pedigree from *Babell* [often viewed as the divine original of commerce] and confusion" (64). Forty years before the publication of Locke's *Second Treatise* and with only traces of Scripture left in his text, Ascham already intimated the ties between consumption and consensual government.

Arguably the single most important apologetical work of the century, Edward Stillingfleet's *Origines Sacrae* (1662), takes ruptured sacred origins as its subject matter. In it he contends that departure from a unified and, hence, true history—when the Greeks, "who had been *traders* for *knowledge* into forraign parts" (principally Egypt)—caused philosophy to degenerate.[87] Stillingfleet's characterization of Greeks as essentially unscrupulous merchant-monopolists—importers rather than exporters—is telling, because by understanding their character we understand practices that corrupted history: "for the certain *tradition* of the *world* was now *lost* in a *croud* of *Philosophers* whose *aim* was to *set up* for themselves" (30). A decade later Charles Wolseley employed the same kind of referential-historical analysis in *The Reasonableness of Scripture-Belief* (1672), in which he attempted to defend the historical veracity of the scriptural master text against the growing skepticism of his age. Accordingly, Scripture fulfills the same role that was commonly attributed to the commercial economy, the supply of deficiencies. " 'Tis not imaginable that God should make a *Revelation* to the world, and not make it proportionate and sufficient to all the *Ends* of Revelation. The great *End* of Revelation is to supply the *Deficiencies of Nature* (for if Nature were in it self perfect and without defect, these needed then no Revelation)."[88] And, toward the end, we learn that in its plenary role Scripture serves as a repository of wealth: "the Scriptures appear to be Designed as a General *Store-house* of *Instruction* and *Satisfaction* to all Sorts of *Capacities* and *Conditions*" (442). Not everyone, however, could partake equally from its stores. In other words, with the introduction of want and demand, a form of economic discrimination settles in, which is attributable to the differences between the original production of Scripture and its seventeenth-century consumption. "Many passages in the *Scripture*," Wolseley observes, "relate to things *past*, and long since transacted, of the *circumstances* of which we are not fully informed; And many passages were accommodated to things well known, which we in these After-Ages are ignorant of. . . . Many parts of the *Bible* relate to the *Customes* and *Laws* of particular *Places* and *Countreys*: Without the knowledg of which, No man can be a competent judge" (442–43). Although Wolseley does not resolve this problem, its import is clear.

In the following decade Samuel Parker, at the time Archdeacon of Canterbury, faced similar problems with historical continuity, though he played a variation on this theme in *A Demonstration of the Divine Authority of the Laws of Nature and of the Christian Religion* (1681). In part 1, under the rubric the law of nature, he urges that to find God it is not "needfull to appeal to the Testimony of *sacred History* or *any other ancient* Record concerning the Original of Mankind, humane Nature it self is a demonstration of its own beginning."[89] With this premise he quickly steers his argument to property matters and follows with comments on commerce and its relation to "the limitedness of every Man's own nature." In this setting, "the convenience of [one's] own life invites [the individual] to trade and transact with others . . . for that is the proper advantage of Commerce to emprove and enlarge the comforts of life by mutuall Exchanges" (41). When, in part 2, Parker leaves the laws of nature behind for the Christian religion, he becomes preachy and moralistic, recalling the value of miracles and tradition as the instruments of faith, neither of which obtains any longer—or, as he says, "the true spirit of our Religion seems to be fled to Heaven with its primitive Professours" (424).

This same economy, as both dispensation and exchange, also influenced scientific discourse. In the period's masterwork of physico-theology, *The [Sacred] Theory of the Earth* (1684–90), Thomas Burnet attempted to reconstruct the earth in its original form from its pristine shards and fragments in order to explain the physical properties that had to compound for the final conflagration to occur. But, as far as Burnet was concerned, the commercial economy simply confirms the condition of the world in a fallen state, so that a global "perpetual Æquinox" no longer exists. "[N]ow one great part of the affairs of life," he determines, "is to preserve our selves from those inconveniencies [of climate], by building and cloathing. . . . [T]hus the Civil order of Things is in great measure constituted and compounded. These make the business of life, the several occupation of Men, the noise and furry of the World; These fill our Cities, and our Fairs, and our Havens and Ports;

Yet all these fine things are but the effects of necessitousness, and were, for the most part, needless and unknown in that first state of Nature."[90]

We can see through these examples how the narrative of commerce, in effect, competed against the master narrative so that in some ill-defined manner it began to assume all the tracings of a "new" cultural origin. This competition stretched in other directions as well, more certainly than what I have detailed thus far or can detail—the ancients-moderns debate, the four-stages theory of historical progress, the great feudal divide, and others—so that the conditions of suspense—resistance to predetermined meanings, superimposed teleologies, and simple identities—had rooted themselves deeply in the cultural contexts of history-making. By and throughout the eighteenth century the secular upswing in historiography was already in motion. That this commerce-accommodating history would seek new and more recent heroes and champions only made sense. Commentators, for instance, routinely lionized Elizabeth for preparing England to compete for the world's vast commercial wealth. Nearly two centuries removed from the Elizabethan Age, Thomas Mortimer (*The Elements of Commerce, Politics and Finances* [1772]) could still observe that "the rise and progress of the domestic trade and foreign commerce . . . continued in much the same situation, with little improvement, from the time of William the Conqueror to the accession of ELIZABETH," because he was trading in one of common myths of modern history.[91] Among the greater lights of the period, Bolingbroke repeated the same point, and George Lillo (*The London Merchant* [1731]) depended entirely upon the applied historical significance of Elizabeth's role vis-à-vis national trade to set his play in motion.[92] The history that mattered increasingly was of a recent vintage and defined according to the needs/wants model of culture.

Not everyone accepted Elizabeth as the standard of a new age. Others promoted William and the Glorious Revolution as the more recent and relevant benchmarks. In claiming "the Constitution new modelled" with the Revolution and "the Sting of Prerogative . . . taken away," the anonymous author of *The Ancient and Modern Constitution of Government* (1734) not only ridicules the Ancient Constitution as "arbitrary" but also accuses Elizabeth of the same, who "governed in a most arbitrary Way." Even so, she employed her power "for the Safety, Honour and Welfare of the Nation, so that they became insensible of the Servitude they were under."[93] By the end of the eighteenth century, no matter what one's political stripe, it had become much more difficult to argue in a convincing fashion that the past, whether real or imaginary, supplied models of "political perfection."[94]

Nor is it a coincidence that, fifty years after his reign, William and the revolutionary order for which he was made to stand were commonly associated with the material advancement of culture: "THAT the Trade and Commerce of the Kingdom has been increasing since the REVOLU-TION, can hardly be doubted"—and its effects positive: merchants now rival "the ancient *Nobility* and *Gentry* of the Kingdom"; and "others of inferior Rank" live more prosperously and decently. "[T]o construe all these into false Appearances, *as some do*, is to suppose a Confederacy among all Ranks of People . . . which is . . . an Absurdity so glaring as to merit no Answer."[95] Needless to say, those who proposed the confederacy had a quite different attitude about 1688, seeing it as a new order of decay and civil degeneration. If Elizabeth was the titular, mythic leader of the new history, William was its *de facto* champion.[96]

Those who stood for an original and pure polity, such as Charles Davenant, did not do so without also being tested and assailed. William Wood disputed the corruption/decay thesis in general and Davenant in particular. As an opponent of civic republicanism, Wood writes: "I know there are a Number of Gentlemen, who Right or Wrong, will be against me for speaking in Behalf the *Trading* Interest. I must desire those Gentlemen who are so much in Love with the Husbandry and Agriculture of their Ancestors, to consider the different Figure we make now to what we did then, and the Change of Affairs and Manners of *Europe* since that Time; our Acquisition of new Riches, Strength and Power, and the additional Value and Worth derived to our natural Product and Possessions by *that Trade*, of whose Increase and Incouragement they are so jealous."[97] In the process he contends that fears of luxury, indulgence, and effeminacy are counteracted by the wars that naturally occur in the arenas of international commercial competition. Even more important, he maintains that the only measure of determining the "decay" of a nation is not by comparing it to older models of history but by tax revenue, scarce money, high interest, cheap land, cheap labor, and a fall in rents (60).

The difference between early and late commercial theory, in effect, is the difference between Lewes Roberts's invisible hand and Adam Smith's. In *The Treasure of Traffike* (1641), Roberts remarks of the "judicious Merchant" that his "labour is to proht himselfe, yet in all his actions doth therewith benefit his King, Countrey, and fellow Subjects."[98] The actions of the merchant become embodied in definable beings and objects; thus, there is no need to name an economic principle. Smith, on the other hand, names and identifies the invisible hand as the agent of an individual's self-interested pursuits: "by directing [his] industry in such a manner as its produce may be of the greatest value, he intends only his own gain, and he is in this, as in many other cases, led by an invisible hand to promote an end which was no part of his intention," one that advances the "public good."[99] Here the invisible hand dissolves into an abstract concept and the world of its operations exceeds the individual self only by default.

This same pattern is repeated in matters of providential commerce—the belief that God ordained the climatic and geographical composition of the world to encourage commercial transaction. Thus, the writer of *A Discourse Consisting of Motives for the Enlargement and Freedome of Trade* (1645) notes that "The Terrestrial Globe is cut out into *Islands* and *Continents*, both [of] which are created to be a Mansion for men; . . . And though the Earth and Sea be of themselves, as differing Elements as any of the rest, yet Divine Providence by a speciall foresight hath so indented as it were, and embosned them one in the other, that they make but one perfect Globe, to render them thereby more apt for the mutuall Commerce and Negotiation of Mankinde."[100] This type of language falls into disuse essentially by the first quarter of the eighteenth century, though many of the most important commercial theorists did not forget the lesson; it is just that they could not duplicate the specific language. Josiah Tucker refers to it in his *The Elements of Commerce and the Theory of Taxes* (1755), though only in passing; and in the introductory matter to *The Elements of Commerce, Politics and Finances* (1772), Thomas Mortimer stops in the middle of things to insert a providential reminder.[101] Although George Whately recalls the model of providential commerce in his *Principles of Trade* (1774)—"the all-wise Creator has ordain'd that *a mutual Dependence* shal run thro' al his Works"—in his next paragraph he has already shifted that responsibility: "by this Investigation we shal find, that our Wants, whether real or ideal; our Passions and our Habits; are the Springs of al our Actions."[102]

We need to be cautious about advocating a one-sided view of the economy, however. Both Joyce Oldham Appleby and William Letwin are too quick to rid economic theory of moral concerns.[103] There can be no doubt that during the seventeenth century theorists were already trying out the possibility of an autonomous economy, but moral watchfulness did not disappear by fiat. Civic republicans during the eighteenth century, for instance, kept a close eye on commercial proceedings, as did many others. But, no matter what form this watchfulness took, it was the act itself that was important. On one level it meant that attempts were made to control and govern the uncertainty and suspense that were figured through the narrative of commerce. And while I have suggested that this metanarrative form of cultural storytelling was antagonistic to authority, it too was a form of governance that fashioned social coherence through disparate parts, divisions, and contradictions that had come to characterize the modern age. One of those parts was the realistic novel, which owed its originality to the narrative of commerce.

3

The "Suspended" Character

Because the capitalist engine could not run without gener-ating heat and friction, the interests of parties, groups, and individuals ensured that the gears and wheels of productivity kept turning and that the capitalist engine itself did not stall. Parts not only rubbed against parts but also increased in number as the economy developed into a more complex machine. With the advent of industrialization, toward the close of the eighteenth century, the dynamic tensions of capitalism were already abundantly clear both in deed and word. The outpouring of labor-focused publications, for instance, along with the emergence of clubs, associations, corresponding societies, and unions, introduced a new factor into the economy, the radical incorporation of labor, which, though resisted, marked a determined leap forward in the otherwise un-enviable history of the British laborer.[1] While the meaning of this devel-opment is subject to dispute, the act itself signaled that the economy could grow in proportion with its contributing parts. This fact was spelled out at the time by an anonymous writer who employed current fictions about China and its economy to reinforce the dynamism of En-glish capitalism: "in governments, where the expences of the state are stationary, as in China, and neither increase nor diminish, the state may continue to exist with a stationary degree of industry; but, in such a progressive increase of expence as that in England, expence of individu-als must be increased, and it becomes the object of the legislature to do it, by every means. While men do not encroach on the accumulated cap-ital that supports trade, the more they expend the better."[2] Although the representation of this economic system is full of bends and turns, we do not fail to notice that the interests of consumers, the pursuit of goods, and the necessity of spending play a key role in fueling expan-sion and change.

But as we talk about the size and scale of the economy, we can, once that economy grows large, become entirely swept away by its propor-tions and other impersonal mechanisms or even begin to assume that every manifestation of economy is political economy. These lures are difficult to resist. As I indicated in chapter 2, the dominant theme of the narrative of commerce is both broad and vague—social cohesion, the invisible glue that held disparate, contradictory, and competing elements together, including political partisans who disputed progress with "origins." As I also indicated, this modal abstraction of cohesion was already in place early in the seventeenth century because, from the start, economic theory organized itself around representations of "nation" as its principal character and tended, therefore, to discourage or exclude other characters and points of view. In this respect, the "natural progress" of period commercial theory moves, as it were, from anthropology to economy, from needs and wants to the narrative of commerce, from the simple to the complex, from the literal to the figurative. Reversing this progress is much more difficult. But the fact is that just as needs and wants were mirrored in the commercial narrative, the cultural and intellectual impact of the latter was mirrored in the former. The consequence was that the foundational premises of character began to erode and crumble, and it is from these bits and fragments of upheaval that the representational structure of the realistic novel managed to produce the inner distinctiveness that differentiated it from earlier forms of novel writing.

The common ground between needs and wants and the commercial narrative was suspense. As a by-product of this narrative, suspense, perhaps appropriately, meant many things—from historical discontinuity to a sometimes fractious coherence—but, in its functional capacity, operated by dismantling and then restructuring the known around the uncertainties of interpretive exchange and negotiation. This same process replicated itself in needs and wants. With the collapse of the subject into the object and the object into the subject clear categorical distinctions no longer obtained so that what was known or could be known was subject to dispute—held in suspense, in other words. Although Francis Hutcheson did not use the word "suspense" to name this epiphenomenon in his *An Essay on the Nature and Conduct of the Passions and Affections* (1728), he was certainly aware of its effects: "the *Laws* or *Customs* of a Country, the *Humour* of our Company may have made strange *Associations* of *Ideas*, so that some Objects, which of themselves are indifferent to any Sense, yet by reason of some *additional* grateful *Idea*, may become very desireable." By way of illustration he inventories a melange of consumption "items" that, curiously, cloud the distinctions between physical objects and psychic import: "Thus *Dress, Retinue, Equipage, Furniture, Behaviour*, and *Diversions* are made Matters of considerable Importance by additional *Ideas*."[3]

It was this muddied distinction and all that it signified in a material culture that factored into operations of suspense. The temptation of course is to read dress, retinue, equipage, and furniture as the material "excesses" that determine the "disfigurement" of character, but, as I would contend, these are visible symptoms of a much broader historical shift that led not to the disfigurement of character but to its "dis-figuration."[4] Through dis-figuration, character becomes a limitless repository of semantics and interpretation rather than a prescribed identity or equivalence. The latter conforms to character types, which, as Paul Korshin has demonstrated, participate in a system of representation that depends upon historical repetition and prediction, as well as duplicable and received identities.[5] Even though Deirdre Lynch relies upon "disfigurement" in her provocative examination of character, she concludes by noting that "by mid-century, by the time its 'realness' had come to depend upon its indeciperability, 'character' had begun to signify its own opposite."[6] That is to say, character in the old sense of the term as an imposed identity ceased to be tenable. Robinson Crusoe, Joseph Andrews, Clarissa, David Simple, Arabella—The Female Quixote, as well as Sir Charles Grandison govern their identities by recurring to types, but it is clear to their readers that these forms of self-representation are only partial portraits because something remains unknown, unrecognized, and, hence, suspended through these acts of narrative self-disclosure. In truth, these old attachments could no longer serve: characters who resisted complicated systems of representation were swallowed up by them.

As Bakhtin has observed: "[t]he novel took shape precisely at the point when . . . the object of artistic representation was being degraded to the level of contemporary reality that was inconclusive and fluid."[7] Although Bakhtin's idea of the novel is expansive, this comment in particular, other than for the word "degraded," is pertinent to the novel central to this study, not for what it resolves, but for what it leaves up in the air. "The object of artistic representation" in the realistic novel, for instance, is the subject—a character—and "reality" is a fiction, a method of narration. In light of the topics discussed in chapter 2, these paradoxes should surprise no one. Yet for readers to imagine that some causal explanation exists or that some point of origin can be identified that will *directly* tie the realistic novel to a culture of needs and wants mistakes what is possible under the narrative of commerce. Instead, we know the impact of needs and wants through effects that are recoverable *from* the narratives themselves. Our inability to detail precisely how this connection came about, yet did, tells us in no uncertain terms of the necessity for parts and divisions, heat and friction, in a capitalist economy. That these parts had a striking resemblance to one another, moreover, is an even stronger indication of the uncanny coherence that bound the material culture together under the narrative of commerce.

But the novel was not the only genre affected by commerce and con-sumerism. Journalism, for instance, with its emphasis on novelty and contemporaneity, seems in many ways to owe an even greater debt.[8] By virtue of its subject matter, journalism is also a discursive genre: the news of the day or week does not purport to tell a coherent story but a series of stories drawn from the facets of daily life. While the realistic novel also stresses novelty and contemporaneity, its discursiveness is of a different kind, a much more amplified and expanded version of the sort that journalism trades in, because its parts and points of view are funneled through a central character who orders narrative action and imparts some coherent sense to it. Without the binding powers of this character, the novel might as well be journalism, even a year's worth of it, or some other form of writing. What is obvious is that among the genres only the novel could branch out and expand at the will of the writer to adapt to the proportionately larger and more complex repre-sentational requirements that needs and wants stimulated.

Discursiveness and the Economy of Narrative Realism

My insistence that the suspended character lies at the heart of the realistic novel—or even defines it—requires further explanation. I want to proceed initially by reexamining three key aspects of the debate sur-rounding the period novel in order to color in some of the features of the suspended character: romance versus novel, narrative discursive-ness, and origins. The last of these, while attractive in theory and endur-ing in fact, places students of the novel in an uncomfortable spot. Something must be done with those "unoriginal" novels that precede the first real novel(s), and typically what happens is that they are as-signed a discrete classification or a disparate nomenclature. Why gener-ically equivalent narratives must undergo such subordination is baffling, particularly in that the act of subordinating not only creates classes, ranks, and hierarchies but also fuels strife where such things seem not to exist in the first place. If, on the other hand, the realistic novel fills in one sector among many others along the productive net-work of its material culture, then questions about its generic uniqueness lose some of their intrigue. Whatever is distinctive about this novel, under the circumstances, falls in line with other like products, especially the female-authored novel that came before. The operative term in this relationship ought not to be hegemony but difference.[9] Writers who in-troduced realism to the genre attempted to improve the novel, to give it a moral role to play; or, in market terms, to expand its stock in ways that would appeal to an audience previously unreached or unmoved.

As critics have recognized, the principal feature of the realistic novel is its discursiveness. In general, the ways in which a novelist applies discursiveness distinguishes the long novel from the short—or the novel from the romance—as Ian Watt implies when he comments that "the function of language is much more largely referential in the novel than in other literary forms; . . . the genre itself works by exhaustive presentation rather than by elegant concentration"—a point of view shared more recently by J. Paul Hunter.[10] John Richetti's *Popular Fictions Before Richardson* (1969) also alludes to this narrative trait, when, in his appraisal of Manley and Haywood, he laments that in "works such as the *New Atalantis* or Mrs. Haywood's *Memoirs of a Certain Island* . . . [t]here is in them no attempt to render that sense of a conditioning milieu, that biographical density and verisimilitude which make characterization possible and relevant."[11] Together, Watt, Hunter, and Richetti draw attention to those features of the novel that, in retrospect, we now take for granted.

By any standard, however, Aphra Behn's *Love Letters Between a Nobleman and His Sister* (1684–87) is a long novel, though not nearly so discursive as it is repetitious. A similar pattern holds for Eliza Haywood's first novel *Love in Excess* (1719–20), a longish effort that not only duplicates the method of *Love Letters* but also borrows from its language. In Behn's novel Sylvia writes to Philander, "my love is now arrived to that excess," which could just as easily serve as the epigraph for the whole of this epistolary novel.[12] No one, however, points an accusatory finger at Richardson for the length of *Clarissa* (1747–48) or censors him for loving words too much. Admittedly, in their designs, *Love Letters* and *Clarissa* are different enough, but the point is this: if we judge the "novel" by what it becomes, then there seems no doubt, at least to me, that women novelists forecast later developments of the genre. If we take another example, Manley's *The Secret History of Queen Zarah and the Zarazians* (1705), it too is a long novel, even an experimental novel, but there is an appreciable difference in the way she manages length as opposed to, say, Fielding in *Amelia* (1751), a novel that also engages the subject of clandestine sexual affairs. Manley's problem is that she seems incapable of drawing the discursiveness of her story together. Thus, rather than resolve the tensions of her characters, she simply stops with an unsatisfactory gallery of painted types.

Manley also follows a similar pattern in her theory of the novel genre, which she articulates in the preface to *Zarah*. There she lays out the modern requirements for novels by distinguishing her work from French romances and "*Historical Novels*," yet never seems entirely settled about the proper role of discursiveness.[13] Throughout the whole of this piece, she darts from one point to the next, one label to the other.

Among her concerns are the unities of time and character, as well as unbiased narration. In the process she dismisses ancient heroes for lacking "reality" and for having *"nothing in them that is Natural"* (A6r); whereas she endorses *"Heroes of the Modern Romances [as] better Characteriz'd, [their authors] give them Passions, Vertues or Vices, which resemble Humanity. Thus all the World will find themselves represented in these Descriptions"* (A1v). She is also mindful of readers' requirements, but without pandering to or overly taxing them as the French romancers and writers of historical novels are inclined to do.

In the end, she intends *"to instruct and inspire into Men the Love of Virtue, and Abhorrence of Vice,"* which is *"the chief End of History"* (A6r)—so does Defoe some years later. But as we try to fix her role or find the one label that she applies, it shifts from passage to passage: she is at once a writer of *"Little Histories"* (A2r), a modern romancer, a writer of either true or false history, an *"Acute Historian"* (A5v), or finally just an unadorned historian—perhaps, even, none of the above because there is no settled identity to account for the role Manley assumes. It is evident that she is unable to find a happy medium between fact and fiction and winds up torn between both. Yet, in terms of conception, little separates *Zarah* from *Pamela*. Although Manley would probably contemn the comparison, she would also have to eat her words in light of the following reflections: *"the Authors of* Romances *gave Extraordinary Virtues to their Heroins, exempted from all the Weakness of Humane Nature, and much above the Infirmities of their Sex . . . It wou'd in no wise be probable that a Young Woman fondly beloved by a Man of great Merit, and for whom she had Reciprocal Tenderness, finding her self at all Times alone with him in Places which favour'd their Loves, cou'd always resist his Addresses"* (A5v-r).

In other words, the categorical distinctions we use, novel and romance, can be made to blur virtually on command, whether we look at romance from the point of view of the novel or reverse the perspective. *The Mercenary Lover* (1726), a novel attributed to Haywood, offers an example of narrative more likely to earn the label of romance in institutional circles because of its brevity. Yet, like Manley, this author is also torn by a commitment to facts in the play of fiction. In the preface she ridicules those *"many Stories"* purporting to tell *"real Facts"* that, in truth, are products of overheated imaginations. Her story, she assures us, is true: it *"happen'd in the Neighbourhood of a celebrated Church, in the Sound of whose Bells the Inhabitants of that populous City think it an Honour to be born."*[14] The mercenary lover himself, a "literary" personage named Clitander, lives in the city "tho' [was] of no higher Rank than a Trader" (10); his real gift initially is that of a Lothario, who woos and marries for mercenary reasons one stick figure of a sister, the ever gay Miranda, the exact opposite of Althea, the dour sibling. From this unpromising start, *Mercenary Lover* takes quick and unexpected turns that reverse the roles of the sisters, introduce and play out the theme of adultery, exploit the psychology of guilt and retribution, and delve into the intricacies of contracts and other legal devices. In many ways, this narrative proves to be discursively rich, in the "novelistic" sense of that term, despite its length of only sixty-two pages. If generic labeling is in order, *Mercenary Lover* is perhaps best classified as neither romance nor realistic fiction, as it is pulled in both those directions simultaneously. But, as far as the about-face in characterization is concerned, it passes without mention. A quarter of a century later, the year after the publication of *The History of Miss Betsy Thoughtless* (1751), a novel we know Haywood wrote, Charlotte Lennox published one of the most intriguing novels of the century, *The Female Quixote* (1752). In it she manages to tease out in the most explicit terms possible the sometimes arbitrary distinctions drawn between romance and novel, as the Female Quixote, Arabella, lives her life lost in the pages of French romances of the previous century and finds it utterly impossible to distinguish between fact and fiction as cognitive categories.

Generic distinctions, as these examples suggest, better serve us than they do the narratives to which they are applied. In truth, however, the so-called "romance-novel" tends to be short more often than it is long. In market terms, these less capacious novels recall the stationary and uncomplicated "Chinese" economy I referred to at the beginning of this chapter, in which presumably the exotic prevails and the body dominates as the focus of intercourse and exchange. Desire, in this sense, appears in its unsublimated forms in contexts that often do not move beyond the pale of court circles. The evidence suggests that, at least at this earlier stage in the history of the period novel, women appeared uncomfortable with discursiveness. Thus while Manley praises modern romances for their exploration of the *"Passions, Vertues or Vices"* detailed in character that *"resemble[s] Humanity,"* she goes on to criticize historical novels because they are, in effect, expansive texts, overloaded with characters: *"a vast Number of Actors who have such different Interests, embarrasses [the reader's] Memory, and causes some Confusion in [the reader's] Brain, because 'tis necessary for the Imagination to labour to recal the several Interests and Characters of the Persons spoken of, and by which they have interrupted the* History."[15] Similarly, *Love in Excess* appears to be discursive, yet closer inspection reveals that length results from the forced juxtaposition of its three parts, each of which could stand by itself as a novel with only slight modifications. The discursiveness of Haywood's novel thus collapses into its known and familiar pattern.

This want of an integrated and coherent discursiveness yields characters that must remain only potentially interesting, due in part to the essentially fixed and one-dimensional desires or interests they embody. In short, these characters lack suspense, with all the semantic properties that term implies under commercial capitalism. The implied differences between romance and realistic novels, however, do not disguise some even more insidious form of schematization on my part; nor do I intend even the faintest whisper about writerly merit. The only criterion I employ for evaluating difference is the marketplace and its impact upon narrative practice. In this vein, neither Defoe, Richardson, nor Fielding wrote the original novel because the market in which they operated precluded that possibility. But they did "improve" a capital stock by repackaging it as a moral instrument and, to that end, were bold enough to risk the reader's embarrassment by engaging the discursive possibilities of the genre. What resulted were the first formulations of the modern character. For this work to proceed, more was necessary than just the promise of character and realism—after all, women writers had already earmarked those narrative needs and wants implicitly as well as explicitly. Defoe, always ready to steal an opportunity or borrow an idea, was the first to exploit such market demands.

But why "he" and not "she"? The answer is not easy, though surely it has something to do with access to the marketplace. As Ros Ballaster has stated, "feminist critics . . . cannot be accused of failing to take note that women writers were differently situated in relation to epistemological and ethical questions by virtue of their sex."[16] It would follow that their divorce from active roles in the economy at large also had a major impact on what they were able to express. Even though the vast majority of any population has no hand in shaping either truth or virtue, we can be certain that injustice, inequality, and discrimination arise when access to institutions and marketplaces is restricted. But within the constraints of the novel trade alone, there is no evidence to indicate that women novelists of the seventeenth and early eighteenth centuries suffered. Their contributions are a matter of record. Even Richardson's Pamela dipped liberally into this genre—and if she did, he did. Whatever grievances spill over cannot be blamed on the trade itself.

The "fathers of the novel," as either a market or a biological entity, could not assume that role without the "mothers of the novel." Defoe, Richardson, and Fielding did not give birth to the novel, nor did they define it; but they did coax and train it, by investing in its structure and organization in order to address the generic wants that had already been called for.[17] Under their management, the appearance, functionality, and economy of the novel changed. Most of all character grew large and complex. Although Haywood's "return" to the novel with *Betsy Thoughtless* makes her effort look like a Fielding novel, not a Haywood novel, this tie is one determined by the market, not by some unwelcome form of discrimination.[18] At the same time, the novel market was complicated, not nearly as illiberal and oppressive as some make it out to be. Sarah Fielding, sister of Henry, attests to this fact. She wrote long novels and short. Her best known, *The Adventures of David Simple* (1744; 1753), has many of her brother's touches, but her most successful effort was *The Governess* (1749), a slim novel directed mainly at young readers, that is replete with romance and fairy elements, while *The Countess of Dellwyn* (1759) borrows from seduction novels from earlier in the century. When Francis Coventry's *The History of Pompey the Little* appeared in 1751, the same year as *Betsy Thoughtless*, he did not so much mimic Fielding as he acknowledged a borrower's debt to him. In his dedication he writes: "I desire to be understood in general, or more particularly with an eye to your works, which I take to be master-pieces and complete models of their kind."[19]

That Frances Burney, Frances Sheridan, Charlotte Smith, Ann Radcliffe, and a host of other writers continued to write after the "interregnum" of Defoe, Richardson, and Fielding underscores how the market continued to reward novels of a type, adaptation, or a combination of both. But in writing their novels these women did not have to forsake amatory themes or the intrigues of romance in order to see their words into print. They did, however, choose to amplify the scope—the discursive economy—of their novels and characters for the sake of meeting the needs and wants of the market. Or perhaps better, they were determined to compete for a market share; for, among other things, they could have continued to write "romances," the more compact and stripped-down version of the "novel," since this genre continued to be written and published.

For as long as we commit ourselves to a rigid definition of the novel, however, we will inevitably think of its history as arced or teleological: it can never be what it is supposed to be until it assumes its one proper shape and form. That is the consequence of dialectical prehistory. Thus the search goes on endlessly for those ingredients of culture that when blended and mixed yield the NOVEL, as if the genre itself could be defined once and for all. Genres and forms, accordingly, become studies of imperfect trajectories that in the fullness of time or the dialectics of history are supposed to get righted.

The history of the eighteenth-century novel makes clear that once the market exerts its influence a competition over form and content ensues. But after the first episode of a discursively complex realism was over, the novel did not settle into a stationary economy. It continued to change. The impact of Defoe and his followers, however, echoed on, particularly in terms of character representation, because this corps addressed large-scale issues of a needs/wants economy that were not about to go away. Although Defoe, Richardson, Fielding, and Sterne have withstood the caprices of systematizers, moralists, and academics, their endurance should not mean that they speak a truth eternal or, under baser motives, conspired to monopolize a discourse. Their importance lies in what they added to the genre in its own time and place, especially the semantically complex "suspended" character, which, because of its persistent centrality to narrative realism, tells us just how much the narrative of commerce still filters into quotidian life.

The Body of Suspense and Its Interests

Narrative/moral realism gave vent to the suspended character because of the way it tailored the body to suit the demands of the commercial narrative. Although implicit in period commercial theory, the physical body could only really haunt the economic corpus. Part real, part insubstantial creation, the body, acknowledged only through its needs and wants, signified sublimation. The provisions that regulated its conduct fell to the office of character, which in its external dealings assumed the shape of *homo economicus*, what might be called the organized ego of the suspended character. But with this code of governance imposed upon it, the body could not play Lear on the heath; it had to be dressed to undertake the business of exchange, which, in defining the ethos of material culture, submitted the body to new forms of discipline. The extreme case is George Barnwell, the merchant-apprentice in Lillo's *The London Merchant* (1731), who, after one night of sexual liberty, sees himself as a debased Satan.[20] The same principle applied to the romance or amatory novel tells us that its exchanges were subsequently devalued for indulging the body alone, which is to say, too much *homo* or *femina* and not enough *economicus/a*.

The same kind of limitation applies to the theory of "excess" in the "disfigurement" of the character type in that only visible, external objects and bodies can be disfigured—it would be incorrect, for instance, to talk about a disfigured soul. Nor can we place too much faith in the otherwise interesting and important analogy that translated the excesses of the body politic to the body natural—for two reasons: the first is that the analogy was not restricted to any single interval of time after the Restoration; and the second is that, as an image, the analogy only served the body politic, a body that existed and exists in metaphor alone.[21] For the transformation of character to occur, especially from a fixed identity to something more plastic, it could only *appear* to "exceed" its corporeal constraints for the simple reason that it could never do so in fact. These changes had to be imperceptible—invisible—and thus required psychic adjustment. The same paradigm also affected consumers, the purveyors of character, who, in needing and wanting goods, aligned themselves directly to the body and to desires that could not stand unmediated. In both cases, desire had to be rewritten and rendered more abstract, even though the body would remain what it always was, other than for the goods that adorned it. As I want to propose, "interest" embodied this sublimated form of cultural desire, which had the effect of suspending the body from the things it desired.

From the outset of its usage, beginning around the Restoration, interest seems almost to have written its own genesis as an economic and political term. It had done so, in part, by obscuring its connection to usury. Only in sixteenth-century England did the long tradition proscribing this practice begin to abate, when Henry and Elizabeth saw fit to establish legal rate ceilings on borrowed money. Appleby has read this substitution of interest for usury, during the middle of the seventeenth century, as the "moral economy in retreat," noting that the issue of interest-bearing loans turned on pragmatic, not moral concerns: namely, whether the practice itself would inhibit economic development.[22]

Even though virtually every major statement of economic theory after the Restoration dealt either explicitly or implicitly with interest, especially the interests of the nation, this concept played a complex role in the commercial polity. Yet in advancing national economic goals, interest also promoted consumer designs, despite the fact that most mercantilist theory either voiced its suspicions or registered its condemnation of consumption practices through a variety of ways. Marchamont Nedham first introduced "interest" to the English political vocabulary via his *Interest Will Not Lie* (1659). As a number of his published works suggest, Nedham was himself something of a political chameleon, which may account for his interest in "interest." At any rate, there is something curious in his analysis of the subject. "One sense [of interest]," he notes, "may be this; That if you can apprehend wherein a man's Interest to any particular Game on foot doth consist, you may surely know, if the man be prudent, whereabout to have him . . . and so his Interest . . . *will not lie* to you, it will not deceive you in your judgment concerning the man's Intent and Proceedings." This is pure Machiavellian theater. "The other sense of that Maxim," he continues "is, that if a man state his own Interest aright, keep close to it, [which is to say, remain prudent,] *it will not lie to him* or deceive him, in the prosecution of his Aims and ends of Good unto himself, nor suffer him to be misled or drawn aside by specious pretences . . . of other men."[23] This second form borders on solipsism and implies that strength of interest is enough to thwart political opportunists skilled in the craft of knowing the enemy.

In his reading of Nedham, J. A. W. Gunn has noticed a curious breach that subsequently developed in the early history of interest between political caution and commercial enthusiasm: "[w]hatever reservations lingered in political literature, commentators on economic life were certain that most people would see their interests."[24] He goes on to enlarge the scope of interest, making it in effect the catalyst of suspense: it "destroyed the predictable nature of social relations, hence challenging an order infused with transcendental meaning. Eventually, though, interest came to be recognized not merely as something disruptive of social peace but as a force necessarily considered for the orderly fulfillment of expectations."[25] James Steuart makes exactly this point in 1767, "were a people to become quite disinterested, there would be no possibility of governing them."[26] Within a century interest the destroyer had become interest the bringer of domestic peace.

If we use Nedham as our standard, interest enacted a duality from its outset, between the public and the private, the outward and the inward. Although Roger Coke welcomed the freedom that commerce had inspired, including the waning of "the wild Tyranny of furious Pedagogues" that the advent of international trade and the promise of *doux commerce* had brought, the same kind of duality colors his representation of trade in his *A Discourse of Trade* (1670).[27] Before branching out into an analytical investigation of trade in the main body of his work, he turns to personification in his preface to dress up its form: "*Trade is now become the Lady, which in this present Age is more Courted and Celebrated than in any former by all Princes and Potentates of the World.*"[28] After all, it is in the interest of nations to do so; yet, in England, he writes, "*we undo our selves by banishing this Lady we so desire and contend for*" (B2r). The solution to the problem of "*this Ladies strangeness to us of late*" is simple, for it entails consumers to encourage her with wide-open purses: "*Trade if it be well managed no where thrives better than where men spend above the ordinary means of living*" (B3v). We note, however, that only princes and potentates do the "courting" and, by extension, only the nation-as-cad, embodied by rulers and monarchs, would treat her ill. The mere mention of "men" summons forth a different kind of language; men show their support of trade by "managing" their pocketbooks in a freer manner. They do not court or woo because either of these would more directly intimate desire. Even though Coke was an avowed free trader and ardent supporter of English trading interests, his language betrays the decorum, good face, and stiff lip that the liberal consumer—a body signified as a pocketbook—must evince in commonplace transactions.

Other writers, those less receptive to a consuming culture, found new ways to censor spending habits, but the old ways also worked just as well. By the 1690s the floodgates of commentary had broken open as consumerism, consumption, and money-dealing had become conspicuous enough to warrant repeated notice. For those worried about these practices, virtually any purchase, so it seems, was enough to inspire fulminations or to be denounced as a vitiated taste for luxuries. These complaints did not discriminate along political lines, nor could they easily disguise the interested motives of their authors in an age already inclined that way. In a short pamphlet, written anonymously and entitled *An Essay, or, Modest Proposal* (1693), an obvious partisan of land and woolen manufactures lashed out at "the meaner sort of People" who adorn the body by wearing "extravagant and expensive Apparel," among them the children and spouses of farmers or tradesmen.[29] About these tradesmen, we learn that they "must for Quietness or Pride, habit their Wives and Daughters as if they had *500 l.* a year inheritance: Yeas, when they dare appear in their Shops; and it is become a very great charge upon the inferior Gentry, to appear now like such, considering how Servants and other mean People are set out" (2). He goes on to alert readers about how among the fashionable the straw-hat has replaced the woolen chapeau as the preferred headdress, but we recall that, a half-century later, when Richardson's Pamela thinks she is about to return to her parents, she examines her appearance in a mirror with a straw-hat atop her head.

Even the free-trader John Briscoe worried about consumption practices. In *A Discourse of Money* (1696), he recognizes the groundswell for material betterment: "The love of Riches and desire of Gain thus growing upon us, becomes a greater incitement to ingage in all sorts of Difficulties, to despise Perils and decline no means whatever that are likely to conduct us to our profit."[30] Still, he cautions about the drawbacks of this movement: "the farther Men wander by Ambition, Violence, Luxury, Avarice, Sloth, and the like Irregularities, from the Innocence and Simplicity of the Original, the harder it is to conceive and propound Remedies for the Evils such Errors produce" (60). In the end, it is interest, not moral codes, that he trusts, because "in Interest we know there is no hypocrisy" (136) — in short, it does not lie. But for moralists who had no recourse to or tolerance for the ambivalence of interest, all consumption became indictable as "luxury" — too much attention to the body, not enough to the soul; or, for the author of *Modest Proposal*, too little regard for God's providential bounty to England, its wool, and too much regard for the modes that threatened the woolens market.

The conflict that interest provoked, however, had nothing to do with "the moral economy in retreat." What interest demanded was not the negation of morality or its slipping out the back door, but a morality that originated in interest. Even guardians of traditional morality, those whose ethical orientation did not reach much beyond the Seven Deadly Sins, were implicated by interest, as is apparent from the author of *Modest Proposal* or the legions of others who excoriated luxury. If, as I have suggested, the sublimation of the body was a nearly spontaneous development of *homo economicus* and the suspended character, then all of the pieces for this reconceptualization were in place during the seventeenth century. What was missing from the equation was the philosophical hard work of figuring out how morality and interest could be integrated. That took time but is evident in the moral-philosophical tradition which includes writers such as David Hume and Adam Smith.

The foundation of this tradition began as early as 1690 with the publication of David Abercromby's *A Moral Discourse of the Power of Interest*, which is a tortured reflection on the dilemmas and suspense that an interest-generated morality had provoked. Surely it is no coincidence that he wrote this work when consumer demand was first being isolated as a cultural problem. In his study he wrestles with how "the Almighty Power of temporal interest so absolutely rule[s] over mens minds," at the same time the soul owes its "very Life" to interest."[31] At one moment he pities the trader whose plight it is to live according to interest, only to condemn him for doing so. Yet, for Abercromby, it is the universality of interest that moves the soul and binds common enterprise. That same interest also compels him to express faith in terms of doubt and to reject the fictions of selfhood wrought from the acquisition of "Great Riches" (155). So entwined does he become in his investigations of the interested self that he is left to doubt even avowed demonstrations of faith: "as we are not sensible of our own strength so long as we live in Plenty, 'tis easie for a man in the actual possession of Two or Three Thousand Pounds of Yearly Revenue, to pronounce such grave Christian Sentences" (117). He concludes with a note approaching despair. "So unsatisfied we still are with the plentifullest Enjoyments of this World. Since then, in all our Attempts, we pursue always our own Interest, notwithstanding our pretences sometimes to the contrary, we shall be reckon'd to act like Politicians, if we mind what particular advantage every man aims at, that so knowing what he may be gain'd by, we may take our measures accordingly, for our own ends" (158).

Even though interest theory may have taken only fitful steps in the early stages of its history, its practical side, demand theory, was not nearly so cautious. This theory inverted the characteristic top-down approach to economic thought and began to emerge during the 1680s and 1690s. Advocates of consumer demand tended to be free traders, whom Appleby, toward the end of *Economic Ideology*, labels as presumptuous, self-indulgent, and naive for imagining that the "human race" shared the same entrepreneurial values that they had embraced. Their "egocentricity so long stigmatized as selfishness appeared to them in a new and acceptable guise as legitimate self-interest in a society run by the pervasive pursuit of profit."[32] But Appleby errs in her characterization and goes on to micromanage the fate of free trade and consumer demand by submitting both to what must be construed as the pervasive caution of politicians. Free trade and the new gospel of economic freedom, according to her, wither on the vine early in the eighteenth century when, through the script written by "bullionists" (supporters of intrinsic value), mercantilism exerts itself for the first time as a government-directed policy designed to organize the economy under "national power."[33] But the organization of national interest through economic power merely followed the logic of extant discourse and the development of an increasingly more complex institution-based economy. The "power" of the state could not exist apart from the "plenty" of the people; the key was to integrate the poles of interest into a system of coherent interest.[34]

Consumer demand/interest, in this context, was not some loose cannon apt to blast holes in the ship of state. When Nicholas Barbon wrote, in 1690, that "It is not Necessity that causeth the Consumption, Nature may be Satisfied with little; but it is the wants of the Mind, Fashion, and desire of Novelties, and Things scarce, that causeth Trade," he identified the kind of psychic adaptations consumers had to make in a material culture.[35] That is, he sublimated desire by rendering the needs and wants of the body invisible and psychological. And by insisting that "Prodigality is a Vice that is prejudicial to the Man, but not to *Trade*"; or that "Fashion or the alteration of Dress, is a great Promoter of *Trade*" (62, 65), he engaged the paradoxes of an interest-centered morality against morality as an imposed system. Neither position, however, compromised national interests or worked against or was inconsistent with the unfolding plot of the commercial narrative. In the following year Dudley North reinforced the same perspective, noting that "The main spur to Trade, or rather to Industry and Ingenuity, is the exorbitant Appetites of Men, which they will take pains to gratifie, and so be disposed to work, when nothing else will incline them to it, for did Men content themselves with bare Necessaries, we should have a poor world."[36] The character of the citizenry, annealed by access and reward, thus generated a heat sufficient to distort or even to melt in a few spots an otherwise rigid social order. "The meaner sort seeing their Fellows become rich, and great, are spurr'd up to imitate their Industry. A Tradesman sees his Neighbour keep a Coach, presently all his Endeavours is at work to do the like" (15).

We can also dispute Appleby's other point: that the interests of state in advancing its own "power" slammed shut the steel door on money. Granted, the historical "origins" of interest were inseparable from money, but that history became increasingly less singular and focused as the cultural semantics of interest branched out after the Restoration. Although interested parties debated how to determine the value of money at the end of the seventeenth century, the history of money itself did not grind to a halt during the recoinage crisis. Money was one interest among others that continued to cross-fertilize with each other. Thus when we consider the work of celebrated eighteenth-century monetary theorists, we see that their conceptualization of money forsook the kind of literal attachments that advocates of intrinsic value had promoted at the end of the previous century.[37] In effect, the character of specie changed so that the monarch it once stood for was devalued by the functional invisibility specie came to represent, a line of thinking that reaches back to the recoinage crisis itself. Jacob Vanderlint, one of the most important monetary theoreticians of the first half of the century, in fact disregards intrinsic value altogether in *Money Answers All Things* (1734). Instead, he posits money as a largely variable agent of the economy, conditioned by the laws of supply and demand to improve whatever ills the economy experienced. Under his terms, money no longer indemnifies regal authority, as it did for the bullionists; rather, its signifying properties spread throughout existing social grids so that if retrenchment were to become necessary its consequences would prove severe: people would have to do with shabby clothing, avoid marriage, and consume less; families themselves would deteriorate and the numbers of poor increase. To avoid these punitive circumstances, he recommends that "instead of urging the People to be less Consumers, Things should be made so plentiful, that they might be greater Consumers, that Business might increase, and not abate. . . . And then Luxury would find its natural and proper Bounds, when if any Man transgressed in any extraordinary Measure, he would be sufficiently whipt of his own Rod."[38] It is not difficult to see in this passage how, by suspending the moral absolutism of luxury, Vanderlint is already working toward the desired reconciliation of the two interests: self- and social.

Later in the century, Joseph Harris observes that the "comparative riches and strengths of nations" do not, as the populace believes, lie in money reservoirs; instead, fertile soil, the availability of products, industry, and skill, and, most important, a "well-administered government" define national wealth.[39] Under these terms, "the whole amount of [a nation's] cash or bullion, cannot make so considerable a part, as people are apt to imagine"; by way of illustration, he goes on to cite the gold-rich Incas of Peru, who would have improved their lot had they transformed their gold into iron (28). Not surprising, Harris also neutralizes the egregiousness of luxury as a moral category. Whatever residual disgrace one can attach to this word, Harris's judgment, like Vanderlint's, derives essentially from economic considerations: "the word *luxury* hath usually annexed to it, a kind of opprobrious idea; but so far as it encourages the arts, whets the inventions of men, and finds employments for more of our own people, its influence is benign, and beneficial to the whole society" (30). Only when it fails to perform these national services can it be said that "luxury . . . degenerates into evil" (30).

The sure measure of an interest-based morality, however, can be gathered from traditional moralists who resorted to shouting down material displays, probably out of frustration more than anything else. Through their eyes we see how *homo economicus* signaled the inadequacy of moral types as the means to fathoming character. In *Of Luxury* (1736), an otherwise revealing critique, J. Philemerus takes 1 Timothy 2.9 as his text. The bodies he implies throughout are not disfigured, merely adorned. Collectively they signify the confusion of ranks and, as far as he is concerned, ought to be legislated out of existence. The purpose of clothing, we learn, is threefold: to hide nakedness and cover shame; to protect and defend; and to mark distinction, this in an age in which "Extravagance . . . [has] descended to the lower Ranks of Men" in a historically unprecedented fashion.[40] He concedes, however, that "it is not *always* criminal, *to plait the Hair, to wear Gold*, or *Pearls, or costly Aray*. This our Saviour Himself seems to allow, [but only] to *Those who are in King's Houses*, to Persons of Quality and Distinction" (4). Erasmus Jones makes similar conjectures, though his lack the Gospel embellishments. His estimates indicate that only one family in ten keeps within its budget and that "the grand Controversy among all Ranks and Degrees, being only who shall *Out-Dress, Drink* or *Eat* his Neighbour."[41] Jones goes on to censure parades of consuming individuals, mostly those of the lesser ranks, for the moral depravity of their dress, furnishings, and even their upstart names: a proliferation of *"Anna Maria's, Charlotte's* and *Hariot's*, in the Family of almost every *Farrier* and *Shoemaker"* (11). Likewise, People where they are not known, are generally honour'd according to their Clothes . . . from the *Richness* of them we judge of their *Wealth*, and by their ordering them we guess at their Understanding" (12). Most significant of all is that these practices and conditions prevail "especially in large and populous Cities, where obscure Men may hourly meet with fifty Strangers to One Acquaintance" (12). What he objects to, in short, is that the characters who fill the streets and hover around the stalls resist classification.

Behind this state of unknowing and dis-figuration lies the workings of suspense. Through its undetectable channels it altered character in profound ways, ensuring that it could no longer be construed as the sum total of its surfaces or determined by its conformity to preexisting types. From the direct impact of interest upon it, this new "suspended" character began from a point of invisibility and moved outward, as it challenged a culture untrained in the art of deciphering the invisible at its core. Visible appearances and public faces, already altered by imperceptible interests, became all the more disorienting. Some writers could finger the source of their confusion, but, with historicisms or teleologies left unsummoned, they demonstrated moral helplessness in staring at what they feared. In an essay that recalls Swift's "A Description of a City Shower"(1710) or Gay's *Trivia* (1716), *London, What It Is, Not What It Was*, published anonymously during the 1720s, recoils at the public-health debacle of metropolitan life. Blight and stench accordingly become the physical manifestations of reckless and irresponsible self-aggrandizement. Civic participation in turn becomes defined by "how profitable [the] Administration has been" to those whose interests are at stake. "But however general Custom may hurry us away in the Stream of common Error," this author cries, "there is no Evil, no Crime, so great as that of being cold in Matters which relate to the common Good. Can then the most generous Motive of Life, the Good of others, be so easily banished from the Breast of Man? Is it possible," he utters plaintively, "to draw all our Passions inward?"[42] When subjects and objects dissolve into one, the answer is yes. But for David Hume, whose philosophy was predicated on this dissolution, this yes requires amplification: "There is no passion . . . capable of controlling the interested affection, but the very affection itself, by an alteration of its direction."[43] Which is to say that where material acquisition is at stake, desire itself must undergo deferral and sublimation; otherwise, as he alludes, Hobbes's state of nature would prevail.

Suspending the body from the things it desired, as we judge from Lorna Weatherill's research on consumer behavior, was central even to eighteenth-century domestic life. If we can assume that the period domicile, in its literal capacity, provided for the orderly fulfillment of interests, then its configuration of space becomes all the more noteworthy. Weatherill has observed that research indicates "one response to living near other people would have been a greater desire to look inwardly, to the living space and to make this as aesthetically pleasing and comforting as possible through the addition of furnishings and goods."[44] Within this refuge existed an even more important bridge to and partition from the world at large. Weatherill notes that period domiciles were divided into a "frontstage" and "backstage," so that callers entering a home would find themselves admitted to its "public" area—or "frontstage"—in which acquired ornaments, furnishings, and bric-a-brac greeted the outsider.[45] Yet, in the conduct of their private lives and within the interior of their own homes, urban dwellers retreated from these public areas, leaving behind the bridge that symbolically connected them to the outside.[46]

This configuration lends itself to many speculations and a range of analogies.[47] Perhaps the most important is that from it we can apprehend in architectural detail the blueprint of the interests and the work that they had managed to accomplish. As visitors to such a home, our admission would be restricted to the part set off for our reception, a place, given its familiar look, in which we would discover a common ground, the goods of the world. But behind the familiar lies another domain to which, for customary reasons or other like conventions, the visitor would not go—the invisible portion of the house. Only the occupants of the house would know about this part of their residence. Yet, if the energy of a commercial society is dedicated in its most literal way to acquisition, even this end serves as something from which the private individual retreats. The paradoxes of consumption and interest, it seems, are woven from an endless skein of contradiction.

Suspense, Character, and the Adam Smith Problem

Those paradoxes and contradictions persist even in places we do not necessarily expect to find them. Adam Smith, perhaps of all writers of the age, should uncomplicate the riddles and mysteries that lie at the heart of the period material culture and the character it produced. He does not. But his extensive reflections on topics central to this study— interests, progress and divisions, trade and commerce, and invisibility, among others—do coalesce as the most directly rendered period representation of the "suspended" character that we can find outside the novel. We do not get this representation whole—assembly is required— which seems fair enough in an age that first measured productivity in bits and jigged pieces. For Smith, we gather, the suspended character occasioned no celebration.

This much is certain: suspense did not lend itself to unanimity or consensus; it thrived instead in the divide—between what was known and unknowable, between representation and misrepresentation. Yet the long-standing debate about Adam Smith, *Das Adam Smith Problem*—the attempted reconciliation of the moralist of sentiment and benevolence in *The Theory of Moral Sentiments* (1759) with the jurisprudential student of selfish passions in *Wealth of Nations*—hinges on the belief that somehow his writings should yield a coherent *oeuvre* and that none of the pieces should be left over.[48] I want to propose instead that the debate is meaningful in its own right and that, in effect, the Smith who resists reconciliation is the Smith we ought to value. In this way his character embodies suspense for having divided its time between moral philosophy and political economy. Clearly the connection between sentiment/ benevolence and commercial gain did not have to wait for Smith; this strain of thought is apparent in writers as early as Addison, as well as a long train of successors, including figures such as Josiah Tucker. That this forced attachment had no lasting impact can easily be tested if we simply think of the associations that come to mind when we hear the word "capitalist"—the list would grow long before we got to benevolence. The point I want to stress is that Smith's divided interests of morality and economy were just that, not for some unacknowledged contradiction within the man himself but because of the circumstantial nature of period productivity.

J. G. A. Pocock writes that "the Scottish theorists were not far removed . . . from the hypothesis that men create themselves in history through their modes of production."[49] Indeed, one of the hallmarks of capitalism is that it invites people to re-create themselves, if for no other reason than the self-made individual evinces no great debts to the past or its potential entanglements. By the time he published *Wealth of Nations*, Smith had already been retired a dozen years from his public life as Professor of Moral Philosophy at Glasgow, and perhaps it is no coincidence that for Smith the first order of business he tackles in *Wealth* is the acme of human productivity, the division of labor, which, as we learn four hundred pages later, means that the undivided personality could no longer hold in a society that depended upon complex systems of delivery and teemed with divided interests and competing passions. In this regard, character underlies system in Smith's thought.

While it is perfectly reasonable to study Smith as the producer of moral and capital systems, we must also acknowledge that both were dramatic stages that he peopled with characters. As David Marshall has prompted, Smith's earlier work, *Theory of Moral Sentiments*, in particular "explores the role of sympathy in a world in which people face each other as spectators and spectacles."[50] Given the centrality of moral concerns in *Moral Sentiments* and the role of the spectator in it, Smith's 1759 study includes a larger cast of characters and one quite prominent one, the impartial spectator, who is made up of bits of God, Stoicism, an internal censor or projector, social conscience, and the demands of the status quo, to name only a few. This "man within" either changes character at whim or wears many masks. Either way the figure is at once ideal, imaginary, and invisible.[51]

No matter what its composition or guise, the impartial spectator was a character both slippery and essential to Smith's moral philosophy. In

Wealth of Nations, by contrast, spectating has a diminished role to play. The nearest cognate we have of it is the person of the speculator, identified in 1, 1, who appears under the chapter heading, "Of the Division of Labor." There Smith talks of "philosophers or men of speculation, whose trade it is not to do any thing, but to observe every thing; and who, upon that account, are often capable of combining together the powers of the most distant and dissimilar objects."[52] Unavoidably, this role is one that Smith assumes for himself. *Wealth of Nations* includes other characters as well, the merchants, farmers, laborers, and the poor among them, though they get lost in the productive grid that is spread over a commercial nation.

But whereas the character of the impartial spectator is an informing spectral presence throughout *Moral Sentiments*, this figure is more akin to a *deus absconditus* in *Wealth of Nations*. The gap is filled to a certain degree by the invisible hand, a kind of administrative synecdoche for the impartial spectator, that, in service to the self-interested and profit-minded individual, "promote[s] an end which was no part of [that individual's] intention."[53] The invisible hand itself is a carry-over from *Moral Sentiments*, in which Smith describes its operations as follows: the rich "are led by an invisible hand to make the same distribution of the necessaries of life, which would have been made, had the earth been divided into equal portions among all its inhabitants, and thus without intending it, without knowing it, advance the interest of society."[54]

Even before this occurrence, he first uses it in his essay on astronomy, albeit indirectly, when he characterizes the governance of ancient natural phenomena as consistent with their own regulatory properties rather than the jurisdiction and intercession of the gods: "the invisible hand of Jupiter [was never] apprehended to be employed in those matters."[55] In effect the pagan world already had a "division of labor" with its specialist gods. But it is Smith's direct and extended treatment of character in *Moral Sentiments* that is particularly significant because the world implicit in his study is modern. Were it otherwise, spectatorship and the convoluted path to public spirit that the invisible hand implies would be rendered unnecessary. In this modern world, watching is allied to emulation, which would be feckless if the "great purpose of human life [precluded] bettering our condition."[56] The equally great spectacle of property distributed unevenly summons into existence the culture of paradoxical passivity. "To be observed, to be attended to, to be taken notice of with sympathy, complacency, and approbation, are all the advantages which we can propose to derive from it. It is the vanity, not the ease, or the pleasure, which interests us" (50). Under these terms the wealthy become Jupiter's offspring. Their possessions conspicuously signal "the industry of mankind" (181) to cultivate, build, and create systems that perpetuate either human happiness or their own. They are the agents of the invisible hand. The needs and wants of all social ranks remain roughly the same, except that the wealthy pick "from the heap what is most precious and agreeable" (184).

Yet, as if to undermine the very system he has created, he goes on to sentimentalize the least desirable spectacle, poverty and destitution, as the best: "the beggar, who suns himself by the side of the highway, possesses that security which kings are fighting for" (185). Even though Smith affirms that the "love of system" is characteristic of the extremes, wealth and poverty, we are left to imagine that the purportedly indifferent and otherwise "impartial" beggar he cites subscribes to a system devoid of those anxieties that grip seekers after observation and attention, which is nonsense. But, then, as if to steady his teetering system, Smith next expands his list of characters. This time, however, he deals only with character types, contrasting those that promote the public welfare (the prudent, equitable, sober, etc.) with those that epitomize self-interest (the slothful, effeminate, voluptuous, etc.). These sharp delineations that set off the morally upright, the indulgent, and the consumer from each other dull quickly as he investigates the process by which vanity results in impartiality and self-interest turns in a socially useful direction. He demonstrates how self-command, a form of prudence, engineers the repression of immediate gratification. This process does not negate want but, consistent with Hume's pronouncement, defers it for a "greater pleasure to come." The character capable of such sublimation, however, is one that Smith regiments under his system in order not to "feel the solicitations of . . . present appetites" (189). A character so ordered may appear to conform to a moral and public-minded type but is actually a mixed and more convoluted character who profits in the end from a system that rewards repression.[57] This character of the modern economy, so foundational to the underlying premises of *Moral Sentiments*, is one Smith cannot begin to fathom.

His character types seem rather like stone guardians in the temple of the living, placed there to allegorize classifiable tendencies in human nature and to enshrine a system of morality that first gives meaning to character. At every turn these representations fail to articulate the more complicated and ambiguous "suspensions" within the psychic economy which he himself has outlined. One may also suspect that detachment alone spares the ideal character, the "impartial spectator," from the kind of circumspection that would have implicated such an individual in system-making—and that blinds the self from recognizing what can only be a proprietary and self-interested projection of moral desires upon others.

Apropos, Smith also has little good to say about the novel, which he addresses in *Lectures on Rhetoric and Belles Lettres* (1762–63). Its uncertainties of character and action are considerable impediments to edification for him. By contrast, classical writers are much more precise in their intentions and purposes, with their characters predetermined from the outset. Virgil, Homer, or any of the tragedians hid nothing from their audiences. For modern readers they still elicit pleasure upon rereading. Novels, on the other hand, have just one merit: "newness" and its readers only one motive: "curiosity," played out according to the demands of suspense: "One method which most modern historians and all the Romance writers take to render their narration interesting is to keep their event in Suspense."[58] By contrast, "in [classical] Tragedy where it is reckoned an essentiall part to keep the plot in Suspence this is not so necessary *as [it is] in* Romance" (my emphasis; 97). When held up to the mirror of classical literature, accordingly, the novel bears only a faint and distorted resemblance to that type of writing. In surprising ways, however, the action of the novel mimics the prudence Smith speaks of as necessary for the acquisition of pleasure in the commercial state—it is deferred rather than immediate. Nor do its characters fit clear and unambiguous types. Both action and character are in addition occasioned by the unorthodox narrative methods and content that form the novel. Had he been more circumspect, Smith would have seen how in his lectures he had been implicated by thoughts first formulated in *Moral Sentiments*.

It might be said, then, that Smith attempted to conceptualize and situate a seamless character in the modern commercial economy—a "somebody," a personal figure who was ultimately as capable of self-governance as the economy itself. The probability of success for this project was sealed, however, when the dominant character to emerge in *Wealth of Nations* is the one removed from barbarism by the progress of history and the division of labor in order to wind up being catapulted into "a civilized and commercial society." What results is that the invisible hand grows to a disproportionate size, distorting the shape of the impartial spectator. The impersonal "part," not unlike the huge helmet that crushes Manfred's son in *The Castle of Otranto* (1764), overwhelms the dispassionate "whole," except that with Smith it does not serve to prove the "horror of the spectacle," the Gothic twist, but its domestication.[59] Self-governance therefore proceeds indirectly through the operations of the economy as the specter of "nobody"—the figure resistant to governance—haunts Smith's moral world.

It would be wrong to conclude that Smith fails in his designs of reconciling the moral and commercial realms. Instead, we need to recognize that the commercial system doomed to failure the kind of reconciliation we seek in him, just as it created a coherence by default through the narrative of commerce. Division—discrete examinations of morality and commerce—inevitably followed, because in all likelihood, the residues of civic humanism and jurisprudential thought had no real place in the moral and commercial aesthetics of novelty. And, in this light, while suspense and the suspended character participated in systems of thought, they were ill-equipped to reconcile them. To this point we should add one final qualification: with the advent of suspense the sure-fire methods of exegesis yielded their place to the less tidy and certainly less assured methods of interpretation, methods that the novel invited with its range of characters, thick verbal economies, and multiple points of view.

The Suspended Character in Theory and Practice

The discursive void in character I refer to above resembles what Catherine Gallagher terms "nobody," which she describes as "the pivot point around which a massive reorientation of textual referentiality took place, and the location of this pivot was the mid-eighteenth-century novel. Far from being the descendant of older overtly fictional forms, the novel was the first to articulate the idea of fiction for the culture as a whole."[60] But this "nobody-ness"— the "overt fictionality" of the novel—could never be an end unto itself, particularly for a culture of expanding needs and wants.[61] Nobody, as I reconceive the term, inscribes suspense, which in turn signifies a missing discursive center, a vanishing point that all characters are subjected to. It cannot be the term itself that makes nobody plausible; only historical circumstances do that. In light of these circumstances, nobody could only be "fictional." As David Hume recognized, fiction satisfied human needs, even when a particular fictional representation—the Golden Age, for example—had no basis in fact.[62] The most detailed characters of the period novel have these vanishing points and can fruitfully be labeled nobodies, but that is because they have ceased functioning as identities or equivalences. To understand them, we must *interpret* their represented lives, which is itself a vanishing act since two readers or interpreters can scarcely ever agree with the other's point of view. In this way the detailed vagueness of the novel character—its apparent representational fullness—parallels the always incomplete or necessarily partial interpretations that readers supply.

Clear differences, however, do separate those novels written earlier in the century (or in the seventeenth century) from those by Defoe, Richardson, and Fielding. For one thing, earlier novelists generally treat character as incidental sketches, so that story, rather than character, determines representation; whereas character dominates story among Defoe and his followers. This refocusing process occurred for a variety of reasons, among them that assumptions about the privileges of fixed property and the ordained separation of social ranks by virtue of birth could no longer be assured. Nevertheless, the simple existence of realism was no guarantee that its narrative practitioners could successfully govern their characters, as chapters 4 and 5 will detail. The truth is that Defoe, Richardson, and Fielding mistakenly believed that they could master the commercial economy they represented without vanishing into it. If commercial capitalism is responsible for "nobody," then that spectral figure did not yield itself easily to comprehension or predetermined classification. For the moment let me rehearse this problem by looking briefly at *Tom Jones* (1749), initially through the lens that Patricia Meyer Spacks provides for its viewing.

In *Desire and Truth* (1990), one of the best and freshest examinations of the period novel, Patricia Meyer Spacks has chosen a decidedly "after" approach to the novel—the novel *after* Richardson and Fielding—in order to trace the demise of the "truth" or "dominance" plot these male novelists perfected and the rise of the "desire" or community novel that women novelists replaced it with. "Desire," according to Spacks, is indwelling and variable, manifesting the "energies of the mind," and, with subsequent writers, eschews the kind of architecturally ornate plot that Fielding had mastered. This "truth" plot, by contrast, is an imposed, externally ordered structure, manifesting a "desire for dominance, that is designed to contain desire itself." Accordingly, the "competitive structures [that govern] the imagined social universe [of the novel], money, social authority, and erotic energy" are all subordinated to "the narrator's power of plotting."[63] Spacks's arrangement of terms perhaps retells an old lesson about Fielding's powers of narrative management, though it certainly makes us want to believe that narrative management is a leak-proof container. But by redirecting our eyes from plot and turning to character, we discover that the power of telling is not nearly as compelling as the power of doing. Granted, Tom Jones is a controlled representation, a product of the narrator's (and author's) larger intelligence. Yet through his deeds he evinces the capacity to sabotage dominance and to raise doubts, finally, about whether plot can serve as *the* explanatory mechanism for this novel or any that followed.

In particular, I am thinking of that portion of the narrative when Tom and Partridge light upon the Man of the Hill's house in the wee hours of the night. Strange and ultimately inexplicable problems arise. Once Tom and Partridge bribe their way into the old Man's home, Partridge immediately fears witchcraft in the person of the Old Woman, who keeps her misanthropic Master's home, because the interior is "furnished in the most neat and elegant Manner."[64] Tom is also surprized by the tasteful appearance of the interior—the "frontstage" as Weatherill would call it—though, unlike Partridge, he has no fear the woman is a witch. Immediately his eyes fix on specifics, "a great Number of Nicknacks, and Curiosities, which might have engaged the Attention of a Virtuoso" (445–46). As he stands, virtuoso-like, "admiring these Things" (446), he also unveils a curious interest in the hoard and its ownership that the preceding seven-plus books do not even vaguely anticipate about his character. After dwelling over these objects for some time, he concludes "by this Collection of Rarities . . . that [the Old Woman's] Master had been a Traveller" (446).

With this surmise, Tom not only gropes to order and organize the objects he stumbles upon but also makes oblique inquiries into the origins of the bric-a-brac he sees on display. Here we have not the Tom of old—the citizen of Paradise Hall and its penumbra—but the new Tom—the citizen of the world—whose eyes glint in appreciation of acquisition and possession. To explain this fascination, other than by voilà, takes us beyond the evidence of his character as it has been ordered. Around the same time, moreover, other acquisitive instincts have begun to surface in him. We do not readily think of Tom as a man hungry for knowledge or particularly keen about acquiring it, a view that Thwackum has a hand in shaping, yet we cannot help but notice that he reads the *Spectator*; has committed both Milton and Otway to memory; knows his Latin; has been attentive enough as a pupil that he has no need of seeing *Erasmi Colloquia*, *Ovid de Tristibus*, and *Gradus ad Parnassum*. In addition, Stowe's *The Chronicles of England*, Pope's Homer, Echard, and the *Craftsman* have all passed his way at some earlier stage, though *Robinson Crusoe*, Thomas à Kempis, and Tom Brown have not (421–22). It is one of the latter unknown pieces that he calls for, not the old and familiar, when faced with another night at a public house. As this and other events unfold, he demonstrates that his passions extend well beyond carnal attachments, Molly and Sophia, and that he is faithful to more than just Allworthy. Fielding, in the process, seems more intent upon conserving a character who has little resemblance to the active fellow he first sets before us.

Once Tom drives off the yobs who are assaulting the Man of the Hill not far from the door of his home, he learns nothing more about origins than what he initially surmised: the Old Man has indeed traveled. Although we may assume that dynastic succession will eventually be secured for Tom because of his advantageous marriage, we can never be sure that he will carry out his role in exactly the same manner that the illustrious Allworthy does his, quite simply because he does not pass through the commercial thoroughfares without disclosing other dimensions to his character. In short, the open road marks Tom as having a refined aesthetic sense. As James H. Bunn has argued, "if the economics of gathering commodities induces bric-a-brac as a side effect, as well as a subsequent aesthetics that self-consciously points to the occlusion of native foundations, it engenders a philosophical stance as well. For the same economic advantage that allows a merchant to accumulate expensive bric-a-brac also engenders the enlightened accumulation of knowledge . . . the best that has been thought and said in the world by a Citizen of the World." Bunn properly holds that aesthetics depends upon divorcing utility from the objects of contemplation and that, in particular, "bric-a-brac misallocates the past."[65] This kind of divorce may explain the misanthropy of the Old Man, but it does not explain Tom's fascination. *Tom Jones* spends twelve books attempting to tie Tom back to his origins and succeeds in answering the social and ethical concerns that attend the biology of human reproduction. But that same luxury is written out of the novel regarding matters commercial. Nevertheless, even without the benefit of travel, Tom already has a keen sense of the finer things.

Tom's needs and wants focus his vanishing point, the nobody-ness and suspense that lie at the heart of Fielding's otherwise guarded representation of him. Their role not only is built into this history of absent or repressed origins but also marks his progress in a life propelled by personal discontinuity. We can appreciate how ingrained this pattern of contradiction and division became during the eighteenth century in manifold ways and from a variety of sources, even from among the socially conservative. We have already heard from Dr. Johnson in chapter 2 about his willingness to impose commercial needs and wants upon the Scots and yet vaunt the commercial self-sufficiency of England, only to consume his dishes of tea after making his boast. This aggrandizement of insularity turns out to be one of those vanishing points, a silent contradiction between claim and facts. Tea in this instance is a bit like bric-a-brac in that it misallocates the past and represses its origin, with its value measured in the gratification of dishes consumed.

These same developments figure prominently in the novels of Defoe, Richardson, and Fielding, as each enjoins the commercial economy in ways that shift existing novels into their "realistic" stage and as each represents a stage in the response to commercial modernity. This is not to suggest that by taking such a step they are any less indebted to the earlier romance or amatory traditions of the novel, but that the desire we associate with this tradition has been refigured or, in some instances, so thoroughly sublimated through the operations of the commercial economy that the novel itself scarcely resembles what it once was. The claim of reciprocal exchange that I am making was not at all alien to the eighteenth century, for in the historical development of culture "from ignorance to knowledge, and from rude to civilized manners," as the argument went, certain changes followed. "As men have been successful in these great improvements, and find less difficulty in the attainment of bare necessaries, their prospects are gradually enlarged, their appetites and desires are more and more awakened and called forth in pursuit of the several conveniencies of life; and the various branches of manufacture, together with commerce, its inseparable attendant, and with science and literature, the natural offspring of ease and affluence, are introduced, and brought to maturity. . . . [Thus,] men, being less oppressed with their own wants, are more at liberty to cultivate the feelings of humanity."[66]

Of all the literary genres the realistic novel requires the greatest investment of time—leisure time, as Ian Watt has told us—as well as the capacity for solitude—among those who courted ambition, aspiration, and mobility, increasingly in urban centers, as J. Paul Hunter has proposed.[67] How, under the circumstances and in the shrinking space of civic virtue, these readers were supposed to cultivate humanity remains a mysterious process but one that undoubtedly is connected to the interested affections and their invisible workings. On the other hand, it is fairly easy to recognize how the novel, if we have judged its readership correctly, spawned even greater needs and wants. That is to say, in form and function the realistic novel mirrored the character of its audience. Far more important were the shapes that it assumed and the phases it passed through in becoming a cultural fixity.[68] The novels I have chosen to examine in the remaining chapters of this study collectively map out a history of progress: from the literary barbarism of *Robinson Crusoe* to the industrial sensibility of *Tristram Shandy*. Within that history, however, lies another and more revealing story about character, the possibility and methods of its governance, in a commercial world where "little depends on the character and genius either of any one man, or a few men."[69] Although the textual richness of the moral-realistic novel may foster the illusion of time unsuspended and undivided, these illusions, in the hands of Defoe, Richardson, Fielding, and Sterne, are not ends unto themselves but testaments to the cohesive powers of the commercial narrative.

4

Primitive Evidence versus Commercial Civilization: The Case of *Crusoe*

VIRTUALLY EVERYTHING THAT HAPPENS AND THAT IS NARRATED IN *Robinson Crusoe* (1719–20) exists in a state of suspense, even though the retrospective nature of this narrative suggests otherwise: after all, Crusoe the memoirist and autobiographer lives to write about his adventures. From the information we are told, a large gulf and smaller ones separate the experiences of the fictional Crusoe from the writing and publishing of his memoirs. This is so for obvious reasons: he spends most of his life far removed from his native country and, even upon his return, can barely sit still long enough before his inner springs uncoil, sending him once again into the unknown. His first major journey, however, is foundational, as his character takes shape during years of protracted isolation. What passes him by in his absence is an England that begins to assume a modern national identity, along with all that is implied in that process, including matters I have discussed at length in earlier chapters. By any standard of measure, Crusoe is suspended in time as a historically dysfunctional being, whose only real frame of reference is an England that exists from before the execution of Charles I. Here lies the source of his failure, the ahistoricism of his civil "origins," which he is not only determined to recover but also bent on asserting, as if to wish his absolutist view of self-governance into existence.

Crusoe is suspended in other ways as well. We like to think of him as *homo economicus*, and he is certainly that. Still, this side of his character is one that he only eventually puts on in otherwise trying circumstances, but with what degree of consciousness is never entirely clear. He falls into a commercial life once he finds himself in Brazil but, whatever his accomplishments in South America, they must wait three decades before he can reap their financial rewards. During the intervening years, he enacts the processes of commercial civilization, passing through the various stages of history that eighteenth-century writers later associated with the progress of history itself. Not long after his arrival on the deserted island, he experiences the pivotal and defining moment of his life,

93

when he passes from a state of doubt, uncertainty, confusion, and skeptical indifference to a state of clarity, purpose, and belief. From this "conversion" his character assumes legitimacy and, decades later, serves as the anchor of his "authorized" personal narrative of history when he publishes his memoirs.

Problems multiply, however, when we examine this testament of faith against the detailed evidence that purportedly documents its authenticity, exposing the deep core of suspense that challenges the presumed with the unknown, faith with delusion. Even his handling of the three volumes that make up his *Life* indicates the operations of suspense. The first volume turns out to be inadequate—suspended, as it were—because as both a narrative and history it must be supplemented and added to. Much the same is true of the second volume, the *Farther Adventures* (1719). Although this sequel volume offers a clearer picture of Crusoe the commercialist, the circumstances it details also demonstrate the divisiveness of his evidentiary standards. In this way, the Crusoe of *The Life and Strange Surprising Adventures* (1719) becomes "suspended" even further from himself. The final volume, *Serious Reflections* (1720), rounds out the life history and its narrative, with all the commercial instincts of Crusoe still intact, but paradoxically so. *Serious Reflections* attempts not only to compensate for the deficiencies of the preceding two volumes but also to rewrite the order of all three, as if to suggest that no single volume can do much more than approximate personal history.

But it is Crusoe's persistent affiliation with a time gone by that underscores the historical suspense that governs Defoe's tripartite novel, which no amount of protest from involved parties, whether fictional or real, can erase. From this circumstance all of the depth and texture of Crusoe's character emerges as a complex creation that unwittingly defies the simple identity that the memoirist wishes for himself. In surprising ways Defoe's other commercial writings explain the reasons for this imprecision, even though we take for granted that Defoe himself was an unequivocal advocate of commercial improvement.

Character and Its Commercial Subtext

Paula Backscheider has written that "Defoe's fictions gave literary history the defining characteristics of the form we call 'novel,'" different from "poetry and drama," and rendered distinct by its discursiveness and single-minded focus on character. She continues, "the form [of the novel itself] serves [as an] exploration of character and becomes a source of radical power because it is the structure of the mind and experiences of the character."[1] Although Backscheider's statement effectively reaffirms that the form of the novel speaks loudly to us, she also complicates matters of novelistic form by introducing a wide range of "biographical" factors that Defoe may have drawn upon as imaginative sources for his fiction. The fact that he participated widely in the affairs of his day, as the "biographical" data evidence, adds to our understanding of Defoe's contribution to the novel, but questions about the obedience of his own sons, Benjamin and Daniel, or the Salters'-Hall controversy about occasional conformity can do little more than to begin to explain the originality of *Robinson Crusoe* (1719).[2] Following obvious leads, we could also turn to spiritual autobiography, sermons, or travel writing as additional sources that played upon and figured in Defoe's fiction. But to do so would bog us down needlessly in matters pertaining to the so-called prehistory of the novel.

This much is certain: that between 1719 and 1724, between *Crusoe* and *Roxana*, Defoe produced his major works of fiction. And while *Roxana* resembles *Crusoe*, the two are, in another sense, worlds apart, though still connected. Formally, both plot the same kind of story, but the transgressions of Roxana differ significantly from Crusoe's, in part because Defoe "mine[s] the popular vein of *chronique scandaleuse*" in *Roxana*.[3] In borrowing from and capitalizing upon this genre, Defoe renders character as such a complex amalgam of social, economic, and psychological factors that he appears to stagger under their weight, in the same way that Roxana is forever burdened by the multiple evasions of her life. Although *Roxana* comes to an end, the sense of closure Defoe provides is hardly satisfactory because no quantity of wealth apportioned to its heroine, which is indeed vast, compensates for the abruptness and unresolved features of this narrative, even if Defoe finished it as intended.[4] *Crusoe*, on the other hand, borrows primarily from itself and capitalizes on the first volume to produce two more. Its slower and more methodical accretions mimic the protracted accumulation of material prosperity that defines its hero's life. Yet, as Everett Zimmerman has argued, the fact that Crusoe does persist evinces "recognition of disharmonies"—that the "religious structure has not resolved the psychological problem . . . [of] behavior."[5]

The value of comparing *Crusoe* to *Roxana*, indicated here only in brief, allows us to appreciate how Defoe peeled away extraneous layers to get to an essential character and, even perhaps, why he turned away from the genre, despite his remarkable productivity, almost as abruptly as he began it. The central problem of character in all of Defoe's novels is regulation, which his interest in the social penumbra and marginal figure only complicates and intensifies. Leo Braudy has contended that "many of the great literary changes of the eighteenth century . . . related to an anguish and uncertainty about human character."[6] He adds that "before Defoe, works that dealt with an individual life usually did not see character as a problem because their intentions were openly didactic."[7] Within the compass of Defoe's fiction, he notes, the unsettled state of character evolves quickly so that, for example, there is already a marked "decrease in providential language in *Captain Singleton* (1720)," which is glaring in light of Crusoe's reliance upon it and suggestive of the "irrelevance of spiritual autobiography" in later redactions of character.[8]

The connection between character and commercial maneuvering in Defoe's narratives is uniformly strong. Although his other publications identify him as a prolific spokesman for English commercialization, the views he expressed did not advance a trade-at any-cost position or anticipate the era of political economy. Defoe's commerce, like that of the characters in his novels, was also a commerce of governance. Yet as I have indicated in chapter 2, by the first quarter of the eighteenth century the regulatory mechanisms of providential commercialism, which ought to have appealed to Defoe, were already waning. In characterizing Defoe's national goals as "nothing less than world domination"—goals wrought by "trade, not military might"—Backscheider targets the most specific feature of his economic thought.[9] Trade-as-conquest does not exactly comport with *doux commerce*, but it is consistent with the power-plenty model of mercantilism.[10] As Backscheider develops her argument she next cites from a page in *The Advantages of Peace and Commerce* (1729): "'if any one Nation could govern Trade, that Nation would govern the World' (6)," which, according to Defoe, would make "Dependents and Subjects" of "the whole World."[11] The next page, however, finds him lauding Louis XIV, who "saw plainly that the Way to make the *French* Nation the Terror of the World" was through commerce.[12] This notion of trade as conquest is, except for the reference to Louis, one that Defoe plagiarized from John Evelyn's *Trade and Navigation* (1674), in which the latter writes: "That whoever Commands the Ocean, Commands the Trade of the World, Commands the Riches of the World, and whoever is Master of That, Commands the World it self."[13]

I draw attention to Defoe's pirating not for the act itself but because Evelyn's work, while dated, is rich with providential imagery and, by implication, the regulatory subtext this discourse of origins supplies. Even so, Defoe proves himself not nearly the skillful manager of commercial affairs as his reputation allows. The language and informing myths of trade cause him no end of difficulty. He toys with these, even teases them, but never makes a final commitment to the expected and unambiguous view. In *A Plan of the English Commerce* (1728), in a chapter entitled "*Of the first Rise, Growth and Encrease of the* Commerce *of* England," he dismisses "dull Speculations of the Nature and Original of Commerce" in a curiously offhanded manner because entertaining them, as he says, "would lead us back into . . . a dry useless Subject, and therefore carefully avoided . . . by which I mean as above, from the Time, *let that Time be when you will.*"[14] Had he not already indicated precisely the opposite, we could take his declaration at face-value.

As it turns out, the comment itself is puzzling to readers of *A Plan* because at the outset he establishes what appears as the biblical pedigree of commercialization. He cites the generations of Adam as "*Mechanicks*" and Noah as the first shipwright. Once he passes on to Babel, the origin of commerce within the providential tradition, he lingers a bit but only to charge its "Brother Bricklayers" as Freemasons (7). Defoe has nothing positive to say about the secret fraternity but, even more important, utters not a single word about divided tongues or the diaspora. Instead, he bounds ahead to the increase of world population as well as the trade and business that rose proportionately with it, then centered in Tyre: "such a Prodigy of Business, as I have good Reason to believe, was never equall'd in the World, except just now, (*viz.*) by the great trade carry'd on at this Time in *England*" (9). From Ezekiel we recall that Tyre, the city God called beautiful, had Satan for its real king. Says God, "I will bring strangers upon thee, the terrible of the nations; and they shall draw their swords against the beauty of thy wisdom, and they shall defile thy brightness" (Ezekiel 28.7). Thus, in figuring his "Beautiful Scheme of Trade," Defoe leaps over the damning, as his history vaults over dispersed people, divided tongues, tribal groupings, and the beautiful city to arrive at the modern world and certainly the central entrepôt on his commercial map, London.[15]

Like Lot's wife, Defoe looks back, but only to discover his own ambivalence. History itself weighs heavily upon his guarded reflections, particularly if we are to accept that the only meaningful origin of commerce figures in Tyre. The same kind of ambivalence, however, plays itself out when Defoe deals with his own modern-day nation and its equivalent Tyre. In his *Tour* (1724–26), for instance, he draws attention to the splendors of commercial success by pointing out the various estates built upon commerce that dot the roads into London. But once his attention shifts to the matter of needs and wants, not in the abstract or as a function of international commerce or providential imperatives, it causes him no end of contradiction, even in publications that seem directly removed from such concerns. *The Complete English Tradesman* (1727) is such a work. This hefty *vade mecum* parsed for apprentices the grammar of trade and instructed them in their obligations to the commercial system as a whole. But it is also more than that; in fact, it relies upon a curious melange of writing styles—the epistolary, expository, narrative, and dialogic—the exact forms that Defoe blends into his novels. While *English Tradesman* lacks the suppleness of the novel form, it manifests all of the latter's contradictions.

At one point Defoe recommends that "A Tradesman," the person directly responsible for catering to the needs and wants of a clientele, "must have no flesh and blood about him, no passions, no resentment; he must never be angry, no not so much as seem to be so."[16] He must, in short, act "dis-interestedly." But sublimation, as Defoe conceives it, has undesirable consequences. He goes on to report, "I heard once of a shop-keeper that behav'd himself thus to such an extreme, that when he was provok'd by the impertinence of the customers, beyond what his temper could bear, he would go up stairs and beat his wife, kick his children about like dogs, and be as furious for two or three minutes, as a man chain'd down in *Bedlam* . . . so absolute a government of his passions had he in the shop" (1, 1:94–95).[17] But the moral we expect from this story is not the one we get: "it is necessary for a Tradesman to subject himself, by all ways possible, to his business" (1, 1:95). To Defoe's way of thinking business inverted the more popular form of the masquerade, but was no less a masquerade because of its inversion. Although the trader who catered to his own pleasures—the trader *"in masquerade"*—provokes him in *Tradesman*, the masquerade of regulation and repression is the one he endorses (1, 1:117–18).

In another place, in what appears as a lapse into mordant irony, he proceeds to depict the honest tradesman as one whose inspiration derives from the emotional attachment he has to his family. "That Tradesman who does not delight in his family, will never long delight in his business; for as one great end of an honest Tradesman's diligence is the support of his family, and the providing for the comfortable subsistence of his wife and children; so the very sight of, and above all, his tender and affectionate care for his wife and children, is the spur of his diligence" (1, 1:125). Defoe uses this unearthly image to spur indolent tradesmen, guided by other realities, to diligence. Lost from memory in the course of thirty pages is the other ideal who beats his wife and kicks his children.

As the impact of commerce upon the social compact became more pronounced, it also excavated new strata of human nature that challenged Defoe in ways he could not fully interpret, other than through trusted categories of moral apprehension and character types. In theory it did not follow "that because a Tradesman is grown rich by Trade, that therefore he must turn a general Devourer and Destroyer of the Trade itself, as well as of his Neighbour Tradesmen" (2, 1:108). It just so happened that practice created new theory unanswered by the "general

Devourer." Purse-proud tradesmen, according to Defoe's analysis, are "bloated-up Animal[s]" (2, 1:233), ill-equipped to enter the human community, yet they too were the agents of commerce. Only the old habits of behest and fiat brought forth governance.

Throughout *Tradesman* Defoe exposes ambiguity without resolving it and reproduces contradictory examples of the type I have cited above. As if by default he had to shoulder the burdens of what commerce had become through its increase and progress, while recognizing all along that "It is very rarely that men are wanting to their own interest" (1, 1:194). On the one hand, commerce checked barbarity and moral depravity, the type the Turks exemplified, who live only according to the primitive barbarity of necessity (2, 2:111–12). Forty pages later, however, he cautions tradesmen not to create fashion or novelty, unless "the Buyer comes and directs him to make this or that thing, of such and such materials, and in such a form, [since] it is his Business to perform it" (2, 2:150–51). Ethical failure in Defoe's trading system stemmed, in the end, from creating demand for things other than necessities.[18]

Robinson Crusoe itself is a sustained, albeit doomed, meditation on origins, of a time passed by, that can no longer be recovered in the contemporary world. It is also, by its counterpoint, a fugue dedicated to the needs and wants of a solitary individual. The dissonances of this composition between prehistory and the present produce a character-centered narrative realism that strains to govern a life that, in the end, it cannot control. By reflecting on the import of just the opening pages of volume 1 or by recognizing that Crusoe is forever searching for new origins, we learn that neither origins nor prehistory can matter, as Defoe himself recognized in *A Plan*, this despite the fact that he revisits them. What had changed so dramatically under the jurisdiction of needs-and-wants capitalism was the evidence by which judgments were rendered through circumstantial-based interpretation. In defining what he calls this "older sense" of evidence, "conceived before the birth of 'epistemology,'" Douglas Lane Patey remarks that "we would now locate [it] somewhere between logic and psychology; a cognate ambiguity governs *opinion*, *probability*, and *certainty*, which in the context of the new theories of knowledge of the seventeenth century betray more clearly than ever before double senses, one logical, the other psychological."[19] Although Crusoe can liken himself to the prodigal or Job, set within a temporal framework that recalls design and purpose, his character is not an imposed identity. That he represents himself in this way tells us much about his needs and wants. But the evidence that ought to substantiate these claims simply does not materialize.

Between *Robinson Crusoe* and *Roxana* the word becomes flesh. Roxanna is "a body wholly body," both whore and mother. Whatever denial she imposes upon her own flesh, it is, significantly, directed at her own daughter, Susan. Crusoe, the dispassionate and sexless man, is "a body holy body," or so he would like to believe. Were it not for Job or God's providence Crusoe would be another Roxana, a character whose life offers no satisfactory resolution. The coherence of *Robinson Crusoe*, in the end, resists the coherence that the narrative of commerce afforded and leaves its eponym to a form of isolation much worse than anything that a quarter-century of literal isolation exacted from his flesh.

Character, Exchange, and Market Mechanisms

The problem of a self-divided Crusoe is a matter that Ronald Paulson has studied in an essay some two decades ago, in which he examined early eighteenth-century narratives split along the lines of journey and theater: a "teleological pilgrimage" versus "a series of provisional structures, roles, and scenes." Of the narratives he considers, the first is *The Life and Strange Surprizing Adventures of Robinson Crusoe*, through which he establishes how journey and theater can become intertwined and mutually compromised: "the converted Crusoe . . . makes it clear that the waves that bear the young Crusoe are the providence of God to which he must entrust himself. . . . The convert can easily become the spectator of his own drama, or even the playwright, imposing providential roles upon those existential events."[20] This same division between God's plot and Crusoe's story, as Leopold Damrosch urges, "stands as a remarkable instance of a work that gets away from its author, and gives expression to attitudes that seem to lie far from his conscious intention."[21]

Although one might argue that the willful manipulation that Paulson refers to differs from the loss of control that Damrosch identifies, both, in effect, imply that artifice abounds to such a degree in *Crusoe* that it infects the truth claims of the novel itself. Readers subscribing to this view sense that the problem with *Crusoe* rests in its evidence, which, in terms of scope and credibility, is incompatible with the significance Defoe attaches to it in Crusoe's life. I have already stressed in chapter 2 how the needs/wants model of commercial capitalism addled some of the standard assumptions about history-based teleologies, which effectively cleared the way for narrative suspense and, as sketched out in chapter 3, the character divorced from predetermined identities. No doubt, Defoe would be hostile to this view, since Crusoe is forever trying to impose identities upon himself.

The reason for this hostility, as I propose, is a function of the moral reservations Defoe expressed about or the divided reaction he had to need/want based demand. In a similar manner, because of his own anxieties about demand, which are partially attributable to dislocations he suffers in time, Crusoe demonstrates how ill-matched his mercantilist proclivities are in the domestic marketplace, defined for him by the book trade of London—the city to which he tells us he retires in 1705. In treating demand, whether in *Crusoe* or other commercial-minded works, such as *The Complete English Tradesman*, Defoe tends to represent it obliquely, trying to keep it out of the range of consciousness, so that its influence always arises from the perimeter, well beyond the main focus of his concerns. In *Crusoe*, for instance, demand generally veers away from its market meanings to signify simple consumption or ingestion, in large part because Crusoe has distanced himself from the marketplace. At the outset, son Robinson fears not only the demands of his biological father but also the perceived threat of being swallowed by his authority. Similar anxieties hound him on his island, as external forces when the earth quakes or the indigenous population shows itself; or psychically, when the angry god visits him in a dream. Upon his return to Europe, however, he responds to consumption in a more complex manner, so that his views intimate with more certainty the positions held by Defoe the commercial writer. In Crusoe's homeward passage through the Pyrenees, ravenous wolves pose a serious threat to survival and are, accordingly, treated seriously; whereas a solitary bear, though equally dangerous, serves as the stuff of arboreal frolicking; after the baiting game is exhausted Friday simply aims and fires. In the civilized world, we conclude, the response to consumption no longer remains nearly so well defined.

Surely the most significant marginalization of consumption occurs in the undisciplined and quite real domestic marketplace of readers and booksellers who haunt the pages of volumes 2 and 3 especially. In fact, we can see how Crusoe responds to this extraneous and unanticipated factor, much maligned by mercantilists, by the way he transforms the overarching conceptualization of the three constituent parts. What is initially "a just History of Fact; [without] any Appearance of Fiction in it," according to the "editor" of volume 1, becomes by volume 3, and according to Crusoe himself, a "story [that], though allegorical, is also historical."[22] The panoptic view of *Crusoe*, in other words, allows us to see that this tripartite narrative is both itself and not itself at the same time, a divided narrative that is simultaneously history and story, fact and allegory. From what we gather, it does not start out that way and, thus, we are left to wonder about how best to explain its apparent generic instability and loss of control. The obvious answer is that we must look to the demands of readers who have challenged the authority and property of the book.

We could accept the exegetical explanation Defoe supplies Crusoe, which occurs in Crusoe's only preface, the preface to volume 3. "[E]verything is said to be first in the intention, and last in the execution, so I come now to acknowledge to my reader that the present work is not merely the product of the two first volumes, but the first two volumes may rather be called the product of this."[23] Although his veiled allusion to the parable about the last being first may soothe Crusoe, the paradoxical arrangement he proposes does little to placate us. Instead we feel annoyed and generally imposed upon by his disclosure. If volume 3 somehow realizes intention, then, we conjecture, Crusoe perhaps did not know what he intended with volumes 1 and 2. By writing both, he not only stumbled upon purpose, which is unconvincing, but also crippled his narrative by resorting to the rigidities of quasi-mystical meditations and quaint allegory. For a life-long journeyer, who has defined himself around the sequences of travel and pilgrimage, his willful reconstruction seems awfully theatrical, if not an assault upon the needs and wants of uncompliant readers.

As it turns out, Crusoe's fiats cannot decree unwavering principle or secure obedience for the simple reason that volumes 1 and 2 already have a market existence. With both sequels, in addition, it becomes clear that a marketplace of needs and wants, literary property, and the variable interpretations that arise from both obtrude upon him and force him into defensive postures from which his market-less island experience has shielded him.[24] Even so, his narrative methods in volume 1 have not prevented critics from unearthing all sorts of "divisions" or "suspensions" that not just vex his account but also suggest its lack of an integrated, coherent view. Some of the most interesting of these readings touch every aspect of composition, from text to self, as if to underscore how fragile the act of fulfilling intention becomes when the mere citation of a necessitarian teleology is all that can be claimed.[25] In this spirit, James O. Foster has maintained that "as the narrative develops, the external and allegorical division between compulsion and authority is gradually internalized into an inner colloquy as Crusoe's father takes on a psychological dimension of the punitive superego manifest in Crusoe's conscience."[26] Thomas Kavanaugh has likewise characterized Crusoe, though in deference to Lacan rather than Freud. "Consciousness for Robinson is circular and oscillatory, never linear. The event is important only as it is susceptible to this constant solicitation[;] this obsessive repetition . . . is the immobile dialectics of a sundered self whose only continuity can be found within this oppositional structure."[27] These examples, among others, begin to suggest why Defoe loses control of his product.

Although volume 1 capitalizes on Crusoe's radical isolation and lack of meaningful circulation, these selling points actually define his loss of engagement with a changing world. As a consequence Crusoe naively implies that Gresham's Law applies to his life and that readers—an essentially amorphous and selfless group, as he conceives them—will assent to his written testimony without reservation. Once the first volume circulates among those readers, its value fluctuates against the artificial worth Crusoe imagines it to possess, just as its uses wind up serving ends about which he never dreamed. Thus the editor in the preface to *Farther Adventures* identifies "envious people" who have disgraced volume 1 as "a romance." He goes on to protest "the abridging [of] this work, as scandalous," claiming an "injury" against "the proprietor of this work" and equating this deed with that of "robbing on the highway, or breaking open a house."[28] The editor/publisher's preface to *Serious Reflections* repeats the same charge. "Those whose avarice, prevailing over their honesty, had invaded the property of this book by a corrupt abridgement, have . . . failed." This time, however, heaven has meted out punishment through the death of the "principal pirate."[29]

That Crusoe himself does not address these matters of literary property in propria persona may strike readers as a curious breach of character, since in the first two volumes he is forever tabulating his rewards in pounds and pence. In making this decision Defoe may want to encourage the belief that his champion would not dirty his hands with such petty matters, yet the Crusoe we know has not been inclined that way before. What Crusoe's detachment emphasizes instead is not only the divided nature of the marketplace but also the continuing self-division that plagues him as he attempts to negotiate the base wants of readers content to read a stripped-down version of his adventures and the barbarousness of those booksellers who would expropriate his property for their own gain. Volumes 2 and 3 thus stress how circumstances beyond Crusoe's control impinge upon his philosophical outlook and draw him into a world of interpretive exchange that he has preferred to flee all along.

By contrast, in volume 1, as Crusoe fashions himself he also fashions his world, the two remaining largely undivided. But even in this narrative we see that he must steel himself to confront and deal with particularly those elements of his island existence that are external to himself, which the cannibals incarnate most dramatically. This feature alone shows how damaging uncontrollable contexts are to his isolationist view. Thus many commentators have studied Crusoe as an exegete and interpreter, since these roles are foundational to what he witnesses and represents about himself, as well as what he fails to witness.[30] Patricia Meyer Spacks untangles the interpretive trials of Crusoe when she writes, "meanings change as feelings alter" and goes on to demonstrate how Crusoe adapts his imagination to reality—but only, I would stress, in controlled and circumscribed environments.[31]

There is no compelling need to replow critical ground already so richly planted. It is important to keep in mind, nonetheless, that although Crusoe divides himself from European civilization he is never far from it, either in thought or deed.[32] Division, in this regard, serves as an illusion, because the literal distance in forsaking family and home does not also entail forgetting. Whatever interest Crusoe's state of nature arouses about "the artificialities of civilization," he can only disseminate the truth of his errancy through the market instruments of civilization. As Daniel Cottom observes, the unaccommodated Crusoe "can only make [his] appearance in terms of some kind of fiction— precisely what the island was intended to sweep away."[33] Trapped as he is, Crusoe may have no recourse but to the familiar, as he plods his way through the strange. But while we concede that Crusoe is a product of environments to which he must adapt and grant that he must interpret his way out of the exotic, we tend to overlook the evidence qua evidence on which he makes his judgments and because of which the suspensions of history and being—the contradictions, inconsistencies, and self-divisions that surface all along—mark his character as no simple identity.

The Evidence of Life: Property and Exchange

For Crusoe evidence is the substance of authority. In lighting upon providential necessitarianism, he borrows from its authority not only to empower himself but also to add credibility to his narration. But while he is away from England, roughly between 1650 and 1690, the "economy" of evidence undergoes a remarkable transformation in terms of its demands and as a system of exchange. Crusoe's unwillingness to adapt to these standards has profound consequences on his self-representation. Evidence, as we discover, becomes meaningful for him only as he is able to connect it to his interests and personal history—to make it, in other words, proprietary. The pivotal episode in this process is Brazil. Having to live in a state of suspense between his first major form of enterprise and his island, Crusoe must learn how to stabilize ownership. This process connects his progress toward commercial civilization with a spiritual justification. That this evidentiary procedure must be *proprietary* satisfies a basic need, but, over time, it also leads him into a state of expanding wants, about which he registers almost no real consciousness. The net effect of this compounding is that, although it forces him to confront changing standards of evidence, his ideas about a commercial economy remain fixed and inflexible, as volumes 2 and 3 underscore.

To characterize just how "suspenseful" the changes in period evidence were, let alone to tie them to commercialization, is impossible in a short space, but a few examples are in order. In *An Essay Concerning Human Understanding*, for instance, Locke addresses the issue of evidence and the difficulties that attend assent in a chapter entitled "Of Probability." That these questions arise within a subtext of international trading, in which the presence of the Dutch East India Company figures, is no coincidence. The illustration he deals with in this chapter is ice—specifically, its familiarity to those living in northern Europe, such that if natives of this region were told that during a frigid winter a man could walk on water "hardened with cold," there would be no reason to doubt the claim. By contrast, as Locke reports, when the Dutch ambassador to Siam told its king that elephants, were they present in Holland during its cold winters, could walk on water, the king fires back: *"Hitherto I have believed the strange things you have told me, because I look upon you as a sober fair man, but now I am sure you lie."*[34]

Although Crusoe travels as far as the Gulf of Siam, where he can attest to the Dutch presence, he has no opportunity to go into Siam itself, let alone chat with its king. And while Crusoe, busy with trading activities, cannot imagine himself in near proximity to evidentiary problems, the contexts of intellectual history station him in their midst. In *Probability and Certainty*, Barbara Shapiro reveals how the divisions of knowledge were all "affected by the changing conceptions of evidence," as well as how probability and degrees of certainty factored in this change. In the area of the law, for instance, she writes about how the trial by ordeal gave way to the law of evidence; and, in the process, how proof beyond a reasonable doubt, exclusionary rules, and other related matters transformed the judicial process, so that what "slowly evolved throughout the seventeenth century was clearly discernible by the beginning of the eighteenth century."[35]

In virtually every other discipline we see the same kinds of transformation unfolding, all of which pertain, directly or indirectly, to the grading of evidence according to the standards of rationalism.[36] Thus, for example, in *Plus Ultra* (1668), Joseph Glanvill defends the advancement of useful, scientific knowledge by decrying the imprecision of existing philosophy: "we are fallen into an Age in which no *Truth* and *Evidence* can secure any thing from the *Captiousness of Disputers*."[37] Hardly godless or atheistical, this same Glanvill, in his sermon "Moral Evidence of a Life to Come," proclaims that "the *strongest* proofs [of everlasting life] are those from the *Scripture*, and all the *Arguments* that demonstrate the *Truth* of *Christianity*, prove also the *certainty* of a *Life after this*. For one of the great designs of the *Holy Jesus*, was to bring *Immortality* to *light*, . . . he gave *visible evidence* of a future *existence* by his *own Resurrection*."[38]

Well over a half-century later, atheistical David Hume relied upon similar distinctions in the gradations, systematizations, and probabilities of evidence to affirm the validity of moral evidence: it "is nothing but a conclusion concerning the actions of men, deriv'd from the consideration of their motives, temper, and situation." Certainly a much more psychologically based and variable form of evidence, yet, as Hume maintains, its use is to establish the facts. Although moral evidence is not the same as natural evidence, both can be "cement[ed] together, and form only one chain of argument betwixt them."[39] It might be said, then, that Crusoe straddles the historical divide between Glanvill and Hume, as he is eager to subscribe to and disseminate the truth of Christianity, consistent with evidence he regards as persuasive, at the same time his "motives, temper, and situation"—the essence of modern character—make us suspicious about any claims to a particular providence.

Changing attitudes toward evidence can all be traced to the new economy of time and history—the evangelical dispensation that I discussed in chapter 2. This dispensation paradoxically bears some blame for the contrarieties and divisions that vex Crusoe, as he indulges suspense but attempts to undo it at the same time. Whether named or not by individual writers, the Gospel economy prepared the soil out of which rationalism flourished. That is to say, the division between Hebrew Scripture and the New Testament marks a shift in rhetorical method that was not merely a function of stylistics but signaled a profound change in intellectual capacity. According to many period writers, Hebrew Scripture relied heavily on poetry and other forms of figurative language to ensure that an uneducated people with a limited capacity were elevated into believers; the New Testament, by contrast, appealed to reason. Isaac Barrow neatly draws out this distinction: he devalues Jewish ritual practices, holding that they "only concerned the body and outward man, and could not perfect the observer's conscience. . . . While moral duties . . . and spiritual devotions (. . . more agreeable to rational nature . . .) were more sparingly delivered."[40] In this way we can see how, under the evangelical dispensation, the turn to time present and the inward person created an ideal match with the self-generating and interest-based economy of needs and wants.

Although Crusoe descends into a state of nature when he first arrives on his island, he has also prepared himself for a new dispensation by effectively stripping away the metaphoric and figurative isolation he claims to have experienced while a plantation owner in Brazil. "I used to say, I liv'd just like a Man cast away upon some desolate Island, that had no body there but himself."[41] Once washed up on the shores of his island, he lives that isolation. Before he leaves Brazil, however, he has already done two things essential to his progress and its governance: he has made the case for the necessity of this new dispensation and at least intimated how the management of evidence is vital to that end.

The most and least obvious feature of Crusoe's Brazilian experience is the commercial success he earns there. Yet Crusoe seems almost to go out of his way to create just the opposite impression when, on two occasions, he details experiences in order to exact moral retribution from them. The first occurs immediately before the passage cited above and pertains to that period after two years of subsistence growing when "our Land began to come into Order" (35). It is at this point that he laments his passage into "the very Middle Station" (35) that his father had promised him five thousand miles away in England. He flails himself with this charge again a few pages later to introduce the slaving scheme that leads to shipwreck. Whereas in the first passage he protests "an Employment quite remote to my Genius" and how it entails the denial of wandering ("the Life I delighted in" [35]); the second passage has him condemning himself for indulging this life, his "foolish inclination of wandring abroad" (38). As is clear to us, there is a world of difference between pursuing a business venture—here, the acquisition of slaves—and aimless wandering. In between he reports "great Success in my Plantation," his "increasing in Business and in Wealth" (37), so that when he departs Brazil for Guinea, about four years after his enterprise began, he is "beginning to thrive and prosper very well upon [the] Plantation" and counts among his "fellow-Planters" acquaintances and friends (38). As it turns out, most of what he relates about Brazil deals with the bare facts of operations: money spent and invested, the quantities of goods produced, and so forth, so that his narration does not even begin to suggest anything odd, extravagant, or immoral in his conduct while he is actually in situ.

We gather from this revealing tableau that as long as Crusoe's proprietary interests are in order and secure, he remains largely untroubled by his deeds; and as long as matters evolve according to plan, he avoids self-incrimination. Only when his commerce appears slow or is interrupted does he chafe under these annoyances. Once converted, he can take the evidence of success and blacken it to create the illusion that the whole of his Brazilian experience was a moral disaster. Yet the facts unadorned by dicta support the idea that after four years he has worked his way well into the middle station, if not already begun to move beyond it, as any "Rebel" of determined "Interest" might (40). We do not hear such recriminations years later when his Brazilian investment pays him dividends. From the lesson of Brazil we learn that evidence is proprietary for Crusoe—his way of undoing suspense—and that the moral truth he wishes to see colors his representations of the facts. Those same facts in turn are either assimilative or dissociative—either they can be made to conform to systematic economy because they are controllable or they become antagonistic divisions and signs of moral failure.

This method of division becomes apparent in the first form of island-writing that Crusoe says he undertakes; through it simple facts grow encumbered as he reads and interprets them. He tallies what has happened in debtor-creditor columns, denominating one entry "good" and the other "evil." On balance, the "evil" column is unembellished and as close to the bare facts as Crusoe can muster. The "good" column, on the other hand, with its more generous quantity of words, tips the scale to its side. By comparing these various entries, we recognize that evil for Crusoe is a privative state, while good is a plenary condition that supplies his "Wants" (66). But in addition these same entries also yield what Crusoe himself calls "Testimony," which carries both religious and legal meanings.

More difficult to determine is whether this testimony or the evidence from which it arises lacks the kind of suspense Crusoe seems so eager to disavow. If we use one of Locke's six criteria of what he calls "testimony," "the consistency of the parts, and circumstances of the relation," problems surface.[42] Although the Journal is itself evidence that writing occurred on the island, it does not corroborate the existence of the good-evil tabulation Crusoe includes. We only have his word that it is an accurate document—"an undoubted Testimony" of his "Condition" (67). Despite his editorial coloring, the document itself is subject to a range of doubts. The "good" side, for instance, contains enough piety of the convert to make us question the date of its composition. Later on, we discover that the Journal certifies the time of Crusoe's conversion some ten months after he has been on the island. We could assume that the tabulation occurs shortly after this point and that Crusoe next compresses a year's worth of events into a two-month spurt of journal-writing, until his supply of ink runs low. If we do, however, we leave unexplained the "evil" or left-hand column of the tabulation that lists attitudes Crusoe has already mitigated during those same two months and afterwards. Under this condition, the tabulation may be a rhetorical ploy that he fabricates for effect, and nothing more.

The other problem that compromises Crusoe's evidence derives from Locke's sixth criterion of testimony: "Contrary testimonies."[43] We would perhaps be less inclined to view Crusoe with suspicion if he had only repressed certain kinds of evidence. Chief among these are the three separate accounts he supplies for 30 September 1659. The first or novelistic account finds Crusoe thankful to God for deliverance, capable of reciting a pious verse, and, on that particular night, sleeping in a tree, where he "slept as comfortably as . . . few could have done in my Condition." The next morning, 1 October, he wakes to discover "the Weather clear, and the Storm [at sea] abated" (47). The second or hypothetical account renders him not the least bit "thankful to God for [his] Deliverance, having first vomited with the great Quantity of salt Water which was gotten into [his] Stomach." He proceeds next to beat himself and to cry out in misery until exhausted and faint, "forc'd to lye down on the Ground to repose, but durst not sleep for fear of being devour'd" (69). The Journal account, by contrast, avoids the embellishment of the novelistic account and the graphic displays of the hypothetical account; it reads: "I slept in a Tree for fear of wild Creatures, but slept soundly tho' it rain'd all Night. The next day, 1 October, "it continu'd raining" (70).

Whether it rained or not, whether Crusoe was pious or not, or whether he slept are matters left indeterminate by virtue of his testimony. In representing himself in full, he reveals the utterly unknown and unknowable about himself through a baroque form of narrative suspense. Simply in terms of evidence, however, his most reliable testimony is the Journal, which, as a document roughly contemporaneous with lived experiences, he purportedly writes for no audience other than himself. Had he only consulted this record to crosscheck facts and details, he could have avoided the appearance of misrepresentation, yet Crusoe never seems to take this step.[44] While it is unlikely that he would choose to represent himself as an individual who plays fast and loose with the evidence, this appearance is unavoidable under the circumstances. Moreover "contrary testimonies" are not limited only to 30 September; many others transpire as we compare the Journal account against the novelistic and vice-versa. In general, life represented in the Journal appears more arduous, discursively rich, and dangerous than what we read about in the novelistic account. Distance from the actual events may have some bearing in this representational shift in that Crusoe, if we go along with the logic of the story, composes his novelistic narration at least some forty-five years after the actual experiences themselves, sometime after his return from his voyage to the Eastern world.[45]

Detection in this area would be eased a bit had Crusoe actually indicated when he began the Journal. It is reasonable to assume that he probably makes his first entry at a point not long after settling his island affairs. In the novelistic account—if we can trust it at all—he mentions that he starts the Journal once he puts his cave in order, which, according to the Journal proper, is sometime toward the end of December, though this period is not the only time frame that has been proposed.[46]

If December is the correct *terminus a quo*, then entries for the previous three months exist as a function of memory, which, however unreliable, lacks the inherent unreliability of a forty-five year interval. No matter what date we finally settle on, however, the Journal itself must stand as the best evidence we have for the time it covers. Yet repeatedly Crusoe edits the Journal as he reproduces it, as if to suggest that documentary evidence cannot stand alone, that it must be made "interested" and proprietary. At moments we suspect the mature voice of Crusoe leaking into the Journal, without any direct indication to confirm our suspicion. At other times we believe we are reading the Journal when he suddenly injects, "But I return to my Journal" (91) — or some variation on this locution.

With these precedents of contrary testimony, we become skeptical about all that follows, even after Crusoe has ceased presenting evidence that invites comparison with itself. That he does eventually desist from his journalistic practice can be accounted for through his own words: "I could not make any Ink by any Means that I could devise" (65). For this task he would need varnish, derived from old nuts or linseed oil, and a coloring medium.[47] Both, we assume, were available on his island, but since he never details his attempts at making ink we can never be sure where he went wrong. Whatever the quantity of ink he has retrieved from the first shipwreck, he husbands it well. Sometime after his first anniversary his supply "began to fail" him and he uses it "to write down only the most remarkable Events" (104), including the letter he leaves for "the sixteen *Spaniards* that were to be expected" (277), some twenty-six years later, when he is about to leave the island.

Perhaps it is unreasonable to expect Crusoe to be ingenious about the manufacture of ink, when there is other evidence indicating his occasional failures at fabrication. Yet the quantity of ink at his disposal is one that cannot be divorced from matters central to evidentiary concerns. Because he does have ink throughout his first documented year, the record of that time is overwrought, protracted, and confused in ways I have already spelled out. The quantity of ink he has is to blame for these obstacles, but does not provide a full explanation in and of itself. Once he returns to the civilized world, in which the supply and demand for ink overwhelm even his productive output, this abundance does nothing to lend clarity to his motives as a writer or our understanding of his character. Thus, the mere possession of ink is not so much the problem as is the evidence that flows from it.

To that end, virtually every act of writing that Crusoe undertakes depends on memory, often as it is stretched by long intervals, which helps to account for his representation of life as a trial by ordeal. As Barbara Shapiro notes, "Trial by ordeal . . . , which dominated legal proceedings all over early medieval Europe, did not involve an attempt to try causes by rational means. Proof of a litigant's assertion was left to God, who would decide which party was telling the truth."[48] Although she does not extend this label to Crusoe, it is one that is especially apposite for the story he tells. In sensibility and outlook Crusoe resists the modern world. Among other things he is singularly apolitical, despite the proximity of pivotal moments in his personal life to salient events in seventeenth-century English history. He departs England two years after Charles's execution, is restored to God's favor in 1660, and returns home shortly before the Glorious Revolution, none of which warrants even the slightest mention on his part.[49] Although many reasons may explain this silence, perhaps the most compelling depends upon evidence that Crusoe only skirts, his early "House-Education" (3) from his father, a man he alternately describes as "wise and grave" (4), "Prophetick" (6), and "very Ancient" (3), who would have been born sometime during the middle of Elizabeth's reign, had he actually lived. Whatever the extent of Crusoe's reading during this period, he fails to mention it. Once on his island he appears to read only Scripture. While there, time stops for him, and he, like Rip Van Winkle, eventually wakes to a new world and a new economy. In this respect trial by ordeal makes a certain amount of sense, since Crusoe knows the past or has only it to fall back on; whereas trial by rational means, which becomes prominent in various disciplines after the Restoration, does not and must therefore be approached with cautious reluctance.

Even so, trial by ordeal has a curious, almost modern twist for Crusoe in that the evidence he assembles about his first year on the island—the longest year if measured by the pages he apportions it—invites us to swim through its murky waters in search of a bottom. Crusoe obviously does the same thing, as he stacks evidence upon evidence in order to grade it and eventually to come to terms with the first year. Still, he is not bothered in the end by rational method. His design is not unlike Glanvill's in this respect or the many others who wrestled with bodies of evidence that competed against the moral evidence of Scripture. Although the moral certainty Crusoe assigns his evidence satisfies his needs as an interpreter and his wants as man of property, it strikes us as not only too determined but also too predetermining when set against an otherwise suspect body of evidence.

The axis of Crusoe's certainty, if not the still point in his journey as a pilgrim, is his conversion experience, which his feverish dream of 28 June 1660 occasions. Only after it does he find the courage and confidence to explore the interior reaches of the island. So armed, Crusoe begins once again to indulge his "wandring Inclination," but this time, rather than finding himself in deeper trouble with a stern father, the pilgrim lights upon a theater of nature. After a detailed inventory of nature's bounty, likened by him to "a planted Garden" (99), Crusoe abandons direct religious allusion in his next breath as he descends into "that delicious Vale, surveying it with a secret Kind of Pleasure, . . . to think that this was all my own, that I was King and Lord of all this Country indefeasibly, and had a Right of Possession; and if I could convey it, I might have it in Inheritance, as compleatly as any Lord of a Mannor in *England*" (100). This discovery happens almost concurrently with the failure of his ink and, hence, marks the formal dissolution of his Journal in a way that his conversion does not. As Richard Braverman has pointed out, the proprietary sentiments Crusoe expresses, in light of his family circumstances, align him with the political theories of James Tyrrell and John Locke, both of whom "concluded that the son possessed a political will, expressed through property."[50] Unwittingly, therefore, property draws Crusoe into the world he has left behind and even imparts to him an abstracted political identity, despite his otherwise apolitical nature.

Once Crusoe cultivates this proprietary sense, the nature of his evidence shifts. No longer does it remain an overwrought and painfully detailed exercise in repetition, so out of character with the methodical and economy-minded individual we think we know. Narrative costiveness that once clogged his passage suddenly breaks up, and in the course of the next fifty pages—roughly the same quantity used to describe the first year—the novel rapidly accelerates through the next fourteen, at which point, during his fifteenth year—and precisely midway through the story—Crusoe spots the footprint. And while his awakened proprietary consciousness may rouse a sleeping and distant grievance that a third son in line to inherit a career, not an estate, has against his father, it serves the more immediate purpose of arming Crusoe's vision so that he does not have to second-guess himself. Without this proprietary sense, as we have seen, he is simply overwhelmed by the demands of the evidence and the uncertainty it engenders. Once property is settled, evidence becomes ordered, secure, and proprietary—as certain for Crusoe as an inheritance duly transmitted. Property, in this regard, settles the evidence needed for its support, as Crusoe himself moves beyond his "Jewish" phase as a wanderer, through his "primitive" stage, prior to conversion, as a scavenger and hunter, to his enlightened state as a farmer, mechanic, and domesticator of animals. With this progress, he has advanced his economy to the brink of commercialization.

Wants, Testimony, and the Reach of Suspense

The next phase of his economic growth takes him beyond need to want and, through an extended and a strategically repetitive history, to the establishment of a "quasi-political" kingdom. Although the nature of evidence changes for Crusoe during these years, it becomes, if anything, even more intensely proprietary, as the stakes of possession increase in significant ways. Between the acquisition of property and the footprint, Crusoe undertakes virtually all of his mechanical exercises, while remaining vocally pious toward his heavenly father and a reader of Scripture. When he discovers that the footprint does not match his own, he fleetingly entertains thoughts of destroying his property, as his sense of trial by ordeal becomes acute. "The first Thing I propos'd to my self, was, to throw down my Enclosures, and turn all my tame Cattle wild into the Woods, that the Enemy might not find them; . . . Then to the simple Thing of Digging up my two Corn Fields . . . then to demolish my Bower, and Tent, that [the trespassers] might not see any Vestiges of Habitation" (159). But, we note, empirical evidence provokes this irrational reaction: that is, Crusoe must measure his foot size against the print before fantasizing destruction. His reflections upon only first seeing the print cause him to imagine that others will consume him and, if not that, "find [his] Enclosure, destroy all [his] Corn, carry away all [his] Flock of tame Goats" such that he "should perish at last for meer Want" (155). "Rational" evidence, in other words, becomes a force he turns savagely against himself—until, that is, strength of belief, now rooted and firmly fixed in property, returns to save him from this destructive course. Were it not so, there can be almost no doubt that Crusoe would begin again to compound the evidence, as he does during the first year and as his twice observing the evidence of the footprint intimates.

With his property and belief secure, Crusoe enjoys as much comfort as he possibly can, while knowing that others do exist and at times violate his territorial domain. Years later, when the Spanish vessel founders off his shore, a curious test unfolds that evinces the stability and certainty Crusoe retains about the evidence of his life. History in effect repeats itself—not for the pilgrim, but for the theatrical spectator. In the short term, and for all intents and purposes, he is again the sole survivor of a wreck. This time, however, mere survival does not spark his reaction to events. Instead, wants that have expanded beyond the compass of the island set him off, as they might, since fixed property has become contingent for him because of the unequivocal evidence of cannibalism. His mind thus gravitates to moveable property. From the second wreck he notices the fineness and features of the goods he recovers—silver-tipped bottles, white linen handkerchiefs, colored neckcloths; he pines for a good pair of English shoes, and, in the process, laments the inadequacy of life without a viable marketplace, so unlike his responses to the shipwreck of some two decades before. When he confesses his original sin, the prodigal wants to return not to England but to another place of origin, Brazil, where he imagines his property and commercial enterprise have grown proportionately with time, to the tune of, at minimum, "an hundred thousand *Moydors*" (193). During this period of repetition and reenactment, he dreams again, but the evidence of the second dream, in which he wishes for a servant, avoids the interpretive rigmarole of the first with its apocalyptic figure about to pass judgment. As the wants of his dream-wish fulfill themselves in reality, Crusoe has before him physical evidence of property in a person—his servant/slave, Friday—the consumer of human flesh brought to governance.

Evidence in the final third of the novel proves to be fairly abstract and often fantastical, but this development turns out to be incidental to a Crusoe whose sense of mastery and control over his property, though under siege from various quarters, is never in doubt.[51] It is also at this stage of the novel that he demonstrates a political nature. According to Braverman, these "final adventures illustrate the origin of civil society, lately grown out of the state of nature."[52] What is remarkable in the process is the degree to which moral evidence, in the face of this emerging political kingdom, is divided off and treated as almost a perfectly discrete matter. I refer to the evidence of a Christian God with which Crusoe attempts to persuade Friday and ensure his docility. The problem he faces is that no amount of simple evidence, the sort of which can be culled from a catechism ("who was his Father," 216), or narrative evidence from Scripture can check Friday's disquieting questions, as the native must first learn the intimidating value of figurative language in the manner of those tribal Jews who labored under the old dispensation. Out of frustration, Crusoe confides that "nothing but divine Revelation can form the Knowledge of *Jesus Christ*" (219). Only out of our hearing, moreover, and in the absence of any documentation, do we learn that "the Savage was now a good Christian, a much better than I" (220). Perhaps as a result of this division, both the incidence and meaningful references to God fall off sharply in the final third of the novel.

While ordeal is not insignificant in this portion of the story, its seriousness in the face of evidence of another kind makes it the stuff of spectacle, theatrical display, and, in the end, a joke. The instrumentality of Crusoe's departure from the island is that English mutineers, who, we assume, are on a trading mission, must first come ashore and submit—an incident that simply expands the proportions of Friday's submission. This process is dramatically charged and filled with twists and turns of one sort or another such that this final island ordeal proves a fitting conclusion to Crusoe's years of isolation. Still, it is not the action as such that matters most during this climax, but the manner in which

Crusoe presents the evidence of deliverance. Like a good opposition attorney, he must anticipate motivations and counter strategic posturing—in this case, those of the mutineer parties as they come ashore. He does so quite successfully, though not without remarking how those prisoners he rescues, including the Captain, wonder whether they are "*talking to God, or Man!*" (254) and not without a passing recollection about how their plight flashes "the first Time when [he] came on Shore" (252). In their eyes, Crusoe serves as "Deliverer" or is cast as a savior often enough that the message is obvious.

At the same time he passes through many other "fictional" roles, first as "a *Spectre-like* Figure," a Prospero-like director of action, a "*Generalissimo*," the Governor's representative, a disembodied voice of authority, and, once investiture is complete, the Governor himself, whose role is to pass judgment and to secure the property of the island as a commercial-based colony, so ordained by Crusoe. However we read this tableau, Crusoe sees it as evidence required for the dissolution of suspense. Once the mutineers have been secured, Crusoe himself figures the English Captain as his deliverer. He says, "I told him, I look upon him as a Man sent from Heaven to deliver me, and that the whole Transaction seemed to be a Chain of Wonders; that such things as these were the *Testimonies* we had of a secret Hand of Providence governing the World, and an *Evidence*, that the Eyes of an infinite Power could search into the remotest Corner of the World, and send Help to the Miserable whenever he pleased" (273; my emphasis). Although the evidence could easily support other testimony, the testimony that matters is Crusoe's alone: he exchanges one form of exegetical evidence for another, Savior = Captain. While we dispute his reading of events, what we lack in this instance, as we do not for the first year, is the visible proof of contradiction. Needless to say, once the mutineers have been defeated, the property of the island attains its highest level of security as Crusoe's colony.

After collecting the profits from his various enterprises, most notably the Brazilian plantation—no doubt moral evidence of Crusoe's justification—he faces one final ordeal, this time in his land passage across the Pyrenees into France. In his crossing he encounters wolves and bears. These creatures have an iconographic function and, as J. Paul Hunter comments, "[t]he episode of the wolves [in particular], like the final dramatic episode in pilgrim literature, demonstrates that man is not really 'delivered' until he is safe at his final destination, a point contemporary theologians stressed tirelessly."[53] Whereas the wolves are to be taken seriously, as Crusoe himself does, calling them "hellish Creatures" (299) and remarking, "I was never so sensible of Danger in my Life," (302), these carnivores are without Scriptural precedent, which is not the case for bears. The most relevant of these is from Amos 5.18–19, in which he forecasts the coming of the Messiah as a day of "darkness, and not light, As if a man did flee from a lion, and a bear met him."

The problem with the bear is that it serves as an interlude, a spectacle, even a joke in an otherwise dangerous situation, which, to recall Paulson, counters the sober-mindedness of the teleological pilgrim. Positioned between two wolf incidents, the bear episode suspends pilgrimage for the sake of sport. Friday tricks the bear up a tree, provoking laughter from the party out of harm's way below, and eventually dispatches the animal. The crux of this passage is not the reportage of evidence as much as it is the divided function the evidence plays. Under perilous circumstances, Crusoe uses the evidence of his travels to enact a divided function, as if, without realizing it himself, he is again both pilgrim and a player in his theater. We in turn are presented the evidence but are more apt to scratch our heads about its import, while wondering what possible function this episode has in the narrative as a whole. When we view it from the pilgrim's standpoint, wolves lack Scriptural authority, but when we turn to the bear, an animal with a Scriptural history, it serves as a theatrical device. Underwriting this exegesis, of course, is the ambivalence it expresses about consumption.

At a more impressionable age Crusoe might have worried over this presentation of evidence, but, some thirty years beyond his first wobbly steps on island sand, he believes in his character and its purpose and thus no longer responds as he once did. John P. Zomchick has proposed that ordeal forces Crusoe to realize his "own judicial subjectivity," which "leads ultimately to a stable sense of self. . . . Crusoe tells the story of laws that direct free and intelligent agents to their proper interests."[54] But the acquisition of a stable character requires Crusoe to treat evidence in a ruthlessly uniform and tenaciously incomplete manner. The *parti pris* and interested designs behind his efforts, in turn, cast a shadow over his reading of character. Thus the pious disciple, viewed through eyes not his, becomes the suspended character, because Crusoe's own written testimony lends itself to more points of view than his alone—his self-interests also become ours. *Farther Adventures*, the next volume, narrates how Crusoe loses his hold even on proprietary evidence, as the world expands before him; while *Serious Reflections*, which contracts into a world of urban retirement, details how his attempt at recovering this evidence brings further isolation upon him. These subsequent volumes in fact go a long way in widening the cracks in his judicial subjectivity even further, if for no other reason than the evidence out of which he fashions that "subjectivity" no longer can indulge itself in a world of bound space, simple need, or imagined want. As someone who feels compelled to look back to rehash and redo the past and origins, Crusoe writes to defy suspense, but his inclinations and personal needs make him only more susceptible to its long reach.

Life's Journey: Divided and Divided Again

Everett Zimmerman has characterized *Farther Adventures* as an "obsession without form," a narrative method that "reflects Defoe's recognition of disharmonies in the earlier work."[55] Whether Defoe actually recognized what he was doing is doubtful, but the characterization itself is eminently fair to the experiences of commercial venturing and capitalization recorded in the sequel, as well as to the state of suspense that underwrites it. James Maddox adds that "Crusoe's farther adventures have not extended his earlier triumphs; they have undermined them."[56] Together both comments indicate that the sense of design and purpose Crusoe relies upon in his first volume to order commercial instincts disappears with the second; hence the "suspense" of the novel. But it is not just the novel that is suspended, it is also his character, which must plod on without a regulatory system in place to define it. Crusoe is lost in the world at large—indeed, he can barely explain why he goes back into it in the first place, as if driven by needs and wants that he dare not confront. Faced with this semantic void, a world not amenable to the recitation of chapter and verse, he begins in earnest to organize his life around commercial venturing. But without providentialism or typology to bind it together, *Farther Adventures* reads like a belabored series of "and thens," because the familiar Crusoe, the Crusoe in control, has been left in and circumscribed by volume 1, an "origin" that assures nothing.

Crusoe's uncontrollable obsession arises early in the sequel. From the conclusion of volume 1, we are aware that he marries. Inexplicably, his wife manages what Crusoe's father could not, which is to keep this son of a Bremen-born merchant homebound for an interval of time. But on his Bedford farm he cannot put aside memories of life upon the island. In a manner reminiscent of the feverish dream he had that brought him to divine knowledge, Crusoe reports that he dreams all night and imagines all day about returning to the place he so eagerly left several years before. Yet this state of mind is one that we cannot attribute to a pathogen, the kind that would have produced an ague. He goes on to talk about "vapours, sick minds, and wandering fancies," only to observe "that my imagination worked up to such a height, and brought me into such excess of vapours . . . that I actually supposed myself oftentimes upon the spot."[57]

The only earlier occasion when Crusoe experienced such torment and mental instability occurred when he stumbled across the footprint. At the time he relates how fear "deprives [men] of the Use of those Means which Reason offers for their Relief," which he personalizes: "the Apprehensions which had so over-run my Mind were fresh upon me, and my Head was full of Vapours."[58] By any standard, the footprint is circumstantial evidence, there to be measured, speculated about, and rendered meaningful by the consciousness that attaches importance to it.[59] For Crusoe it is a diabolical sign as long as he forgets Providence; upon his return to God the print can be put in its place, one link among many in a chain of evidence. Bedford has similar circumstantial value as evidence. Indeed for a mind prone to retrospection as Crusoe's is, his settled life as a farmer in his native country is analogous, in purpose and years spent, to his time in Brazil where he created and settled a way of life, as it seems, for the leaving. In fact, when his wife dies, freeing him at last to depart England again, Crusoe remarks: "When she was gone the world looked awkwardly round me, I was as much a stranger in it in my thoughts as I was in the Brazils" (7). From the standpoint of spiritual progress and history, the analogy does not bode well for Crusoe because, in mirroring his earlier history, it too precedes "conversion." But by the time his nephew offers to take him back to his island and then on to the Eastern world, the second of which he says he will not do, Crusoe now believes "that it would be a kind of resisting Providence, if I should attempt to stay at home" (11). Although the evidence for leaving remains the same, its meaning changes: what we would read as a simple coincidence becomes, for Crusoe, a manifestation of divine purpose. Presumably, he and we are to forget about vapors and the unbalanced mind.

Returning to his island, however, does nothing to quiet Crusoe's demons because the evidentiary makeup of the place has changed. No longer a deserted island, it is, in his eyes, grown into "a little city in a wood" (127), which he is intent upon furnishing with commercial needs and wants. Before crossing the Atlantic he lades his nephew's ship with both useful and pleasurable commodities—those things for which he expressed great want at the time of the Spanish shipwreck in volume 1—as well as a group of specialized laborers—including a tailor, a smith, and a couple of carpenters—to ensure that material needs and wants are met. Crusoe even anticipates the advent of a money economy in his little city, an urban outpost of divided property, when he imagines women denied sanctified marriages left "friendless and moneyless" (144). Crusoe best signals this altered state of his character and his now distant attitude toward the evidence when he disembarks from his nephew's ship. "I shall no longer trouble the story with a relation in the first person, which will put me to the expense of ten thousand Said I's, and Said he's . . . but I shall collect the facts historically as near as I can gather them out of my memory from what they related to me" (40). This kind of self-consciousness never afflicts Crusoe in volume 1, where incidents occur not a few years before their writing, but decades; "I" dots every page; and commercial civilization, by dint of necessity, is only a dream. But with *Farther Adventures* and Crusoe's return to one of his starting points, origins begin to slip from his grasp as the evidence all too painfully documents.

Crusoe's detachment from and loss of purposeful commitment to his version of the evidence are all the more pronounced when the French priest expresses his concern to him about the lack of sanctified marriages and religious instruction among the pagan islanders. Within the past decade he suffered no such lapses when Friday first came to him, but then he did not live under a commercial economy. Now, since he is "bound to the East Indies" (140) and intuits that in an advanced economy preaching the Gospel "fall[s] into the way of [the priest's] profession" (141), Crusoe gladly delegates spiritual ministerings to him. In this way he fulfills the promise of Locke's final chapter in *An Essay*, one that follows on the heels "Of Probability," "Of the Division of the Sciences," in which the philosopher announces in global terms the separation of the "intellectual world" into categories "distinct one from another": natural philosophy, ethics, and semiotics.[60] With his mind turned inexplicably to an adventure that he himself fails to understand, Crusoe unwittingly discloses a profound alteration in his character through his handling of ethics and semiotics and, as a consequence, he can no longer view the evidence before him as he once did.

By the time he leaves the island, the altered perspective and accompanying disorientation that beset his character influence the divided way in which he would have us see the facts most central to his life; history, in effect, becomes a series of partitions. "I have now done with my island," he notes, "and all manner of discourse about it; and whoever reads the rest of my memorandums, would do well to turn his thoughts entirely from it" (197). After his departure, even his little city fails, which not even "doing for [the colonists] in a kind of haughty majestic way, like an old patriarchal monarch" could prevent. As Crusoe confesses, he "had no authority or power to act or command one way or other, further than voluntary consent moved them to comply" (198). This characterization, it should be said, is pure fantasy and does not begin to comport with the facts of his second coming to the island. But it is a revealing fantasy because, whether he sees himself as a Hebrew patriarch or some Filmerian monarch, it is consensual government that renders him impotent.[61]

In leaving one "origin" behind, he sails to another, this time Brazil, where he is unwelcome and even prohibited from disembarking from his nephew's vessel. As he journeys next to the East, the fragmented and episodic nature of his travels, while numbing to readers, serves as the most powerful evidence we have that Crusoe has ranged far beyond his element. The confusing array of evidence that he samples in these alien reaches simply exceeds the controlling mechanism that he could once summon to order an essentially barren and unpeopled island. Hardly an Alexander, but certainly with no worlds to conquer, he trades. At best he reacts to what he sees, as for example in his response to the great Chinese empire. "It seemed strange to me when I came home, and heard our people say such fine things of the power, riches, glory, magnificence, and trade of the Chinese, because I saw and knew that they were a contemptible herd or crowd of ignorant, sordid slaves, subjected to a government qualified only to rule such a people" (273–74). The problem is that from the evidence we see and hear at this point Crusoe's character has degenerated from pilgrim to commercial profiteer. The worth of these travels is the "sale for our goods, as well those of China, as . . . of Siberia," which Crusoe computes down to the penny: "3475*l*. 17*s*. 3*d*" (342). What is missing is the moral evidence of reward, of the Job figure who reaps the dividends of a Brazilian plantation.

Only in *Serious Reflections* do we learn the breadth of Crusoe's reaction to his Eastern travels and appreciate the extent to which an omitted proprietary evidence has determined narrative practice. There, in a burst of spectacular theatrics, he advocates a worldwide Christian jihad, obviously a holy war he could not undertake *solus ipse*. "I am not much of the opinion, indeed, that religion should be planted by the sword; but as the Christian princes of Europe, however few in number, are yet so superior to all the rest of the world in martial experience and the art of war, nothing is more certain than that, if they could unite their interest, they are able to beat paganism out of the world."[62] Despite the blood that would be spilled in such a crusade, Crusoe imagines it "as far as in [Christian princes] lies, a bloodless conquest" (218), because what he encourages depends not on facts, but on the method he establishes in volume 3, allegory: "I propose a war not with men, but with the devil" (220). Accordingly, flesh incarnate cannot be itself, but must embody something other than itself. No statement better explains the manner by which Crusoe deciphers his own character to avoid the semantic uncertainties of suspense.

Crusoe's savage reverie and revelation constitute the final section of his *Serious Reflections*. To it, in a significant juxtaposition, he appends "A Vision of the Angelic World." This flight of fancy effectively undoes the rational being Crusoe tries to represent to us.[63] He presents what he regards as "undeniable" signs—evidences—of the spiritual realm, including "Dreams, Voices, Noises, Impulses, Hints, Apprehensions, Involuntary sadness &c." (249); and prefaces this enumeration with the following instruction: "we are all able to bring *evidence* of the existence of the devil from our own frailties, as we are to bring *evidence* of the existence of God from the faculties of our souls, and from the contexture of our bodies" (247; my emphasis). But if this is the case, such moral evidence is more akin to what David Hume cites when he talks about the need to consider the "motives, temper, and situation" of men whose interests are complex and subject to interpretation.

The simple evidence that undergirds *Serious Reflections* and that we should not forget is that Crusoe is now the ancient mariner returned to his native island. He resides in "London, where [he is] writing this" (4) and which he has visited before, more recently in 1692, just prior to crossing the Atlantic with his nephew. At the time he reports in *Farther Adventures*, "I had no relish to the place," but in due course the great commercial center becomes his home.[64] Although presumably still a father, he does not refer again to his children in *Serious Reflections*, though he does go out of his way to lecture parents, in the name of "honesty," that they owe their offspring "the debt of instruction, the debt of government, the debt of example" (62). How he is capable of any of these things in light of the fact that he has not seen his own children in over ten years is a matter that escapes explanation. But the division between thought and deed runs throughout *Serious Reflections*. It is an effort singularly devoid of any visible evidence and is written by a man who styles himself as a person having "grown old in affliction, borne down by calumny and reproach" (225). Later, in "A Vision," when he refers to his "retirement" on the island, he confesses to having had an "abundance of strange notions of my seeing apparitions there," particularly "by moonshine" (241).[65] One cannot but wonder whether he is similarly affected now that he has retired from his active life to write memoirs that savage readers and booksellers pounce on in broad daylight to the utter consternation of their author—one, especially, who believes himself faithful to the evidences of life. What Crusoe discovers is that, although he can generally control his narrative accounting, he cannot control the marketplace of ideas that enterprising readers give vent to. Indeed, in his character he gives vent to the contemporary problem of confused origins and states of unknowing, which ought to have helped him in his own passage. "There will come an age when the minds of men shall be more flexible, when the prejudices of their fathers shall have no place . . . that our children may rise up in judgment against their fathers, and one generation be edified by the same teaching which another generation had despised" (Crusoe's Preface to *Serious Reflec-*

tions, xiii). That generation had, in effect, already come, and the work of commercialization had made it possible.

Crusoe suffers, then, from the evidence of modern commercial life, which his efforts as a writer in early eighteenth-century England have hastened. In some mysterious way we suspect that the world he has come home to explains, in the end, the division we see in volumes 2 and 3 of his life-history. Which is to say that once Crusoe departs Brazil a second time and heads toward the Eastern world, he ventures into the alien, strange, and forbidden that his character can never control—in the same way he finds modern English life alien, strange, forbidding, and uncontrollable. In it, as he learns, property is never entirely secure. Midway during his three-volume odyssey, at the half-way point in *Farther Adventures*, the representation of his life becomes largely a compilation of facts, a series of suspended evidences, devoid of the interpretive strategies that make them comprehensible to Crusoe.[66] This void is one he attempts to fill with *Serious Reflections*, not by supplying evidence, but by issuing a volley of *obiter dicta* and by retiring into the complexities and unfathomed mysteries of himself. At his earliest stage, in *Surprizing Adventures*, although the evidences of life prove confusing to Crusoe when he first arrives on his island, his world then exists in miniature, remains largely uncontested, and is easily vested as property.

While a belief in the sole ownership of evidence might indict us all, once evidence itself is transmitted into the public domain it must meet standards of scrutiny. We should not be at all surprised to find, therefore, that in Defoe's century new demands were placed upon evidence of all sorts—the value of hearsay, the legitimacy of depositions, and the reliability of confessions, all in the name of not unduly prejudicing those who sit in judgment.[67] The reason was quite simple: certainty and truth became the focus of contest and competition. Through his presentation of the evidence, Crusoe invokes a past that no longer exists and a character that cannot withstand scrutiny. By the end, he becomes what he has been all along: the body invisible, a disembodied voice of remarkable self-interests that cries in a wilderness into which its master has fled. The differences between fact and fiction, past and present, as well as providential teleologies and personal histories translate Crusoe's character into a realm of representation that only suspense could comprehend. At the far end of this journey waits Roxana whose final disappearance is predicated upon circumstances that drive her to disavow her own flesh and blood.

5

Domestic Exchange: Richardson versus Fielding

Even before we get to the text of *Pamela* (1741/40), we find ourselves bombarded with advertising endorsements for the product to follow. Although the polite term for this material is probably *testamonium humanum*, the letters of Jean Baptiste de Freval, William Webster, and Aaron Hill underscore the significance of Richardson's novel in both a literary and economic context. De Freval writes to the editor of *Pamela* that "thou mayst give an Example of Purity to the Writers of a neighbouring Nation; which now shall have an Opportunity to receive *English* Bullion in Exchange for its own Dross."[1] Webster likewise notes that "a Piece of this Kind is much wanted in the World, which is but too much, as well as too early debauched by pernicious *Novels*," a sentiment that Aaron Hill draws upon in his lengthy preface to the second edition: "who could have dreamt, he should find, under the modest Disguise of a *Novel*, all the *Soul* of Religion" (8, 9). How Richardson's novel outfits itself for public consumption and the needs and wants it satisfies in doing so, in other words, become critical functions inseparable from the text of the narrative itself, matters that Hill goes on to elaborate at considerable length.

Fielding apparently could not rely upon this sort of *testamonia*, so he created his own promotional blurb to advertise the originality of his narrative: "having thus distinguished *Joseph Andrews* from the Productions of Romance Writers on the one hand, and Burlesque Writers on the other, and given some few very short Hints . . . of this Species of writing, which I have affirmed to be hitherto unattempted in our Language."[2] The truth or falsity of this claim is immaterial; only the selling point of originality matters. What it does is to introduce an edgy form of competition to the genre and to fix the novel in its domestic marketplace. The fact that this consciousness assumes explicit forms throughout *Joseph Andrews* is indicative of just how dominant a market sensibility had become in the production of the genre, but the role of the market serves other less apparent functions as well. Although one would scarcely characterize the relationship between Richardson and

Fielding as a partnership, it does make sense from an institutional standpoint to propose, as Michael McKeon has done, that their efforts yielded "a form sufficient for the joint inquiry into analogous epistemological and social problems."[3] I would only add as both problems came to be defined through the marketplace and the commercial narrative.

About this market sensibility Colin Campbell has noted, "what separates the traditional consumer from his modern counter-part is his view that [all things] novel [are] to be feared, if not actually regarded as the embodiment of evil."[4] The equally new moral response that emerged from novelty, according to Campbell, developed, as he puts it, from an "imaginative hedonism," which separated the ideal from the real: "the more the hedonistic impulse causes images to be idealized, the greater the discrepancy becomes between these and the real-self."[5] Although he does not refer this matter to the Richardson-Fielding novel, it is as if Campbell has distilled the essence of how those two writers debated and articulated the genre. That is, both traded in the imperfections of realism—its sublimations and contradictions—while promoting an ideal behavior tantamount to moral perfection. The setting of this paradox is a culture of apparent luxury and material indulgence, but its vehicle is character, which somehow is supposed to defy the laws of material gravity. As Campbell goes on to explain, "the concept of character"— how one is perceived, how one perceives oneself—is the binding agent and moral force of a "hedonistic" culture. "It is not suggested here," he comments, "that it is people's direct desire to 'do the good thing' which is most affected by changes in conceptions of the good, the true and the beautiful, so much as the indirect effect exerted via the need for character confirmation. It is the need people have to be convinced that they are good which is crucial."[6]

Under these terms, the power to make this persuasion is subject to a range of failures, but it is exactly this work that Richardson and Fielding undertook as they attempted, like Defoe, to govern the character that functions amid the dilemmas and disjunctions of consumer capitalism. That they willingly return this character to its familiar domestic settings gives it a new stage on which to sport but adds only a little in terms of its progress. Their differences in approach and technique aside, Richardson and Fielding produce remarkably similar responses to the problem of character, which, as I hope to demonstrate, underscores the role of the commercial economy in dis-figuring simple identities via suspense.

A Divided Pamela

That "People have to be convinced . . . they are good," as Campbell remarks, isolates not just a consciousness that is acutely relevant to the post-Mandevillean English economy but also is at the heart of the debate between Richardson and Fielding. Throughout especially the first half of the eighteenth century, categorical forms of "goodness" often surfaced as something superadded to economic theorizing to neutralize the untoward effects of commercial and material seeking. Thus, benevolence and sentiment were sometimes cited as the agents that carried out this neutralizing function; in the process, they demonstrate just one of the ways in which the "ideal" was employed to transform the "reality" of exchange and interest.[7] Nancy Armstrong assigns a similar purpose to those novelists who, "in shaping an ideal woman out of the stuff of novels, . . . did not appear to be assaulting the dominant culture so much as rescuing both the female and the domestic life she superintended from their fate at the hands of degenerate authors."[8] Appearance is everything here because Armstrong subsequently goes on to urge that, "by representing relationships within the traditional country house as a struggle between competing interest groups, Richardson challenged the dominant cultural ideal."[9] In effect, the ideal woman brings down the other ideal embodied in the aristocracy.

There is more to this exchange, however, than Richardson's incorporation of the prescriptive or "nonaesthetic" features of the conduct book into fiction, though Armstrong's argument is both compelling and persuasive. Among other things, it demonstrates the importance of governance in character newly conceived and executed, as well as the departure this form of characterization makes from its more typical representations in earlier narratives. Still, Pamela's conformity to conduct-book codes alone do not make her character interesting; it is her interest in preserving her self-made representation, her mindfulness of this role, that embellishes her character as a suspended form. In addition, although *Pamela* departs from romance, it does not leave it entirely behind—even the sequel engages romance elements. Nor should we be overly hasty in shunting Pamela off into an economy that is no economy, the domain of "domestic woman," while according B. the prerogatives of "economic man."[10] After all, trade is a woman to be courted, says Coke, and credit in Defoe's hands is Lady Credit. *Doux commerce*, for that matter, has so much "woman" in it that the moralist of sinewy virtue feared the feminization of culture under it. Pamela's influence is enough, we recall, to soften B. and to redirect him from active forms of masculinity, with dueling as one obvious example. As Richardson recognized, *femina economica* had to be paired with *homo economicus*. But while a newly conceived character and a refashioned genre began with some sense of the demands that the economy placed upon both, governing even one was a formidable affair. In many ways *Pamela* struggles with this responsibility, competing not only against itself but also against the very system of governance it employs to exact moral coherence.

Richardson's difficulties in finding this coherence were mirrored in his need to control response to his work, as well as his nearly obsessive practice of revision. Why, in this light, he produced a sequel to *Pamela* is a bit baffling, except for the obvious reason that he wanted to undo the spurious sequel that had appeared from the pen of John Kelly. Forced composition does not necessarily produce the most inspired works, which may account for the reason why the sequel has had fewer readers. Yet, like *Farther Adventures* and *Serious Reflections*, it opens Pamela up to circumstances that she cannot so easily control. That is, part 2 makes Pamela more vulnerable, more a character studied than enjoyed, because so much of the narrative suspense that propelled action in part 1 gets left behind. The result is a more extensive paper trail and, in a curious way, a narrative commentary on the fruits of the mésalliance. Events, as we discover, do not gratify Pamela so much as they test her mettle.[11]

In one of the extended panels of the sequel, Pamela finds herself distanced from the gates of her country estates and, through the inexorable logic of a needs/wants culture, winds up in London where she picks her way through a smorgasbord of "high-life." With her descent into the great metropolis readers also begin to perk up, though perhaps for the wrong reasons, as Pamela's routines of domesticity fairly quickly are troubled by a whiff of infidelity. Although Pamela does not welcome this form of narrative suspense, she seems if not relieved, then stimulated by it, as we are too.

In broad generic terms, the sequel is all-London in many ways, diverse in its array and discursive in its practice, a loose network of fragmented parts that is held together by virtue of Pamela's character but that unto itself does not especially cohere. There is movement without action and narrative without plot; whatever coherence we sense borrows from the youthful Pamela, whose skills at sublimation and pleasure denied grow with age into a mature state of moral isolation—the body perfectly sublimated. That she continues on to her grave only intensifies the suspense of her suspended character, just as Richardson, in his dogged fashion, is still pleading the case of the curiously allegorical character to the very end.

The settled Pamela, as we discover, must suffer through a series of humblings and mortifications—the flare-up over breast feeding, the threat of polygamy, and the appearance of an affair between B. and the Countess Dowager of _____ , among others—that, in narrative terms, lead to what Terry Castle has generously called "the pleasure of repetition"—and Freud a compulsion—a surprising re-creation of the dangerous fantasy that the first part enacts.[12] It is certainly true that the sequel replays Pamela's awkward relationship with her inherited social sphere, but it does so with a twist. Later in the novel, after breast feeding, polygamy, and the Countess Dowager have receded and no longer bind her to her husband, B. himself effectively disappears from the last quarter of volume 4, supplanted in the nest by John Locke, his *Some Thoughts concerning Education* (1693), and Pamela's extensive commentary on it. Although she initially shrinks at the presumption needed to challenge an authority and author whom B. values so highly, she proceeds with gusto and at length. Before actually undertaking the project, however, she senses danger in the criticisms she has to offer, lest she offend B., but circumvents this problem by contriving that she conduct her reflections as a kind of one-sided correspondence, since she has not shown him anything "for a good while." Thus he proposes: "suppose me at a Distance from you, cannot you give me your Remarks in the same manner, as if you were writing Lady *Davers*, or to Miss *Darnford*?"[13]

It does not require a great deal of imagination to see that Locke serves as both a paper husband and father in her commentary, a figure worthy of respect but subject to challenge as occasion and circumstances warrant. The note is a familiar one in Pamela's life, but it tells us something enduring about her: all her writing is stippled with reticence and indirection, telling and hiding simultaneously. The truth, for Pamela, is never as it is written, nor could it ever be, as I will demonstrate in following sections. But these facets of her character are not the sort of thing she can admit to consciousness a là Richardson himself. The other side of this coin is the Pamela who guards her precedent scrupulously and with clear interests. Thus she looks through a keyhole to watch her servant Polly frisking with Mr. H., a "foolish Gentleman! — [who takes] Liberties with *Polly*, that neither became him to offer, nor, more foolish Girl! her to suffer" (3:362).[14] H. might just as well be B. Pamela looks in effect at herself but, as an established woman, wants to monopolize the character she gave vent to and, accordingly, remains on the qui vive to ensure that it is neither exchanged nor debased. When she first arrives in London, she is again painfully aware of eyes looking upon her, hoping that her novelty will soon wear off, which is a reaction that deviates from the one she records when, shortly after her marriage, she attends church in her Bedfordshire parish. Indeed, when faced with a living and uncontrollable competitor, the Countess Dowager, she even indicates a willingness to surrender her place to the noble woman by removing herself to her parents in Kent, where she knows she can preserve her virtue. Here the lessons of indignity resonate but also recall an earlier circumstance when, liberated from the Lincolnshire estate, she travels half-heartedly toward her parents until her heart and B.'s letter reveal the impossibility of that journey.

London itself does not swathe Pamela; it exposes her, telling us more about her character than what the insulated world of familiar estates can only hint at. As a consumer of contemporary culture, Pamela is often at a loss, generally for some deficiency she sees in it, to participate. Her reflections on opera are a case in point. While the pleasure of this experience for her is at first undeniable, she guards against this indulgence by unwrapping the package to find an empty box. "The Scenery is fine; The Company splendid and genteel; The Musick charming for the Time;—The Actions not extraordinary; The Language unintelligible; and, for all these Reasons—The Instruction none at all" (4:90). The problem is that Pamela knows no Italian, which will have a pivotal role to play shortly when she cannot understand the Italian that the Countess Dowager speaks to B. at the masquerade. Once she leaves the opera behind, she turns next to the masquerade and, in words either prescient or prejudiced, she anticipates that this "Diversion or Amusement . . . [is one that she] shall like still less" (4:91).

Although Pamela is provoked by a range of experiences, she tends to find those beyond her control the most dangerous. Thus she manifests an almost obsessive need to peel away and pare back until she can reveal her moral self working amid diversions, amusements, or other acts of consumption. That she must avoid the appearance of indulgence is, in part, owing to the role imposed upon her by her correspondents but, on the more personal level, indicates her unwillingness to disclose any sign of want. We find this same pattern affecting the novel clear to its end. There, when Pamela addresses her own students, she recurs to her education under Lady B. who limited Pamela's reading of romances and novels. These narratives—at least the ones that she did read—gave her "no great Pleasure," as she reports, "for either they dealt so much in the *Marvellous* and *Improbable*, or were so unnaturally *inflaming* to the *Passions*, that hardly any of them but seem'd calculated to *fire* the *Imagination*, rather than to *inform* the *Judgment*" (4:426). In the next twenty lines or so she details the features of plot that characterize these narratives. From the length of her description, we may wonder just how long her summary would have been had she actually taken "great pleasure" in what she read. As if to underscore her lesson, she goes on to tell to Miss Goodwin one of the nursery tales she has composed to illustrate the need females must have in order to be "watchful over . . . their Reputation: 'Tis a tender Flower" (4:442). That the story turns out to be an allegory, with characters that go by the names of Coquetilla, Prudiana, Profusiana, and Prudentia, is not unexpected, but its effect is quite odd, stressing the great distance between allegory and *Pamela*, whose eponym is the missing fourth "P" from the list.[15] Even stranger, perhaps, is that the editor's final epitome only *describes* the fate of individual characters, a new practice that deviates sharply from the final instruction of part 1, where the editor *informs* readers about the moral truths they should derive from the various characters depicted in the novel.

Segregating *Pamela* from romances plays an internal role within the two parts of the novel. B.'s uncle, Sir Jacob Swynford, an opponent of his nephew's marriage, injects this element in part 2 when B. speaks with transport about his wife. Sir Jacob cries, "What is it I hear! What is it I hear! — You talk in the Language of Romance; and from the House-keeper to the Head of the House, you're all stark-staring mad. . . . I'm in an inchanted Castle, that's certain" (3:310). We are not to trust his assessment, though we are to believe Pamela's when she remarks to Miss Goodwin that "what principally distinguishes the Character of the [romance] *Heroine*, is, when she is taught to consider her Father's House an inchanted Castle, and her Lover as the Hero who is to dissolve the Charm, and to set her at Liberty from Confinement" (4:426). It just so happens that in part 1, once B. has read through some of Pamela's secreted papers, he tells her that her narration of events has "such a pretty Air of Romance, . . . in your Plots, and my Plots, that I shall be better directed in what manner to wind up the Catastrophe of the pretty Novel."[16] Here B. acts the role of his uncle, seeing romance in her depiction of captivity. Not long afterwards, however, B., in a hero-like gesture, liberates his prisoner from her confinement, granting her the freedom to return to her parents. She travels only part of the way home. Once she returns narrative suspense abates a bit between Pamela and B., as events follow haltingly, though assuredly, to the altar.

In what remains of the first part and then throughout the second, however, Richardson appears mindful enough of his craft as a "novelist" not to forsake narrative suspense *in toto*. In the process, character continues to develop in complexity because of changing circumstances yet also becomes more fixed in deference to a settled domestic economy. The sequel is not exactly Pamela imprisoned in Lincolnshire, though the comparison is not wholly inappropriate. Her role has changed, though, as has her level of consciousness about her obligations to it. Thus, for example, in explaining her reasons for not being severe with Mrs. Jewkes, Pamela confesses to her correspondents: "would it not have been out of Character in me, and against all Expectation of my high-soul'd . . . Master, if I had not?" (3:71). This example, among many others, demonstrates the self-interested and proprietary features that Pamela assigns her character, as well as her skill in biting her tongue. In this respect all of *Pamela* becomes a series of assumed roles that, once acted upon, infect even the genre itself. Neither romance nor novel, *Pamela* is simultaneously both—a romance to which Richardson makes capital improvements, as well as a novel that pays for this investment.

Although Pamela tries to restrict the ways in which her character and writings are "consumed," as did Richardson, that ideal proved impossible because she lacks the simplicity of Prudiana, Profusiana, and Prudentia. We do not have to look far to appreciate how fruitless such hopes were or to recognize how fraught the commerce of reading had become.[17] The author of *Pamela Censured* (1741), for instance, accused Richardson of communicating "*Sentiments* and *Desires* worse than ROCHESTER can" with "Images which in *too many* Pieces tend only to *inflame* the Mind."[18] Ironically, these particular vices approximate those that Pamela, in her capacity as a teacher, singles out as the inexcusable failings of romances. The problem is that, as both novel and character, "Pamela" is a divided representation, never just one thing without being another. As I want to indicate in the next section, it is because of the split between the wants of her commercial identity and the needs of her moral being that Richardson fails, in the end, to govern her as he had hoped.

Cracked Mirrors, Economic Change, and the Suspended Character

The range of responses that *Pamela* stimulated with its publication testifies to Richardson's inability to control his product. Why this problem should have occurred goes to the heart of character representation in the novel, which is not so much a problem of character management on Richardson's part as it is a function of historical change. Foucault identifies a symptom of this change in the paradigm shift between the classification work of natural scientists of the "Classical" period and subsequent scientific investigators, who drew upon the "internal laws of the organism [as] . . . the object of the natural sciences."[19] To wit, internal markings replaced a system of differential characters, an exchange that bears directly upon *Pamela* and helps explain the curious and extreme response that Richardson's novel received in its own time.[20] On the one hand, the Reverend Slocock recommended it from the pulpit of St. Saviour's, while, on the other, Fielding exposed the true Pamela initially as Shamela—an eager, though wily seductress whose mother lodges at the Fan and Pepper-Box in Drury Lane and whose accomplice, Mrs. Jervis, hopes to establish a bagnio in the vicinity of Queen Street.

Fielding's satiric reduction does no justice to the complexity of Richardson's creation; in fact, it is hell-bent on conserving character in reactionary ways so that all he really accomplishes is the substitution of a lascivious and manipulative character type for a more malleable type, the secular-saint. With that said, however, Fielding's "true representation" of Pamela's character creates its own interest, not because it overtaxes the laws of possibility but because it isolates a strain in Pamela's character that not even Richardson's determined representation could entirely occlude: that is, Pamela's great stores of piety cannot negate the appetites and wants of her character. With *Shamela* Fielding simply removed the veil draping these features.[21] Some of the elements of this narrative puncture pretense and serve only the designs of *Shamela*, as, for example, the elevation of Parson Williams as the more adept and desirable lover; others, however, go beyond *Shamela* to resonate within *Pamela* itself, particularly as Fielding deals with questions of self-interest. Although he exaggerates the case, his distortion does not exceed the scope of the character Richardson has represented, especially when the breathless Shamela itemizes the blessings soon to be hers: "I shall be . . . mistress of a great estate, and have a dozen coaches and six, and a fine house at London, and another at Bath, and servants, and jewels, and plate, and go to plays, and operas, and court; and do what I will, and spend what I will. . . . [A]nd can't I see Parson Williams as well after marriage as before: for I shall never care a farthing for my husband. No, I hate and despise him of all things."[22] Money, alas, does not buy happiness.

At the opposite extreme is Jean Baptiste de Freval, who recommended Pamela for her imitable excellence to the votaries of virtue. That is his main point, but he is the one who also conceives of *Pamela* in terms of its exchange value: "*English* Bullion . . . for [French] Dross." Why anyone on the English side would want to make this improbable exchange escapes understanding, though the sentiment is pleasantly unrealistic. But so is the notion of imitating Pamela, since obviously one can only imitate broad patterns of behavior rather than the particular circumstances that help define her character. Richardson himself endorsed the imitative model, via his editor, when in the interlude between Pamela's last letter and the advice to readers, the latter notes of her future that she "was look'd upon as the Mirror of her Age and Sex" (409). Character-as-mirror suited Richardson's desired conception of Pamela as a stable moral type, in large part, because a character so "marked" allowed him to control and govern the otherwise more fluid story of a virtuous serving girl who becomes the lady of a manor. But not even Richardson is capable of sustaining that method of governance. The concluding instructions the editor supplies to readers, for example, implicitly acknowledge that the various ranks of people read and observe in different ways. While one mirror may serve all, everything depends on who looks into it at any given moment—as each observer perceives in ways consistent with personal interest and economic standing.

But not all mirrors are metaphorical in *Pamela*. Literal mirrors figure in the novel as well, the most obvious of which is the one Pamela looks at when, as she believes, she is about to leave Bedfordshire for the home of her parents. There, she struggles to read her ideal character as she peers into the glass, though the reflection is mixed—more so for her readers than for her. While she tries to dress in a manner to suit her homecoming, the whole of her primping indicates how torn she is by her roles as consumer and pious daughter. Everything that she has donned we learn about in some detail: the cap, though ordinary, is adorned with a green knot; her straw hat has not just strings, but two blue ones; and so forth. While presumably plainer than her servant's garb, her country attire still seems out of keeping for a home whose head slogs mud from ditches.[23] In fact, that she wears a straw hat rather than a woolen one indicates her taste for what by 1730 had become, according to Aileen Ribeiro, a "fashionable accessory."[24] Half aware that pride puffs her up even in her fashionable simplicity, Pamela cautions her parents beforehand not to think her "presumptuous and conceited," the same sentiments she worries about as she embarks on her commentary of Locke.[25] And as if to confirm that she "knew how to suit [her]self to the State [she] was returning to" (61), she then acts out a dress rehearsal before her surrogate mother, Mrs. Jervis, who fails to recognize Pamela. B., on the other hand, who is conveniently cast as *"Lucifer"* in this scene, is not so easily deceived by appearances and recognizes her as soon as he sees her face. This moment of operatic pathos in the novel discloses a Pamela who cannot get beyond moral staging or read significance into it, let alone see with the eyes of B. She is in this sense like de Freval who, in his eagerness to find a moral tale, finds nothing but.

Although disposition and circumstances force Pamela to look within and to record in intimate detail her private history, she is after all a domestic servant and later a wife who domesticates a husband who would be domesticated. That constraint placed upon desire limits her powers to penetrate beyond narrative detailing and moral ordering.[26] Had she a more analytically empowering vocabulary to rely upon, however, it is still likely that she would not employ it, as I shall discuss later. In service to the domestic ideal, she has no exotic and uninhabited islands to which she can flee.[27] Without the luxury of reflection, she writes essentially to the moment, devoid of any clear religious frame or ready supply of types.[28] Because of commercial failure at home, she must seek her fortune elsewhere. That she must fend for herself at such a tender age underscores the ruthlessness of economic necessity that Richardson plants in the novel.

As harsh as Pamela's fate may seem initially, economic necessity teaches her important lessons about adaptation and survival and pre-pares her character to adapt to a world of circumstantial necessities. With the death of Lady B. and the passing of an uneventful matriarchy, Pamela finds herself in a situation that forces her to value herself. With-out the goading and chicanery of B., she would have remained a hum-ble, though talented servant girl. Once pursued, she learns the value of competition, no matter how unfair and threatening its manifestations. From her present troubles Pamela retains only one attachment to her past, her virtue. Although divorced from the commerce of the world, she experiences how its valuation process works in an immediate way. Disoriented at first, she quickly learns to adapt to this strange world, which intrigues her sufficiently so that she fixes her place and self in it through her writing. But it would be incorrect to argue that her suc-cessful adaptation is a measure of her parents' influence. Too often we see how their wisdom has little bearing on events or fails to impress her in meaningful ways. For that matter, well before Lady B.'s death, when Pamela mastered tasks that made her service special, economic neces-sity had already shaped her fate by making her overqualified to return home.

The acquisition of this valued refinement under Lady B.'s tutelage, what Pamela calls "Qualifications above my Degree" (25), adds depth and complexity to her character. Through her own admission she ques-tions whether she can resume the more rugged duties of a useful daugh-ter in her parents' household, as the formation of blisters on her hand from scouring a plate suggest not. Fortunately, she is spared the an-swer. From the first page of the novel onward, Pamela instinctively thinks in terms of action, what she is able to do, not motivation, how she does not want to go home. In stopping short of self-discovery, she manages to reconcile herself to a new social sphere without having to mourn for those attachments to an unproductive prehistory that pay no dividends, those that identify her with a lower station. When, in present surroundings, the servant Harry speaks freely to her and grabs her, Pamela reports her disgust to her parents: "I can't bear to be look'd upon by these Men-servants" (30). She prefers instead the company of Mrs. Jervis, "a Gentlewoman born, tho' she has had Misfortunes" (30). Without having to sharpen her quill, she next calculates the cost of a possible relationship with B. in commercial terms: "for I am sure my Master would not demean himself so, as to think upon such a poor Girl as I, for my Harm. For such a Thing would ruin his Credit as well as mine" (30).

Only later, after suffering through a series of indignities and wrestling with her own needs and wants, does Pamela realize her capacity to credit herself differently. In a manner of speaking, her accumulated experience has mustered in her the resources necessary to capitalize herself and to express that potential value to B. in a way that anticipates striking social and political changes. Her program, as might be expected, rejects the aristocratic idiom and any reliance upon an unproductive past. Moreover, she announces it *en passant* at the critical turning point in the novel when she returns to Lincolnshire in effect to marry B. Shortly after her arrival, he reads to her Lady Davers's letter urging her brother not to disgrace the family name through an ill-conceived marriage: "ours is no upstart Family; but is as ancient as them best in the Kingdom" (221). Pamela retorts, "And how can they be assured, that one hundred Years hence or two, some of those now despised upstart Families, may not revel in their Estates, while their Descendants may be reduced to the other's Dunghils?" (222). In this passage it is the work of the commercial ranks that opens the possibility of a different kind of future, which Pamela herself has sampled shortly before her departure from Lincolnshire through B.'s valedictory letter. "This Letter," she cries, "has affected me more than any [new plotting] could have done. For here is plainly his great Value for me confess'd" (214). Raised to his level, despite their differences in rank, she reads her relationship in socially expansive terms and defines her history and future in commercial terms. Thus her inability to penetrate completely to self-knowledge is in part a reflection of the internal competition between what Foucault would call the "*mark* " and "*organism*" of character, as commerce directs attention toward an uncertain future and away from a predictable past—in short, to the mechanisms of suspense.

Through her confusion over the motivations of character and evident self-contradictions, Pamela tacitly expresses her appetite for commercial novelty. From one standpoint the work of the commercial rank was to advance, to get out of the house, and not to look back too often, as was evident in period migratory behavior. To succeed Pamela must internalize this ethos and, unlike Crusoe, leave the past behind. Accordingly, she must accept responsibility for and the consequences of the property of her script, as her writings form the basis of her exchange system as well as the authority it presumes. In this sense, Pamela is forever slipping from Richardson's grasp, as he tries to control her with what remains of moral typology, but cannot succeed because the historical imperatives of commercial progress, as I have indicated, were too great to linger long over an older moral economy.[29]

The Question of Origins

Whether he realized it or not, Richardson placed Pamela in a context that calls to mind the restraints upon liberty and capitalist progress that, in the eyes of period commentators, feudal subordination had perpetuated during its historical tenure. That the bulk of *Pamela* takes place at Lincolnshire, B.'s gothic estate, is no coincidence because, for part of the time at least, Pamela lacks even a basic freedom of movement. Only after the amelioration of her relationship with B. does the gloom lift, the demonic dissipate, and the unnatural become ordered, as Pamela herself experiences mobility of a different kind. Although she remains scrupulous throughout, her moral scrupulosity abates a bit after this amelioration, as she becomes more circumstantial in her judgments, rather than keyed to a system of allegory and types. Indeed, later in the novel, when presented in effect with a secular typology of the ideal wife, we see Pamela's willingness to dispute some of the "sweet Injunctions" of housewifery, while weighing the legitimacy of and her inclination to comply with many others. She has prepared us for such expressions of liberty because easy submission has never been bred in her bone. Indeed, resistance is the hallmark of her virtue. Under the proper set of circumstances, the strength of her character undermines the tyrannical and appetitive designs of B., as well as the history that Lincolnshire recalls.

She arrives in this world because of commercial failure; because without her father's miscarried venture as an operator of a country school, Pamela would likely never have gone into service. Thus, when she establishes a school of her own, toward the end of the sequel, she demonstrates how easily one generation, blessed with mobility, can outdo the previous generation and overwrite prehistory. This rupture of the present from the past bespeaks the breadth of Pamela's needs and wants in the context of family history and social class, but it also underscores the contradictions of her character. When she literally thinks in terms of rupture, she conceives of it as a state devoid of writing, though the rupture in this instance is between her and her friends at Bedfordshire. Upon her return home, as she remarks, there will be "no Writing, nor Writing-time" (82). Despite this wish, she subverts the adequacy of familial restoration soon thereafter when she promises to pen a letter to Mr. Longman and Mrs. Jervis once she is safely home—but only after she first asks Longman, on the point of her departure from Bedfordshire, to supply her with paper, "For I shall want often to be scribbling" (95).

Over time, her attitude toward writing changes, as circumstances themselves change, even though she laments her fate as a writer once imprisoned: "I have now nothing to do, but write, and weep, and fear, and pray" (94). A less determined writer would not endure the ordeals of the pen she suffers, but it is her productivity, sufficiently intriguing unto itself, that lifts her beyond the private and proprietary into the public sphere following B.'s endorsement. As if the invisible hand herself, Pamela, in turn, effects the utter transformation of B.'s private and appetitive self-interest in service to a more liberal public order. Although it is true that B. never entirely abandons his aristocratic pretensions or its proprietary interests, he is enough the student of his times to sense the imperatives of the moment and its association with the commercial ranks. In the sequel he concedes that "as to Citizens, in a Trading Nation like this, I am not displeased in the main, with seeing the over-grown ones creeping into nominal Honours; and we have so many of our first Titled Families who have ally'd themselves to Trade, (whose Inducements were Money only) that it ceases to be either a Wonder as to the Fact, or a Disgrace to the Honour" (3:171).

The history of B.'s transformation entails a gradual process of negotiation that eventually rewrites the terms of domestic economy. After assertion and intimidation fail at Bedfordshire, B. pretends to send Pamela home but, in effect, delivers her to Lincolnshire where she will reconceive his assumptions about domestic arrangements. B. is already aware of the threat she poses to his imaged order because she writes. Accusing her, in effect, of violating caste assumptions, interestingly through "her own romantick Innocence, at the Price of other People's Characters" (162), he proposes the purchase of his desire in a contract he draws up to secure that end. Already knowledgeable about matters that seem to exceed her purview and certainly intolerant of "Power and Riches [that] never want Tools to promote their vilest Ends" (111), Pamela counters B.'s terms by replacing his language of monopoly and excess with her language of sublimated restraint, moderation, and an equitable commerce. "I hope, as I can contentedly live at the meanest Rate, and think not myself above the lowest Condition, that I am also above making an Exchange of my Honesty for all the Riches of the Indies" (167)—itself a locus of monopoly.

Although Pamela is premature in implying that her needs and wants are modest, since she will return to B. later when her journey home has nothing to do with plotting, she already has commanded a position of legitimacy for herself, along with a sense of fair dealing. But the proximity of Pamela, as body and text, has profound implications for B. and, at his darkest moment, he casts her from his sight and house.[30] What we learn is that B. has a guilt-ridden past to hide that must be told in full before Pamela and he can experience a fully settled domestic life.[31] This process begins just prior to her dismissal, when she has a tormented conversation with B. about her fears of a sham marriage. B. most assuredly recalls at this point how he too was the victim of "plotting" when Lady Godfrey attempted to manipulate and coerce him to marry her daughter, Sally. Even though he remains quiet about the subject at this point, his guilt forces him to acknowledge his own "plotting," hence his precipitous dismissal of Pamela. By returning after her dismissal, she assures him that the present can cure the ills of the past and its burdensome prehistory. This same lesson is one that Pamela teaches to Lady Davers who, unlike Pamela, dredges up episodes from her brother's unsavory past, by letting it be known he was a rake and dueler, to humiliate him and to fix his attention on then, not now.[32]

Richardson's representation of the aristocracy, thus, is of a rank weighed down by its prehistory; Pamela's character, for reasons that are obvious, does not suffer from the same kind of strains.[33] Whatever the past signifies to her, it is a matter largely forgotten or simply irrelevant. It cannot matter or, at least, cannot trouble her consciousness. The first page hurls us immediately *in medias res* and thereafter reduces what preceded mostly to conjecture. Even the blow of Lady B.'s death is softened, as Pamela reports, because her former employer recommended the servants one by one to her son, who promised to protect Pamela from her worst fear, to be "quite destitute again" (25). The absence of need and the satisfaction of want explain in addition, as much as anything does, her persistent labor of the pen, and her obsessive practice of ordering the present and the moment through her writing. She confirms her temporal fixation with the present by the simple act of returning to Lincolnshire when called. Were the past and destitution so important to her she would have continued on to her parents.

On the face of the evidence, no one could have predicted that competition, monopoly, exchange, and the terms of a commercial economy would have reached as far as an ancient English country estate or would have mattered much to an isolated serving girl. Excessive attachment to the past, under her circumstances, would ultimately reduce her chances of success and yield a predictable sameness to her life. Accordingly, by deciding for herself that she will marry B., Pamela reaffirms the inutility of past attachments. Goodman Andrews's presence at the Lincolnshire estate, when he comes in search of his daughter, remains "celibate." By the time his daughter marries, he has long since distanced himself from the scene of the ceremony that alters her station. This devaluation of her nuclear family depends on the long series of exchanges she has had with B. Her intrinsic value, while significant, does not define the sum and substance of her being, however. Through her marriage she begins to circulate in expanding circles that only add to her value, as she easily wins the approval of the local gentry and even the assent of Lady Davers. These small victories grow in proportion in the sequel, itself an expansion of needs and wants, as Pamela's opinions diversify and she herself partakes of London's cultural amenities. For the moment at least, she has found in B. someone whose unpredictable deed infuses the old aristocracy, a loveless lot, with the spirit of a new and vital class that B. himself recognizes. "The Perverseness and Contradiction I have too often seen, . . . even among People of Sense, as well as Condition, had prejudiced me to the marry'd State; . . . you see, my Dear, that I have not gone among this Class of People for a Wife. . . . For here is my Misfortune; I could not have been contented to have been *but moderately happy* in a Wife" (368).

Pamela and the Moral Governance of Narrative?

Like the heroine of the fairy-tale romance, Pamela gets the glass slipper to fit—her marriage provides her with a rich husband, three estates, and the admiration of all.[34] But even as a Cinderella story Pamela's rags-to-riches tale drapes itself in disguise. Richardson's heroine is not so far removed from the romance tradition as her endorsers, as well as her author, might want us to believe. In effect, she pays a price because of Richardson's desire to capitalize on originality and to redirect the market for narrative. In practice that meant he took an existing genre and larded it with morality, hoping against hope that the simple moral character would be what readers took away from the story. Only some did. Personalizing the needs and wants of a commercial economy, catalyzing them with social mobility, and then fusing this volatile mixture onto moral selfhood complicates Pamela's representation. Although commercial theorists of the period experimented with much the same chemistry in order to govern the economy, perhaps for no better reason than fear or skepticism, Richardson's attempt at governance yielded a character that not even he could fully comprehend, not by the end of part 1, or in the sequel, where he backs into a final resolution by simply having Pamela die.

But the last Pamela we experience is also the first. She awakens to a world of loss—Lady B. is dead, her parents are elsewhere, and ahead lies uncertainty. From this void she can reclaim literally nothing. Instead, she must anticipate the novelties of suspense by securing herself against those unpredictabilities with the credit of her virtue intact. What ensues subjects that moral absolute and ideal to the vagaries of interest and exchange, as readers ever since Fielding have noted. That Pamela herself cannot acknowledge appetite, aspiration, and acquisition credits her moral sense, even though we find our credulity taxed under the circumstances.[35] At the crossroads between Lincolnshire and home, where B. has struck at the "credulous, fluttering, throbbing Mischief" (217)—her heart—with an invitation for her return, she makes a startling disclosure. "O how I love to be generously used!" (217), she apostrophizes; the *OED* indicates the meaning of "generous" as "munificent" and "liberal in giving," as well as "appropriate or natural to one of noble birth and spirit." None of these definitions could be applicable to her parents, unless a few letters of advice can be counted generous; thus, Pamela has no material reason to go home.

In the final quarter of part 1, however, her moral sense becomes acute, once she can admit that her prison has become her paradise. But the latter entails exclusion. Pamela is unwilling to have her parents settle under her roof, we learn, out of fear that "for, so constantly seeing the Hand that blesses them, they would, may-be, as must be my Care to avoid, be tempted to look no further in their Gratitude, than to the dear Dispenser of such inumerable Benefits" (305). Given their devotion and piety, the Andrewses probably strike most readers as unlikely candidates for perverting the methods of typology. Whether Pamela's concern in this local matter is fair and disinterested or purely interested is difficult to say. Either way her parents become beneficiaries. Still, Pamela must believe that her critical faculties do not suffer from the possible impairments she imposes upon her parents. If, on the other hand, we could be assured that her words reveal the workings of self-interest, then her moral fastidiousness becomes nothing more than a projection of her own inclination upon her parents.

No doubt Pamela would prefer to trust in types. Whether she can, given the unpredictabilities of her personal history, is a matter never entirely resolved. Toward the end of the story, when B. contemplates his death, he tries to soothe Pamela's upset with a poetical effort that depends explicitly on typology: *"The tow'ring Lark . . . / . . . flies / To Heav'n, to type your future Joys."* Inspired by good intentions and little else, this poem winds up disorienting the now vulnerable Pamela and wrenches from her a surprisingly fuzzy metaphysics that reveals the shortness of her memory as she tries to imagine life without that "excellently generous Benefactor of [hers]!" (406). Like Clarissa, Pamela finds a home that is not her father's. Its bounty, benevolence, and generosity furnish what her first home lacked—but not through any predictable means. The same holds true of B.'s two main estates, where, if Richardson intended any prefigurative system at all, its operations suggest that nefarious scheming, interested affections, and the mechanisms of exchange are a necessary prelude to the blessed life. But to remove the means to that end is to reimpose a more traditional structure on society in which predictability and imitation once more reign.

At the conclusion of Pamela's narrative, toward the close of part 1, the editor once again surfaces to address the audience. There he tries to undo the tangle of sociological and moral categories by reasserting moral stratification to the ranks of readers. For example, those of low estate should follow the model of John and Elizabeth Andrews, while servants should scorn the Jewkes type and gentlemen the libertine. These and other characters represented in the story thus invite imitative behavior, duly partitioned according to rank. Pamela herself, however, is not so readily defined and typed as these other characters. We sense editorial exasperation when she turns into an enumeration of moral principles, as if her character must be divided and subdivided to achieve any sense of wholeness or comprehension.[36] These "many signal In-stances of the Excellency of her Mind" allow the editor to conclude that they "[m]ay make her Character worthy of the Imitation of her Sex, from low to high Life" (412) — or, we could add, they may not. In subse-quent editions, Richardson dispensed with the fuzzy by doing away with the readers' instructions. Unlike the other characters he refers to in his codicil to the first edition, Pamela transgresses imposed limita-tions and socially constructed restrictions. At bottom she endorses the revolutionary creed of commerce: from the one Pamela, many Pamelas, a creed of needs and wants that the editor can only attempt to govern through moral appeal.

The mixed and complex messages that *Pamela* communicates depend upon Richardson's choice of narrative form and, within that large struc-ture, his method of character representation. In a similar vein Michael McKeon writes: "There is an inherent tension between the dynamic form in which Pamela's personal merit is manifested — the plastic pow-ers of her mind — and the progressive ideal of meritocracy, which envi-sions the replacement of arbitrary aristocratic culture by a rigorous consistency of moral and social success, not the ethically uncertain force of persuasive self-creation."[37] This uneasy split between the licit and transgressive, between consistency and uncertainty, not only stimulates more probing forms of character representation but also invites more skeptical modes of interpretive analysis. As cautious and scrupulous as Richardson was in his composition and various editions, the "author-ized" version of self that his Pamela records does little to restrict what others see, in his time as well as ours. Pamela, in the end, is merely one interpreter of her character. As Clinton Bond has urged, "early novel-ists and readers discover that an open narrative continually resists the moral and coherent pattern, despite the author's attempt at control." The contingency of realism, he goes on, is "its dependence upon a sub-jective grasp of reality [that] is not capable of being wholly abstracted or moralized."[38] Suspense ensured that fact.

Background: Consumption and Contradiction in Fielding

Fielding's version of narrative realism appears initially to elude the contingency factor that Bond describes. His realism is a special case, it seems, and one that we are apt to qualify with the labels, classical or epical.[39] Fielding's hand in shaping this response is unambiguous, as it was he who deployed classical devices in *Joseph Andrews* to give his work the ironical and satiric edge he sought. From the disparity between the commonplace and the grand he managed to create an aura of moral correction so that his undressing of *Pamela* appears modest, not salacious. However, neither *Joseph Andrews* nor his first assault upon Richardson, *Shamela*, suggests even the slightest tolerance for subjectivity or the semantic confusions of the suspended character. In this regard, his method of undoing Pamela was that of redoing the narrative form she occupied. The result of this effort obviously did not translate easily into Fielding's own life, since, in 1747, he married Mary Daniel, the servant of his deceased and beloved wife Charlotte. Unlike Pamela, as it turns out, Mary was pregnant at the time of her marriage. Fielding, of course, was under no obligation to be a sincere reader of the stories he wrote, but this friction between theory and practice underscores a much more important distinction between the private person and the public man, a division that goes to the heart of how we read and understand his novels.[40] That he does get his hand stuck in the cookie jar may cause historical embarrassment but, for us, also affords an opportunity to look again at the inconsistencies and contradictions in his novels, which, as they surface, we are perhaps inclined to smooth over, as if Fielding himself were a perfectly calm sea despite his many ironical billows.

On the whole and perhaps not inexplicably, the unsublimated body fares better in Fielding's world than the sublimated, with sexual misconduct more apt to be forgiven than material-based appetites. Yet even here his bag is mixed and his yardstick selectively applied. The elect are more likely to benefit. Bridget Allworthy sins, but she also dies. From first to last, Booth remains a blunderer and is unworthy, lucky to have Amelia, though probably more deserving of Miss Mathews. Randy Tom is spared because he is Tom—hence his premarital copulations yield no children; although Joey sheds his sexual reserve, he does so appropriately only after Fanny appears on the scene. Only then does he become the Joseph who tries to shed the watchful eye of Parson Adams. Once the smoke clears, the good-natured man or the virtuous citizen has, by design, no unwelcome embarrassments to face—virtue and reward, when they are earned, are earned by default rather than positive example.[41] While Fielding's larger design seems to be that of teaching through correction and emulation, the fact is that not even unblemished

models tell all—their objective rendering collapses into curious forms
of subjective representation. Moments of discovery or truths at last revealed, in turn, are apt to complicate, not clarify. That he tries to rewrite
the origins of the novel and recover a universal and typologically
fraught history with *Joseph Andrews* only mires him further in the here-
and-now.[42]

Throughout his career, but especially so with his periodical and incidental writings, Fielding remained an active diagnostician of contemporary ills, identifying their underlying pathology as hypocrisy, vanity,
and self-love. Still, he holds forth the remote possibility of cure in the
person of the ideal "character." In "An Essay on the Knowledge of the
Characters of Men" (1743), this character suggests a republican patriot
who can put aside love of self—what Fielding calls "private affection"—and take up love of country.[43] The problem with this public
ideal lies with its proper definition and historical grounding. About the
latter we learn that not even Rome and Sparta can offer much guidance
because Romans were "robbers" and Spartans "very depraved." Historical precedent fails Fielding but, in a fundamental way, so does definition, since at the end of the essay he concedes the desperation of his
efforts: "however useless this treatise may be to instruct, I hope it will
be at least effectual to alarm my reader; and sure no honest undesigning
man can ever be too much on his guard against the hypocrite, or too
industrious to expose and expel him out of society" (178). Given the
range of individuals stricken with hypocrisy Fielding isolates in the
essay, one wonders who will be left in society after the expulsion. The
more relevant linkage here, however, is that of "honest" with "undesigning"; its opposite, the dishonest designer, is simply another way of
labeling the interested party, a figure bent upon the *"Art of Thriving,"* as
it is identified at the beginning of the essay (154). This practitioner of
the chrematistic art, whose opposite is the purportedly virtuous Dr.
Harrison, seeks "his own particular and separate Advantage, to which
he is to sacrifice the Interest of all others." Under the tyranny of this
"crafty and designing part of mankind, . . . the whole world becomes a
vast masquerade, where the greatest part appear disguised under false
vizors and habits" (155). Only after establishing this principle does
Fielding then break into his gallery of rogue types.

That the whole world has become a masquerade—a melange of mis-
representations and suspended truths—indicates the extent to which
needs and wants have dominated contemporary life. By the time Fielding published *Amelia* (1751), he shows signs of a shifting attitude about
the "art of thriving," not that he discountenanced it, but merely inverted
it to recommend the more positive "Art of Life."[44] With this principle he
offers the hope of reform, again by positing an ideal form: "the several

Gradations which conduce to bring every Model to Perfection." While his stress upon art, rather than life, may strike us as a union through catachresis, it is geared in the end toward productivity.[45] Significantly, partitioning or grading requires the detailed observation of "the several Incidents which tend to the Catastrophe or Completion of the whole, and the minute Causes whence those Incidents are produced" (17). How these procedural steps pertain to "life" is unclear, but the echo of the division of labor in this formulation is unavoidable. This division had already been advanced by Fielding's time and its association with increased productivity and the commercial state was inevitable.[46] That such a principle resulted in his darkest and, if it is legitimate to say so, most uncharacteristic novel is intriguing under the circumstances. Indeed, there is a strong anticommercial bias in Fielding's writings so that, for example, when he wants to illustrate the corruption of patriotism in "Characters of Men," he does so by imagining "twenty boys [who] were taught from their Infancy to believe, that the Royal-Exchange was the kingdom of heaven; and . . . that it was . . . god-like to defend it; nineteen of them would afterwards cheerfully sacrifice their lives to its defence; at least it is impossible that any of them would agree for a paltry reward, to set it on fire; not even though they were rogues and highwaymen in their disposition."[47] The Royal Exchange was, in fact, destroyed by fire during the seventeenth century, but also rebuilt. Nevertheless, the likelihood of history repeating itself does not even seem remotely possible in the eighteenth century, as Fielding surveys matters. Still, his choice of imagery is telltale, for the Royal Exchange compresses all of Fielding's antagonism toward material needs and wants into one of the most famous of London marts.

Although he claimed to be no opponent of trade, much in the manner Parson Adams does, Fielding read profoundly unwelcome changes to the constitution of England in its development. Among other things, "the introduction of trade," as he remarks in *An Inquiry into the Causes of the Late Increase of Robbers* (1751), "hath in a great measure subverted the former state of affairs, and hath almost totally changed the manners, customs, and habits of the people, more especially of the lower sort."[48] Although in *The True Patriot* (26 November 1745) he observes that "many thousands have got an honest livelihood for themselves and families" because of trade, he fully believes that trade should alter nothing at all, certainly not the social hierarchy. Corruption, vanity, and vice, however, have written a different script. In their material form, these vices bottom out as luxury—the moral evil of consumption. As a consequence, improved "arts and sciences," ornamented "human life," and available "comfort[s]" not only implicate both the state and private individuals but also fix history on an irreversible course. Fielding's gloom arises, however, from his interest in origins.[49]

The version of an uncorrupted origin that he relies upon perhaps more than any other is the Ancient Constitution, which he either refers to in or has infuse his social and political commentary. Without it or the historical perspective it supplies, he would have lacked the framework on which he constructed the progress of corruption, a state that he detected in virtually every quarter of contemporary life, as well as a movement that had even generated its own philosopher in Mandeville, on whom Fielding heaps special scorn in *The True Patriot*. In *A Proposal for Making an Effectual Provision for the Poor* (1753), he identifies the scope of the Ancient Constitution when he notes that "the great Aim of the first founders of the English constitution [was that] no man whatsoever [could be] exempted from performing such duties to the public as befit his rank."[50] With Italian opera, masquerades, fashion, and a long list of other acts of cultural consumption—almost all of which are a source of grievance for Fielding—the tradition of rank and obligation has evaporated, so that riot and disorder have become "almost too big for the civil authority to suppress." From this chaotic state of suspense he determines: "the constitution of this country is altered from its ancient state."[51]

Commentary such as this makes Fielding sound like a despairing civic humanist or a descendant of Charles Davenant, even though Davenant himself was much more temperate and pragmatic in his examination of republican themes. Given Fielding's perception of the corrupted origin, however, one matter that weighed heavily upon him was authority. I have previously mentioned that the growing strength of a commercial state had weakened the persuasiveness of the argument to authority. Fielding expressed his views on this subject even before he embarked on writing novels, though, with the formal presence of strong narrators in *Joseph Andrews* and *Tom Jones* especially, his concerns about authority play a significant role in what we are suppose to derive from these novels and their characters. Authority, as he remarks in *The Champion* (15 January 1739–40), has also suffered corruption: *auctoritas*, in "its original tongue, . . . convey[ed] the idea of . . . awe and respect"; whereas in its corrupted meaning, it signifies "the capacity or ability of doing such and such things."[52] This translation from a state of being to the capacity to act resonates throughout his exercise of narrative authority, but the application of the original definition to Fielding's narrators is not at all convincing. He manages to spare these figures from any direct action in his narratives and, just as clear, wants his narrators to convey "respect"; however, neither the narrator in *Joseph Andrews* nor his counterpart in *Tom Jones* can be said to command "awe."

And with *Amelia*, the narrator bears only a faint resemblance to earlier incarnations. Something runs afoul in the novels, and all leads tend toward the role Fielding assigns to property.

Whether explicitly indicated or not, the landed estate—both a stronghold of republican virtue and a refuge from the disquieting advances of commercialization—organizes much of his social theory and figures decisively in the plot resolutions of his novels. This prejudice for the land figures as his general willingness to spare the nobility censure in his commentary; whereas the less fortunate, members of the lower ranks in particular, often receive severe treatment. The mob, the tradesman, the laborer, the mechanic, but also the upstart, effectively constitute those who make "depredations on property."[53] Thus the uprooting of the land and its subsequent realignments stood as a sure sign of social corruption. Nevertheless, it is the preservation of *his* property and the integrity of *his* script that plays significantly upon the administration of his novels.

Commentary he makes in *The True Patriot* sheds some light on the disposition of property set against the backdrop of liberty and trade. In Number 4 (26 November 1745), he begins with reference to authorship, partisan politics, and the power of interest, as these matters became more volatile under the threat of the Jacobites. At stake was property itself: for if the Jacobite threat actually lived up to its promise, it would imperil the security "of our estates, properties, lives and families, under the government of an absolute popish prince."[54] Mandeville haunts the central portion of this essay as an author gone bad, but he simply supplies the trappings of a ruinous philosophy that panders to the prevailing ethos: that of "selling ourselves." The chief victim in this poisoned atmosphere is government itself, which, as Fielding describes it, has suffered in proportion with *auctoritas*. Now, "power and government, instead of being the objects of reverence and terror, have been set up as the butts of ridicule and buffoonry." Were the Pretender to assume the throne, as his hacks have urged for "pecuniary considerations," then, as we are cautioned, these sellers of print would find their "whole trade . . . ruined by this man's success" (*True Patriot*, 139).

Whether he realized it or not, Fielding defined the market in terms of its competitive practices, yet lambasted the selling of print he deemed politically objectionable. With an absolute government in place, there would be no marketplace to speak of, which paradoxically appears to be just the kind of print market Fielding worked towards because of his need to muzzle the competition. Nor do we have to overtax ourselves to recognize that, whether it is *The True Patriot* or any of his other writings, the competitive print marketplace was what set Fielding's pen in motion. On one level, *Joseph Andrews* exists because of its own merits.

Yet not unlike the true Jacobite, Fielding tries to uproot Richardson's estate in property vested in *Pamela*. Without it—or, better, without his interest in capitalizing on an existing literary property—Fielding would perhaps not have written *Joseph Andrews* at all. By choosing to compete with the model of virtue Richardson first established in his character Pamela, Fielding asks his readers to consider a new way of consuming what they thought they knew.

Consumption and Contradiction in Practice

Joseph Andrews embodies Fielding's attempt to rewrite the market for novels, if not his attempt at rectifying the kinds of social ills he identifies in his periodical writings, which *Pamela* somehow distills. Accordingly, significant differences exist between Fielding's and Richardson's management of narrative, with the most glaring being the way in which Fielding proceeds self-consciously with the business of crafting narrative. *Joseph Andrews* does not simply tell a story. It also articulates Fielding's theory of the novel, one that he duly partitions within the framework of the narrative via the critical prefaces that head the individual books of the novel. In effect, *Joseph Andrews* is both theory and practice—a novel about itself that also tells a story. On this complication hinges not just the role of Fielding's conspicuous narrator but also the structure of needs and wants that informs his revisionary novel. More than anything else, however, the fascination with *Joseph Andrews* is the sophisticated bungling job Fielding manages to produce in trying to reconcile theory with practice. This process evidences the long reach of suspense in a novel calculated to teach moral certainty through the administration of character.[55]

The last thing we are supposed to think about at the outset of *Joseph Andrews* is the impact of the marketplace on literary productions or the author's self-promotional interests. For a good reason too, he begins with intellectual concerns that force us to think about a still perplexing subject: the origins of the novel. To that end, the first sentence of the author's preface sweeps aside residual associations that may exist between the romance and the novel and, with the second paragraph, has introduced the question of origins. There he discusses the lost comic epic of Homer and from it reconstructs, if not the primal vehicle itself, then its close cousin, the "comic Epic-Poem in Prose," the genre to which *Joseph Andrews* subscribes. Although Fielding nominally connects this genre with the romance, he clearly distinguishes it from romance as it has been transmitted in subject, purpose, tone, diction, and range of characters. As a repository of theoretical principles, the novel, though of ancient lineage, not only risks social discrimination, as Field-ing's representation of hypocrisy makes apparent, but also devolves into a tortured and tortuous statement of aesthetic discrimination, so that those terms that ought to hold the properly formed novel together be-come instead a mishmash of qualifications and stipulations. Who bene-fits ultimately from this theoretical posturing is never entirely clear, but Fielding does go out of his way to discriminate between educated read-ers—whom he calls "the Classical Reader"—and, by implication, low readers, those who will be disappointed with *Joseph Andrews* for its lack of conventional titillation.[56]

Certainly one legitimate way to regard the preface is as "a kind of manifesto of Fielding's conception of his art," but it is also possible that Fielding's beginning thoughts entail a much more determined author-function, so that externally directed concerns about audience composi-tion and the conditioning of ethical response may not matter nearly so much as we think.[57] The preface, in this light, cloaks self-interest, at the same time it advances Fielding's own authority through its formidable rhetoric. Thus, in order to impart the "awe and respect" of *auctoritas* to himself, he must assume a particular type of persona. By distancing himself from narrative action, "author-Fielding" fosters the illusion that his interests lie with literary tradition, not the literary marketplace, or with genre theory rather than literary property. Once we shift to the narrative proper, as author is displaced by narrator, this new persona wastes no time in assigning names to those vague romances the author cautions against. In fact, they have specific names, the most contempo-rary of which is *Pamela*, a tale that passes as biographical writing.

As it turns out, narrative practice modifies authorial theory, subject-ing it to a range of conditions and circumstances that complicate genre and tradition with competitive designs, market concerns, and the prop-erty of the text itself—because surely one of the implicit needs Fielding expresses via the preface is that by controlling and securing his own work he effectively safeguards it from the kind of harassment he used against Richardson. Questions of origins assume a special importance in this context by creating an aura for *Joseph Andrews* that it somehow transcends the limitations of its own historical production. Yet we can-not read beyond the title page without recognizing that origins are not so simple or ennobling as we might assume. There, in print unmistak-able, we read that *Joseph Andrews* is "Written in Imitation of the *Manner* of Cervantes, Author of *Don Quixote*." No matter what its pedigree or implicit claims, however, not even the preface can sustain itself, as ori-gins shade into originality. In the concluding paragraphs of the preface, after having "distinguished *Joseph Andrews* from the Productions of Ro-mance Writers on the one hand, and Burlesque Writers on the other,"

Fielding declares his novel a "Species of writing . . . hitherto unattempted in our Language." Perhaps not surprising is that immediately thereafter the subject of character surfaces once issues from the actual narrative itself, specifically the representation of Parson Adams, begin to impinge upon the author's consciousness. Awkward and even embarrassed, Fielding writes of a Parson Adams, "designed a Character of perfect Simplicity," who participates in "low Adventures" (10–11). Simplicity, we gather, precludes complication and "low" here intends no offense. As we shall see, however, this "origin," like the *Margites*, gets lost in the folds of circumstance and can even be construed as a disguise for self-interested and politically undesirable motives.

Once the theory of authoring shifts to its practice, we find that the premises Fielding has barely sustained in the preface are those he cannot sustain in the narrative proper, as the administration of narrative becomes preeminent.[58] Origins succumb to praxis as the needs of a genre must assume a material form, including action and character; otherwise the intended object, a novel fit for consumption, would only exist as the subjective theorizing of the author. Even though the purported executor of the author's will, the narrator, hovers above narrative action like some bodiless "impartial spectator," his remove does not distance him from either interest or implication in the unfolding of plot. He is to *Joseph Andrews* what Pamela is to *Pamela*—the central character and intelligence, who pieces together whatever coherence can be found in the world as represented. But between theory and practice, need and its supply, origins and praxis—indeed, author and narrator—emerges suspense, which addles the premises of plot, complicates character, and invites uncertainty into a novel predicated on renewal, strong governance, typological models, and predictability.

From the start of the narrator's prefaces, it is the present, not the past, that fixes his imagination. As a result the market figures centrally in his own cultural, theoretical, and generic redactions and undergoes its most explicit examination in the second of the three introductions that he writes.[59] Because of the role that he plays, the "narrator" is much more detailed than the "author" who merely summons principles and precepts throughout his preface. The narrator's obligation differs from the author's, and he says so in the first sentence of book 1: "it is a trite but true Observation, that Examples work more forcibly on the Mind than Precepts" (17). While this *precept* is richly ironic, it prepares us to recognize how the circumstances of administering and executing narrative practice necessitate a different order of consciousness, one in fact that originates in the rhetoric of indirection, irony itself. Once begun, the narrator's work moves expeditiously to contemporary concerns, to Colley Cibber, with whom Fielding settles an old score, and of course to Richardson.

Bits of the narrator's second preface, however, appear to slip beyond the orbit of the contemporary when, perhaps in deference to author-Fielding, the narrator recalls the classical epic and its traditions, citing Homer, Virgil, and Milton. Whatever their worth as independent practitioners, they are quickly brought back into the fold of the contemporary.[60] Thus we learn that Homer once "hawked" his epics, probably a book at a time—very likely "by Subscription" (91), and Milton, fired by hubris and the need to compete with Virgil, expanded *Paradise Lost* from its original ten books to twelve. These book divisions matter now more than they once did because of their commercial value: "there are certain Mysteries or Secrets in all Trades from the highest to the lowest, from that of *Prime Minstring* to this of *Authoring*. . . . Among those used by us Gentlemen of the latter Occupation, I take this of dividing our Works into Books and Chapters to be none of the least considerable" (89). In this climate division is associated with productivity, but while the "authoring"-narrator cannot rival the output of Virgil or Milton, let alone Homer, he still intimates enough competitive hubris to suggest that his work, consistent with simple mathematical computation, has one-third the merit of Virgil's and Milton's and one-sixth the merit of Homer's.

The narrator's third preface recalls the romance tradition once again but to gainsay it in favor of biographical writing, the sort that the narrator-storyteller himself produces. At the heart of biography lies character and, in this sense, the third preface echoes the concerns of the author's Preface, where the latter steadily draws upon the abstract principles of character in order to direct them to their fulfillment in Parson Adams. Here, in *"Matter prefatory in Praise of* Biography," the process is reversed. Instead of the Parson, the narrator, in looking back upon his story, not ahead, seizes upon the lawyer, a scoundrel, and follows him with unhappy reflections on Mrs. Tow-wouse. Both, we learn, are characters of vice; both, moreover, extend beyond their incarnate form to represent the corruption that attends universal history, a period of some "4000 Years" (189). To that end, the lawyer typifies all those who have "made Self the Centre of the whole Creation"—he is not "an Individual, but a Species" (189). And like Mrs Tow-wouse he is figured as appetite and avarice. The narrator, however, cannot reconcile these creatures of hyperbole by steering our attention toward "perfect Simplicity"; whatever complications exist or remain, that knot is left for readers to untie. The novel itself, along with its representations, serves as a mirror—a "Glass to thousands in their Closets, that they may contemplate their Deformity, and endeavour to reduce it, [in order to] avoid public

Shame" (189). This solution solves nothing. The language of conveyance is at best tentative, and the method of reform Richardsonian. In a
profoundly contradictory way, this instruction shifts the authority of
the book to the "Self," which anchors the "Centre of the whole" reading
experience. Moreover, via its interpolated tales, the novel has by 3, 1
already exposed the defects and imprecisions of "private" readings and
will continue to so.[61] This sense of the unrelenting contradiction between theory and practice is underscored one last time in book 4, where
the narrator simply abandons his pattern of beginning a book with theoretical posturing.

Had he done otherwise, Fielding would have been forced to negate
the principles expressed in the prefaces to books 1 and 3. What occurs
in book 4 is that practice quite overwhelms theory. As the resolution to
the novel, book 4 descends to the level of romance as the narrative calls
upon the services of a peddler (often regarded as the bane of domestic
commerce), a changeling story, and a secret birthmark to unknot its
mysteries. The broad import of this development suggests that no resolution is possible until the narrator loses final control of his product;
and that by not governing his product, by failing to have it live up to
the demands of an imposed theoretical model, only then do characters
earn their individual rewards. Through his final omission of a preface,
the narrator proves that not every want is fulfilled in a commercial
order.

What we witness in book 4, however, has had a long preparation.
The need to govern character certainly figures prominently in the design that the novel assumes from the beginning of book 1. There the
debt to Richardson is great, as Joseph, the chaste-male, lives up to the
character of the woman he assumes is his sister, Pamela. Later, once the
beloved Fanny appears, Joseph evinces the sexual vigor of a Tom
Jones but with the open displays and compromising situations omitted.
As an oblique demonstration of his vigor, Joseph subsequently legitimizes his need to cleave to the flesh—namely, Fanny's—during a testy
exchange with Parson Adams, when both are tied back-to-back in an
upstairs room of the last public house they pass through. As the chaste
male *ab initio*, Joseph also recalls his biblical prefiguration and name-
sake. The problem with his typological identity, however, is that the
narrator fails to sustain it and to fulfill its predictions. True, Joseph is
later reunited with his father, but there is little to recall the Scriptural
model either by the end of the novel or in its middle sections.

This same failing has relevance for other characters as well, particularly as the narrator occasionally attempts to live up to the recommended representation of character that the author's preface prescribes.
"Surely," the preface informs us, "he hath a very ill-framed Mind, who

can look on Ugliness . . . as ridiculous in [itself]" (9). In a similar vein, author-Fielding rejects caricatura: "its Aim is to exhibit Monsters, not Men; and all Distortions and Exaggerations whatever are within its proper Province" (7). Mrs. Slipslop, for instance, scarcely fits the mold; her not "remarkably handsome" person is "very short, . . . too corpulent . . . , and somewhat red, with the Addition of Pimples in the Face. Her nose . . . too large, . . . her Eyes too little; nor did she resemble a Cow so much in her Breath, as in two brown Globes which she carried before her; one of her Legs was also a little shorter than the other" (32). Although her physical description does not stay with us, when we read it we understand why she transmogrifies the language. At the opposite end is Fanny, "tall and delicately shaped," set off, not by "brown Globes," but "swelling Breasts;" "her Neck, [of] a Whiteness [that] appeared which the finest *Italian* Paint would be unable to reach." On and on it goes. But to find this creature, according to the narrator, we "might say to ourselves, *Quod petis est nusquam*" (152). Fanny is not perfect nature; she is utter "Exaggeration."[62] Thus, even in its most elementary representation, the practice of character in the narrative proper is already an act of defiance.

There is, in fact, much more at stake in narrative practice that goes to the heart of the commercial ordering of *Joseph Andrews*. The crux of this matter concerns the way in which the narrator deals with the two male principals in the novel, Parson Adams and Joseph. We know of Adams even before we meet him because of the author's character blurb on him in the preface as "perfect Simplicity." The travails of his character hardly need restatement; it is worth noting, however, that his first appearance in propria persona is formed out of the shadows, a kind of chiaroscuro, that lends dignity to his person. The narrator casts him as "a grave Person" (61), at once sympathetic to the downtrodden and instinctively attuned to the nuances of petty tyrants. In daylight hours, he becomes something else. A later campaign in preservation of Fanny's virtue finds the Parson victimized by the random *asperges* of a chamber pot, the contents of which "trickle down the Wrinkles or rather deep Furrows of his Cheeks" (258). Near the end of the novel, once night settles, the call to virtue rouses him again, though he must first do battle with the bearded Slipslop, before he winds up spending the remainder of the night in Fanny's bed.

These adventures are, as advertised, "low," but they are also demeaning—gratuitously so, one suspects. Nor does this pattern of erosion abate. By the end of the novel Parson Adams has forsaken his parish for a living of £130 that Mr. Booby has proffered. While Adams's pursuit of money is novel-long, his financial woes precede the novel. And in what is the only excursus in narrative action—neither interpolation nor anything else that we can classify—he divulges the history of his money problems to a stranger-patriot. There, in 2, 3, we learn of his self-interested and political nature, via his dealings with his nephew's vote, a rector, Mr. Fickle, Colonel Courtly, and Sir Oliver Hearty, which unearths a side of Parson Adams we do not recognize. The narrator himself prepares us for the oddity of this disclosure, calling it "not only the most curious in this, but perhaps in any other Book" (132). If, somehow, we are obligated to recall "perfect Simplicity" throughout this novel-long unravelling, it is never clear what the term signifies other than an authorial need.

The needs and wants of the narrator, however, subvert that end. Still, we must recognize that Parson Adams, by virtue of his Christian office, poses a threat to the material the narrator trades in, which is to say, authority—not *auctoritas*—but his capacity to do certain things. Adams, we recall, is the only figure in the novel to decry trade as it is managed in the contemporary world, echoing in this regard the position of Fielding. He is not without material needs, as his interest in the sale of his sermons and his consumption of ale and tobacco make evident. These needs, however, often figure in exposing his character to ridicule. The point is that by devaluing Adams in his person or office the narrator helps to inflate his own worth as a competitor in the marketplace. Among other things, he is not foolish enough to leave his literary property behind—we are not, after all, reading the shirts and shoes packed by his wife; nor are we reading a sermon for which, according to the bookseller, no market exists. We read, instead, the product of someone who knows the market and can capitalize on its tastes—and who is, therefore, also subject to its machinations of suspense. As a practitioner he functions best within the restraints of his own division of labor as a trader in literature; accordingly, he disadvantages legitimate competitors by manipulating his textual economy to attract credit and confidence in his own product, not the product of others.

Joseph Andrews, as such, does not pose the same kind of risk to the narrator.[63] He is, in effect, the raw material—the capital—out of which the novel takes its shape. His change from modest brother to heroic lad, however abrupt, reaffirms a progressive capitalization process, which builds up rather than tears down. Unlike Parson Adams, moreover, Joseph displays little concern for material needs or wants. At the beginning of the novel, while under the influence of Lady Booby in London, he turns to the consumer pleasures of the town—operas, plays, assemblies—which give us a glimpse of Joseph in *"High-Life,"* but the general progress of his life retreats from "party-colour'd Brethren" and "the newest Fashion" (27).[64] This is not to suggest that he is without needs, though most of them are Fanny-centered. Despite this fact he is rewarded not only with the woman he has sought but materially as well—handsomely so, in fact, since, through the bounty of Mr. Booby, Fanny comes with an estate or at least one that Joseph can purchase with Booby's £2000 gift. We are a bit surprised by this Horatian solution because all along Joseph has not been one to cry "*O rus, quando te aspiciam,*" as if his Sabine farm awaited him. Thus, this resolution is curious in a couple of ways. First, the acquisition of property never uncomplicates a life and, in this regard, its purchase seems especially out of place for a character who has wanted so little. Second, although this "literary" resolution brings the novel to a close, it fails to address the "real-life" problems that it portends. While it may be that Joseph becomes the hero returned to the plow, the better alternative is that, by forsaking the open road, he loses his heroic character to domesticity. Nor does it seem possible that his retreat will spare him subsequent commercial intercourse with the world at large. Among other things, we learn that his property contains a dairy that Fanny, like Mrs. Trulliber, will manage; and, like her again, she will no doubt follow "the Markets with Butter and Eggs" (162). Joseph, in the meantime, will not sit by while his wife works; his role will be that of husband, father, and husbandman. Whatever surpluses accrue will go to market. The only commerce we know for sure that he has ruled out is the book trade, which the last lines confirm: "he will [not] be prevailed on by any Booksellers, or their Authors, to make his Appearance in *High-Life*" (344).

This detail, yet another barb directed at Richardson, addles *Joseph Andrews* as a whole, suspending it, in its last utterances, between fiction and factual fiction. We have been prepared for this kind of departure earlier in the novel, but the narrator's receipt of a letter from Wilson and his awareness of the unsuccessful attempts by booksellers and biographers alike to broker a sequel gives Joseph a life apart from the story told about him. The precedent for this practice is the skewering in 1, 1 of Cibber and Richardson, who purport to write "from authentic Papers and Records" (18). In this regard, *Joseph Andrews* comes full circle in order to settle on an unresolvable contradiction; it ends because there is nothing left for the narrator to turn into capital. Silence is preferable to that, and silence is what we get.

Fielding did not manage to undo Richardson. He merely turned his methods upside-down. Although the principals in *Joseph Andrews* lack the texture and depth of portraiture that Richardson evidenced in *Pamela*, Fielding's relatively flat characters are not without a range of complications and a broad band of "suspensions" all their own. But even in flattening these characters as he does, the narrator appropriates their hidden textures and stored energy and makes them proprietary in ways that his own invisibility cannot obscure. In his suspended state on the margins of narrative, the narrator acts out the consummate role of character in a commercial culture—a body that is not a body—a role that we cannot imagine he would intentionally choose for himself. The coherence he imparts—the progress of discarding the unworthy or objectionable and shepherding others more deserving back home again—is admirable. But it is a coherence, as I have tried to demonstrate, that settles nothing; not even the elect receive a full accounting. It is the type of coherence that only the narrative of commerce could generate. More than any other character in *Joseph Andrews*, Fielding's narrator stands by himself as the most complicated, complex, contradictory, and suspended figure we meet.

Neither Richardson nor Fielding resolved the problem of the character in suspense, though both tried unsuccessfully to govern it. That we can trace the operations of commerce and of material needs and wants in these characters is certainly no coincidence because the questions that commercial civilization posed to the eighteenth century and the realistic novel were ongoing. While it is never entirely clear what the answers were finally supposed to be in a progressive state that accommodated no positive definition, one answer was already clear: that returning to the older moral character in order to impose it upon the circumstantial did little to solve the enduring uncertainties of commercial life. Sterne pursued yet another answer to the riddle. Instead of resisting suspense, he indulged it in ways that demonstrate a marked advancement in attitude about the economy of narrative and the place of character in it. To him I now turn.

6

Sterne and the Industrial Novel

Underlying the calculus of period needs and wants was a simpler, almost arithmetical progress, from things "natural" and necessary for survival to things "artificial" and inessential. The importance of this progress for the economy is self-apparent. Not so obvious is its application to the set of novelists I have studied thus far. Of the many common denominators that link Defoe, Richardson, and Fielding, the most critical is that, while they all produce (realistic) fiction, they do not acknowledge this fact in the same way. To visualize the "progress" of fiction among these writers we could, if so inclined, assign coordinates to each along "natural (factual)/artificial (fictional)" axes. If the x-axis stood for the "natural" and the y "artificial," then the graph of progress would be an ascending line segment that would reflect the following relationships: Defoe disclaims fiction and pretends fact; Richardson pretends fact but is suspected of fiction; and Fielding broadcasts fiction except for those moments when reality impinges, for example, booksellers knock on Joseph's door. Defoe's realism is "natural"; Richardson's ambivalent; and Fielding's generally, though not entirely, "artificial." Sterne goes one step further. *Tristram Shandy* (1759–67), by comparison, is all fiction, at once unabashed artifice, perfect luxury, and complete indulgence, occupying the highest coordinates relative to the y-axis.

At an early stage in the novel Tristram epitomizes his approach when, in describing his father, he describes himself and, in turn, the fiction that is unfolding before us: "for he had a thousand little sceptical notions of the comick kind to defend,——most of which notions, I verily believe, at first enter'd upon the footing of mere whims, and of a *vive la Bagatelle*; and as such he would make merry with them for half an hour or so, and having sharpen'd his wit upon 'em, dismiss them till another day."[1] *Bagatelle* is the key to Sterne's fiction—stuff and nonsense, trinket and trifle—the makeup and material of *Tristram Shandy*. No household in the eighteenth-century novel is filled with more; no eighteenth-century novel toys with us as much or contains as many toys. *Tristram*

155

Shandy is in this respect a novel whose economy depends utterly upon the bagatelle and toy. As Maxine Berg notes, the center of toy manufacturing during the period was Birmingham. By 1759, the year in which the first two volumes of *Tristram Shandy* were published, Birmingham employed 20,000 workers in the toy manufacturing trades, and "the value of the ornamental part of the trade was estimated at £600,000 per year."[2] The reason for this vast enterprise was Birmingham itself: its "geography, its unincorporated political status, and its role as a haven from religious persecution."[3] Machinery was essential to this type of industrial development, which, as I detail subsequently, is also essential to the productive consciousness that informs *Tristram Shandy*. Although the introduction of machinery during the century was not untroubled (as we shall see in some of Walter Shandy's observations), the common view held that if machinery did not imperil the labor market it was critical for continued economic growth. The author of *Reflections on Various Subjects Relating to Arts and Commerce* (1752), for instance, argues that "*People without Commerce*, may safely refuse to admit" machinery of any type because it will create unemployment.[4] But even commercialized countries, the author contends, must be careful when introducing machinery, particularly if it "would *lessen* our *home* Markets ... [or create] a shameful *Monopoly* to enrich one or two" (27). Such, however, is not the case in England, where "all our *Staple* ["natural"] Trades are greatly extended and advanced; we have also invented and imported a Variety of new ones, particularly in the Toy-Manufacture, to which alone Birmingham owes its vast Increase of late Years" (77–78).

James Steuart (*An Inquiry into the Principles of Political Œconomy*) was a bit stronger in his endorsement of machines, arguing that their "advantage is permanent, and the necessity of introducing every method of abridging labour and expence, in order to supply the wants of luxurious mankind, is absolutely indispensable."[5] The risks he cites pertain to the unknown: "The consequences of innovations in political œconomy, admit of an infinite variety, because of the infinite variety of circumstances which attend them: no reasoning, therefore, however refined, can point out à priori, what upon such occasions must indispensibly follow" (1, 19:165). Or, in Tristram's case, write the first sentence and trust the rest to God. Machinery also had an impact on the processes of reproduction and thus complicated the idea of origins and originality. In his *Conjectures on Original Composition* (1759), Edward Young alludes to this connection when he associates originality with "natural" processes: "an *Original* may be said to be of a *vegetable* nature; it rises spontaneously from the vital root of genius; it *grows*, it is not *made*." By contrast, "*Imitations* are often a sort of *manufacture* wrought up by those *mechanics*, *art*, and *labour*, out of preexistent materials not their own."[6]

When he draws the two together, he echoes the seventeenth-century mercantilist who figured additional supplies of bullion as the solution to a weakened currency: "thoughts, when become too common, should lose their currency; and we should send new metal to the mint, that is, new meaning to the press." This retrograde solution is one that he traces even further back to "the division of tongues at *Babel*" (8). Those who fared well in the search for "original" standing were the ancients and, then, only by default: they "had no merit in being *Originals*: They could *not* be *Imitators*." In other words, underdeveloped markets and a lack of consciousness explain their originality. "Modern writers, [by contrast,] have a *choice* to make; and therefore have a merit in their power" (8). They face, in short, congested markets inhospitable to originality. Thus, as Young implies, the very notion of originality in a market society creates a psychological barrier too formidable for the majority to overcome (9).

Young's reflections typify the moral crisis that commercialization had occasioned throughout much of the eighteenth century and that we have seen acted upon in the novels of Defoe, Richardson, and Fielding. That the commercial economy had fashioned a range of "artificial" needs and wants was already commonplace by midcentury; its "fiction"-making capacities went hand in glove. But even as Young imagines a kind of pristine origin, the mechanism of productivity—the division of labor—structures the amelioration he conceives. "[C]onsider, my friend!" he urges, "knowledge physical, mathematical, moral, and divine, increases; all arts and sciences are making considerable advance; with them, all the accommodations, ornaments, delights, and glories of human life; and these are new food to the genius of a polite writer; these are as the root, and composition, as the flower; and as the root spreads, and thrives, shall the flower fail?" (33).

This particular image of progress through division, found in other period sources and related to industrial productivity, figures prominently in *Tristram Shandy*: "Thus,—thus my fellow labourers and associates in this great harvest of our learning, now ripening before out eyes; thus it is, by slow steps of casual increase, that our knowledge physical, metaphysical, physiological, polemical, nautical, mathematical, ænigmatical, technical, biographical, romantical, chemical, and obstetrical . . . have, for these two last centuries and more, gradually been creeping upwards towards that Αχμὴ of their perfections." The next clause informs us, in characteristic Shandean fashion, that, in light of "the advances of these last seven years," the crowning achievement of all knowledge, to wit, the dissolution of reading and writing, "cannot possibly be far off" (1, 31:71–72). As the prelude to a rather lengthy excursus even by Shandean standards, some forty pages in the Florida

Edition, these reflections occur at that instant when Elizabeth begins her labor. Occasioned by the footfalls and noise heard by the worthies assembled in Walter's parlor below, Tristram's thoughts about the division of labor form a natural association with and follow from the labor of his mother about to give birth to him. According to the productivity model that the novel supplies, this complex union of parts signifies an "origin," at once literal and figurative, that suspends narrative action for the sake of narrative originality, including the reproduction of birth and its sequelae. Sterne's approach to originality is more manufacturing and machine than flower and, in this regard, defies the model that Young proposes.

Jonathan Lamb has identified this more complicated approach to originality as one of the principal components of the "double principle." In its broad outlines, this notion defies Aristotelian logic because Lamb fixes an acute eye on how the thing is itself and not itself throughout *Tristram Shandy*. By pursuing the republican notion of *patria*, for example, he takes us through the public/private paradox to make a strong case for its reconciliation, though Lamb's terminology does not do justice to his method. The larger point that he asserts depends on his sophisticated understanding of literary language, as that understanding has been at least partially refined by Derrida, de Man, J. Hillis Miller, and others. Thus he declares "the fact that language is resistant to any notion of identity, and splits it along the lines of imitative originality . . . , explains why Shandean pleonasms seem to be founded on tautologies of perfection."[7] The eminent Sternean Melvyn New has taken exception to this approach, as practiced by Miller, Iser, Markley, and especially Lamb himself, by arguing that this quadrivirate has found "indeterminateness" in *Tristram Shandy* where none exists. Sterne's activity is "ontological," not "epistemological," he contends, and thus urges that "every attempt to create a world of certainty and truth will fail, the attempt is what ties us to the community of humanity . . . to create, if not God's world, then our own world in imitation of His."[8]

There is no doubt that, as the principal agent behind the Florida Edition, New has a remarkable gift for, among other things, identifying the sources and references buried in Sterne's novel. He also has the ability to range over textual examples and order them in such a way that even the most skeptical—or epistemologically inclined—among us would have to agree that Sterne seeks "determinateness," not its opposite. Yet I believe it is not only possible but necessary to draw these two camps together: that is, while Sterne pursued certainty, he did not succeed in producing it because he could accept, as others before him did not, the consequences of suspense. *Tristram Shandy*, I propose, is the first novel that not only has no qualms about the commercial economy but also

adapts to the "machines" of its productivity, especially through the vehicle of character. Our tendency is to take Sterne's novel as *sui generis*—
off by itself. This habit, certainly basic to the critical program of Watt
and others, strikes me as a bit curious, since what is essential to this
novel is its debt to precedents, including earlier novels. It would be fool-
hardy, however, to imagine that we get our Montaigne or Burton, Richardson or Fielding, unalloyed in *Tristram Shandy*. Because these writers
can only circulate through an alien context—the economy of Sterne's
novel—they assume whatever value the Shandean textual machine accords them. By way of illustration, we acknowledge the ridiculousness
of male chastity in *Joseph Andrews*; in *Tristram Shandy* it becomes another
of Tristram's book-debts, but one that he revalues and legitimizes
through his representation of Uncle Toby.

If we think of political economy as a more autonomously functioning
economy—more detached in its operations and disburdened from moral
concerns—then it marks a clear advance over the I-win-you-lose strat-
egy of mercantilism. From the perspective of the ordinary citizen, this
type of economy was not one so easily meddled with or subject to moral
persuasion. Brown expresses this historical dilemma in his *Estimate*.
Others did too. Sterne's solution was not to imagine a different order of
state, a nation miraculously purified, or a morality universally spread.
His novelistic microcosm is humble not proud—an offering, not a sermon. What we get is a Walter Shandy who, in orating on the state of
the nation from just beyond his armchair, exposes the condition of state
and citizen in which neither paradox nor bridge exists to span the divide.

It is not determinateness that fixes such enterprise, but approxima-
tion—leaners rather than ringers in the parlance of horseshoes. Neither
Defoe, Richardson, nor Fielding could tolerate this sense of approxima-
tion, though they failed with brilliance in their attempts to govern the
narrative forces they resisted. Sterne plots an altogether different
course, such that even the manufacturing of a book is as much the story
of *Tristram Shandy* as bulls that fail to live up to their reputations. In
the process, machines move, direct, and govern the economy of Sterne's
novel, just as they were beginning to do much the same work in the
economy as a whole. They were, one suspects, sure signs that the
Golden Age could only be imagined. Even James Steuart could muster
disapproval of the machine, though only under a precise set of circumstances. "If you can imagine a country peopled to the utmost extent of
the fertility of the soil, and absolutely cut off from any communication
with other nations; all the inhabitants fully employed in supplying the
wants of one another, [without the possibility of] increasing either circulation, industry, or consumption[, then] in such a situation as this, I

should disapprove of the introduction of machines, as I should disapprove of taking physic in an established state of perfect health."[9] That perfection can scarcely be claimed of the England inhabited by the Shandy family. Hence, in its domestic miniaturization of nationhood, akin to Toby's bowling-green model, approximations, revisions, and revaluations become the Shandean order of the day. Behind each lies those "wants" that must remain unsatisfied, though tantalizingly so, precisely as the material culture dictates for its survival.

Narrative in the Machine Age

More so than any other eighteenth-century novel, *Tristram Shandy* forces us to confront the idea of narrative originality—it is, after all, an "odd" book. Still, Dr. Johnson's characterization was mistaken on one score in that Sterne's novel has lasted. While no one is likely to mistake Johnson for an ideal reader of *Tristram Shandy*, that he would react to it as he did tells us something important about the enduring resistance to novelty and change that persisted in some quarters throughout the period. We too are susceptible to the same disposition. By habit and training, we do not typically associate Defoe, Richardson, and Fielding with Sterne because, quite frankly, this sequencing does not favor the seemingly eccentric or anomalous writer. In theorizing the "rise of the novel," we have in practice sided with Johnson. If we reverse the sequence, using Sterne as a way of organizing his precursors, then the apparent discontinuities from first till last are not nearly so glaring. This is not to suggest that *Tristram Shandy* lacked originality, but to urge that its originality, which we all acknowledge by segregating it from other novels, was manufactured from pieces near and far.[10] Indeed, it is difficult to see Sterne's work as anything other than a response to recent narrative practice, the legacy and transmission of which are, I believe, unmistakable: the first-person narration of *Tristram Shandy* recalls Richardson, while the chattiness of Tristram himself echoes the Fielding narrator; and, on the thematic level, matters of birth, parentage, travel, and (à la Crusoe) miniaturization suggest strong ties with Defoe. Ronald Paulson, in putting a finer point on these matters, has maintained, "Sterne apparently saw the same difficulty as Fielding in *Pamela* and *Clarissa*—a discrepancy between the moral structure of the novel and the psychological reality portrayed," so that, as he claims, we ought to regard *Tristram Shandy* as "a satire on novels."[11]

Sterne's method of course is not Fielding's—nor is it Defoe's or Richardson's. Sterne's approach is to dismantle preexisting novels, not to junk them, but to reuse their parts in a novel "machine." The image is his, not mine, and, though it appears on a number of occasions, Tristram employs it globally shortly after Elizabeth goes into labor in order to justify his own method of narrative labor. Although the machine image may trigger thoughts of literary machines—the *deus ex machina*, for instance—common associations have no place in Sterne's designs. "[T]he machinery of my work," says Tristram, justifies what is essential to the narrative: namely, the "digressive-progressive" (1, 22:81) tension that accounts for his productivity. The exploded view of this machine allows us to see even more clearly the relationship between parts and the whole. "I have constructed the main work and the adventitious parts of it with such intersections, and have so complicated and involved the digressive and progressive movements, one wheel within another, that the whole machine, in general, has been kept a-going;—and, what's more, it shall be kept a-going these forty years, if it pleases the fountain of health to bless me so long with life and good spirits" (1, 22:81–82).

While the idea of novel-as-machine seems, at best, to have only dubious merit—a far cry from, say, the dramatic intercession of a god on stage—the model itself indicates Tristram's commitment to the historical legacy that has shaped him. From the start, the role of the machine figures prominently in his life—indeed, bears much of the blame for the peculiar set of circumstances surrounding his personal origin. I refer in particular to the clock at the beginning of the novel, which retains a kind of primal authority, with a tick that is at once regularly irregular, ubiquitous, and cumulative. By book 7, this clock, figured as Death, has almost caught up with Tristram, who, in his need to survive, spares his own life by racing across the Channel to France. Of special note about this book is that Tristram begins it by recalling the machine. Before naming it as such, he reintroduces his production rate (two volumes per year of life), yet worries about meeting this self-imposed quota because of a "vile cough." In this state of distraction he cannot "recollect" where he spoke of his "book as a *machine*," but is mindful enough to craft a *memento mori* by crossing his "pen and ruler . . . upon the table" (7, 1:575). Like time itself, as it is represented in the novel, the clock is blamed for "dispers[ing] the animal spirits" of Tristram the homunculus, even though the tick-tock sexual commerce between husband and wife better explains Walter's recourse to damning a machine. The most elementary machine, the pulley—or, better, the defective pulley—accounts for Tristram's genital trauma, raising questions about his manhood, while Dr. Slop's forceps is instrumental in crushing the infant Tristram's nose—a symbol of manhood as we later learn—to a jelly. Even the most benevolent and gentle-minded of characters, Uncle Toby, cannot do without his assortment of machines and engines.

Through their aid, he is able to re-create the siege of Namur in scaled realistic detail to effect the recovery that bed rest and reading would not allow. Machines, in this regard, structure history as Tristram knows and lives it.

This intimate commerce between machine and history, enacted through measured time, yields a narrative chiming with historical references of one sort or another that, in turn, resonate in and for the moment. The scholarship and learning of the novel, otherwise so out of place in fiction, contribute to this effect. As a bookish novel, *Tristram Shandy* fosters the illusion that movement beyond the armchair is unnecessary, but this impression makes us forget the ways in which external history forever impinges upon the present to expose character defects or to introduce narrative conflict. King William's Wars, long since passed, animate Uncle Toby in the present, allowing his old wounds to heal properly. Indeed, the most incongruous action in the novel, Tristram's circuit of France in book 7, rouses us from the insulated comforts of historical Shandydom to expose the adult vulnerabilities of its son, the narrator, who after a protracted delay finally occupies a place on his own stage.[12] But we do not have to read far in order to appreciate how time, even mythic time, collapses itself into the present moment. Book 1, chapter 1 finds Walter reacting to Elizabeth's question about the clock: "*Did ever woman, since the creation of the world, interrupt a man with such a silly question?*" (1, 1:2). It is difficult to think of another novel of the century that so thoroughly exhausts the breadth of human imperfection and so completely fractures history into shards of contemporary moments.

What is striking about this conjunction is the reorientation of time that it effects. Through the instrumentality of the machine, Sterne detaches the "narrative of history" from its teleological base and, by doing so, opens his novel up to other forms of inquiry and interpretation that depend upon historical progress and suspense. There can be no doubt that the machine, along with its human equivalent—the division of labor—accelerated the commercial revolution in England, as both conditioned a more efficient use of time. The consequences of this progress tell us much about the formal and thematic properties of *Tristram Shandy*, but only as they are pulled by the "digressive" pole of Tristram's self-declared "digressive-progressive" axis. We get a good sense of this tugging when he makes sport of the "*icals*," those consequences of the knowledge explosion and the intellectual division of labor. In a most profound sense, however, even though Tristram may protest the advances of his age, he is powerless to alter the forces behind the industrial economy or to dispense with the uncertainties that attend suspense, even in the most elementary way. One of the strangest admissions he makes—and that initially invites skepticism—deals with his pen. He claims no responsibility for his productive output, while prompting us to blame the implement and not the person for any affronts we may experience to our sensibilities: "ask my pen,—it governs me,—I govern not it" (6, 6:500). Although the passage readily lends itself to metaphorical understanding, it does the same on the literal level, if we can appreciate how Tristram's mind, like the economy and the machine, is geared toward parts, not wholes.

James Steuart sounds the requisite cautionary note about progress in the machine age when he comments on the inappropriateness of the machine for a self-contained, self-sufficient community that already meets the material needs and wants of its members. The Shandy family is not that unit, nor is the England of its residence. Both assume parts in a fiction of imperfection that no quantity of *mea culpa*'s can undo. It was the genius of the industrial mind, however, to offer remediation for imperfection with its opposite: perfection. In part 4 ("Of Consequences that result from the Advancement of Civil and Commercial Arts"), section 1 (*"Of the Separation of Arts and Professions"*), of *An Essay on the History of Civil Society*, Adam Ferguson remarks "that the more [the artist] can confine his attention to a particular part of any work, his productions are the more perfect, and grow under his hands in the greater quantities."[13] He follows this notion with a more precise elaboration that connects it to the machine: "manufactures . . . prosper most, where the mind is least consulted, and where the workshop may, without any great effort of imagination, be considered as an engine, the parts of which are men" (183). Yet, despite this union of man and machine, the facts belie the mechanical incarnation, as Ferguson goes on unwittingly to indicate: "some employments are liberal, others mechanic," with each requiring "different talents, and inspir[ing] different sentiments" (184); as a result, "thinking itself, in this age of separations, may become a peculiar craft" (183).

There is no reason to blame Ferguson for leaving a complex paradox unexamined, since the genre of history writing, as he knew it, did not require him to measure it in human terms. But while his reflections on the mechanical age overlap with Sterne's, the latter does not have the luxury of avoidance. The impact of the machine, of manufacturing processes, and of the division of labor must be gauged by individual characters through the workings of history. Even though Tristram may have no inclination to participate in a system he does not choose, he participates nonetheless. While machines have no minds, they have a powerful influence on perceptions of productivity, demand, and work itself. For Sterne, the machine organizes the most basic unit of work as it is represented in the novel, with every other manifestation of work developing out of it. Thus, when Tristram refers to the cabbage planter at the beginning of book 8, defying "him to go on cooly, critically, and canonically, planting his cabbages one by one, in straight lines . . . especially if slits in petticoats are unsew'd up" (8, 1:655), he alludes to his own writing practice, which, in the orderly arrangement of a printed book, is a series of words "planted" generally in straight lines. Behind this analogy lies the machine, either the printing press or, for the cabbage planter, the plow. That Tristram implicitly thinks in terms of an agricultural implement may suggest, in addition, that, at root, the printed text is the first stage of a multistaged progressive unit of labor; though in a more perfect world—one in which progress plots an undivided course and the stages of history are an unequivocal measure—book 1 should have sown the seeds of this idea, not book 8.

The Shandy family is similarly ordered according to the simple-to-complex process. Tristram reflects, "Though in one sense, our family was certainly a simple machine, as it consisted of a few wheels; yet there was thus much to be said for it, that these wheels were set in motion by so many different springs, and acted one upon the other from such a variety of strange principles and impulses,—that though it was a simple machine, it had all the honour and advantages of a complex one,—and a number of odd movements within it, as ever were beheld in the inside of a *Dutch* silk-mill" (5, 6:427). Tristram's machine, by contrast, is more productive, as well as more sophisticated than his family's. And with a number of volumes already published, all of them contributing to the economy of letters, he can afford to say, "All . . . we can do, is to turn and work the machine to the improvement and better manufactury of the arts and sciences" (6, 17:525). Here Sterne seizes on the perceived benefits to the polite arts and knowledge in general that, as others confirmed, occurred in conjunction with the fourth or commercial stage of history. Ferguson, for example, alludes to this phenomenon. Earlier, David Hume said much the same thing in "Of The Rise and Progress of the Arts and Sciences" (1742): *"That nothing is more favourable to the rise of politeness and learning, than a number of neighbouring and independent states, connected together by commerce and polity."*[14] The difference, however, is that, for Sterne, the machine intersects the rise and progress of the arts and sciences; it is, after all, their "manufactury" that he stresses.

To imply that Sterne is a product-based novelist is not to slight him or his creation at all. This classification, however, sets him apart from Defoe, Richardson, and, to a lesser degree, Fielding, who invest heavily in character to carry their fictions. The latter two, especially, are keen on representing the ideal character or even, in Richardson's case, the perfect character. The commerce they effect with their readers is, by contrast, one-sided, as if the only acceptable response were the homogenized and intended response. Sterne's approach is not only different but also accommodating. At any given moment he divides his labor among grave critics, Christians, anti-Shandeans, fellow laborers, worships and reverences, Nosarians and anti-Nosarians, Mesdames, Sirs, parents, governors, and assorted others, not to separate them according to economic rank, as Richardson and Fielding are inclined to do, but to address the particular persuasions and interests of audience as classifiable readers.[15] As such, these readers perform double-duty: they anchor Sterne's novel-machine internally as a literary genre and secure it externally in the marketplace of available literary goods. Sterne himself realizes that in an age capable of mass production—the machine age—the best audience is the broadest audience, for without consumers the productive output of the novelist would be tallied as a cipher. To that end, he summons the liberal marketplace—the comprehensive and varied audience—at the beginning of the novel, as we begin to hear the first turnings of the machine itself: "my life and opinions are likely to make some noise in the world, and . . . will take in all ranks, professions, and denominations" (1, 4:5).

Yet we should not assume that Sterne's model of divided labor produces undivided perfection. Although he makes Tristram proud about his composition and its masterful arrangement of parts, these forms of perfection, if to be tolerated at all, inhere in the product, not the person, as each character represented in the novel is flawed in some way. But even if perfection is possible beyond the novel, let us say in a body of "perfect" readers, then knowledge of this possibility is suspended from our view; for as Tristram concedes, "no author, who understands the just boundaries of decorum and good breeding, would presume to think all: The truest respect which you can pay to the reader's understanding, is to halve the matter amicably" (2, 11:125). Not even the God of truth can do much to alter this relationship. Tristram discloses that he writes his own first sentence and trusts God for the next (2, 8:656). Whether this is God's idea or Tristram's is beyond our knowing. The only certainty the passage allows is that the division of labor is universal.

Although the sophistication of Sterne's craft belongs to his consciousness of machines, manufacturing, and the commercial age in which he lived, his indebtedness to authors before him is as intense and open as any we can find in the period novel. These matters were precisely those that invited questions about origins and originality, as we have already seen in the case of Edward Young. David Hume addressed similar concerns in his essay on the arts and sciences when he comments that "it may not be for the advantage of any nation to have the arts imported from their neighbours in too great perfection. . . . So many models of ITALIAN painting brought into ENGLAND, instead of exciting our artists, is the cause of their small progress in that noble art." To read Waller, concludes Hume, is to remember Horace, as well as to recognize that, had they both written during the reign of Tiberius, Waller could not have competed with Horace. Though the past may be burdensome and trigger anxiety, Waller is not devalued because of it. "We esteemed ourselves sufficiently happy, that our climate and language could produce but a faint copy of so excellent an original."[16] We do not recover "origins" from *Tristram Shandy*; if anything, we recover the remanufacturing and corrected retransmission of them in order to count ourselves "sufficiently happy." At his most literally "original" moment, at the outset of the novel, Tristram tells us he subscribes to Horace's *ab ovo* beginning, from which all else shall be traced. But there is a problem. The transmission of the "begetting" derives from Uncle Toby, whose sensitivity and modesty about sexual matters make him the *least* likely source of such embarrassing information. Needless to say, this mystery is not solved, but the ambiguity that lingers after, about words and their possible meanings, applies equally to *ab ovo* or origins. Through the passage of time or even at the beginning of a novel, the literal and metaphorical become clouded, so that the truest measure of the evidence is the moment before us, not the long history that precedes "I wish either my father or my mother . . ." (1, 1:1). A compromise is "Waller-ization," which adds to the "*bulk*—[and] so little to the *stock*" (5, 1:408).

This commitment to the present—to the craft of fabrication and to the business of manufacturing a novel—makes Sterne acutely aware of his literary property. The typography and layout of the book itself, production schedules, self-promotion, sales concerns, indeed audience as market all contribute to his proprietary sense, and underscore the strategic role the machine plays in the consciousness of needs and wants. Earlier I referred to Adam Ferguson's passage on the division of labor, in which he says the more attentive the worker is to discrete tasks in the manufacturing process the "more perfect" his productions become, growing "under his hands in the greater quantities." This language is nearly identical to that used by Tristram, whose father Walter borrows his son's name as part of a larger project on education, the *Tristrapaedia*. Of its history and author, Tristram tells us this: "—he imagined he should be able to bring whatever he had to say, into so small a compass, that when it was finished and bound, it might be rolled up in my mother's hussive.—Matter grows under our hands.—Let no man say,—'Come—I'll write a *duodecimo*'" (5, 16:445–46). The life of Walter, as we see it, is one filled with frustration, dissatisfaction, and of needs and wants never satisfied. The curious thing about the culture of mechanical perfection is that it is of a type that must always defer gratification—no one individual will ever fashion the whole; the strength of the machine is that it quantifies perfection, not in the person, but through the product. Under these terms, and with Walter as a model, *Tristram Shandy* is a novel about infinite needs and wants, omnipresent but forever suspended, because the sum total of its parts, given the impossible demands of its production model, never amounts to a completed whole or finished product. The system of political economy that provokes this kind of uncomfortable suspense is not easily subject to governance, and perhaps it is no coincidence that the phase of economy that England moved toward at the time has been labeled laissez-faire.

Obviously, Defoe, Richardson, and Fielding could never quite accept the full implications of the commercial economy and were bold enough to suggest that their principal characters had the moral strength to govern it themselves. The result, as I have contended in earlier chapters, is the suspended character. By effacing virtually all traces of teleology from his design, Sterne accepts not only the already divided character as the essential feature of his narrative but also the environmental factors of suspense that made this character so. This practice does not preclude moral self-discovery and, for that reason, addresses the implications of character that Defoe, Richardson, and Fielding failed to examine. But while Sterne could protest the presumptions of progress, he could only answer bluster with digressions. The map of progress remains largely unchanged. So too does the consumer capitalism that defines its land masses and seas. For what the commercial revolution was predicated on, particularly as it was enhanced by the machine, was a Fibonacci sequence of needs and wants and a crude calculus of deferred gratification.

The Old Economy Versus the New

It is one thing to be told about the division of labor and another thing to experience it. Sterne not only forces that experience upon us but also expects us to live up to its conditions. By any standard of judgment, *Tristram Shandy* is labor-intensive for its readers, precisely because we are not told everything, a fact that Tristram himself admits. Yet its omissions and shadings only compound that sense of obligation Tristram exacts from readers by dubbing them his "fellow labourers" (1, 21:71). Although an odd way of defining audience, this locution occurs early and often, either implicitly or explicitly, so that we take the role seriously even when Sterne uses it in playful terms. In one such incident he goes out of his way to tease a reader about her careless and inattentive labor when she misses the fact that Elizabeth Shandy is not a Catholic. Such a reader, Tristram contends, comes armed with a view of what a narrative is supposed to be rather than what *Tristram Shandy* actually is: "'tis a rebuke to vicious taste which has crept into thousands besides herself, — of reading straight forwards, more in quest of adventures, than of the deep erudition and knowledge which a book of this cast, if read over as it should be, would infallibly impart with them" (1, 20:65). An accusation of this sort virtually indicts us all, for who among us is capable of reading anything perfectly?

Although this passage arises from the parochial matter of intrauterine baptism, its significance goes well beyond the administration of rites. Sterne expects from us an attention to details and parts that either elude us or seem not all that important or relevant. Our ability to accomplish what he demands of us is further complicated by our habitual interest in getting from point a to point b. The Shandean system, however, does not tolerate indolent or single-minded readers. In fact, through its most elementary form of exchange, the one between reader and writer, this system advances an industrial sensibility. Yet the passage underscores another, equally important issue. If we are conscientious about our labor and internalize the prescribed method of reading stipulated in *Tristram Shandy*, we begin to question our ability to read any of its passages or episodes with even the basic skill asked of us. Because, as conventional readers, we make certain assumptions about the intelligibility of language, ordered action, and the existence of closure, these needs and wants are routinely frustrated in Sterne's novel which is predicated on an elaborate system of sublimations, deferred gratification, and protracted suspense. The incarnate form of this industrial design is Tristram Shandy himself, who constantly withholds information about himself, and, although conceived on page 1, defers his birth and legitimacy as heir apparent until books later in the novel. If *Tristram Shandy* did not purport to be an autobiography, perhaps we would not find its atypical narrative parts so disorienting; yet it is because we are thinking in terms of a conventionally administered *whole* autobiography that we react to Tristram's invisibility.

This effacement of the self stands in utter contrast to character delineation in Defoe, Richardson, and even Fielding, whose named central character, Joseph Andrews, is fully detailed. The characters of these earlier novelists become intelligible through direct apprehension and as we watch them perform in a series of largely continuous actions. The desired end of these delineations is emulation. This model does not work in *Tristram Shandy*. Whatever we know about Tristram we gather from bits and fragments, displays of wit and ingenuity en passant, or the tales he tells of others, not himself. There is no indication, however, that Sterne perversely or willfully obscured his character simply for the purpose of concealment. We must remember that his novel machine includes many wheels, one of which happens to be the narrator's method of self-representation. This particular mechanical operation is of course powerful because its propels us through the novel. But even more than that, Sterne's invisible narrator stresses not only the influence of the narrative of commerce and its demands for the invisible character but also the generational conflict between father and son that fuels the narrative. Earlier novelists sometimes included parents in the stories they told, though these same writers tend to kill them off or get them out of the way quickly. A good portion of Clarissa Harlowe's ills are attributable to the fact that her father survives as long as he does; in fact, the whole Harlowe family is infected by his tyrannical disease. The holy Sir Charles Grandison is spared such indignity, since his father is dead, yet there is nothing kind about the son's remembrance of a father who, among other things, was quick to unsheathe his sword. Walter Shandy, by contrast, occupies a central place and remains eminently likeable, once we appreciate his eccentricities, even though there are enough philosophical disagreements between father and son to suggest that their relationship could easily have soured.

Walter remains in place because he too is a wheel, though a wheel that wears out over time and must be replaced. In the most literal sense, he is the father of the storyteller; but he is also the figure of the older economy—the economy of Defoe, Richardson, and Fielding—who resists all that commercial capitalism signified and political economy was beginning to signify. Although Walter is curious about the machine, his interest is only in its theoretical applications. The particuiar machine that supports this view is Stevinus's sailing chariot, about which Uncle Toby is knowledgeable, Dr. Slop purports to be, and Walter registers his opinion. About this Stevinus Walter offers that "the inventor of [the sailing vessel] must have had a very mechanical head; and tho' I cannot guess upon what principles of philosophy he has atchiev'd it;—yet certainly his machine has been constructed upon solid ones." Dr. Slop is the one who suggests that investors ought to seek land applications for Stevinus's chariot because, compared with horses, it costs nothing. "For that very reason," counters Walter, " 'Because they cost nothing, and because they eat nothing,' —the scheme is bad;—it is the consumption of our products, as well as the manufactures of them, which gives bread to the hungry, circulates trade,—brings in money, and supports the value of our lands; . . . if I was a Prince, I would generously recompence the scientifick head which brought forth such contrivances;—yet I would peremptorily suppress the use of them" (2, 14:136–37). While the conversation comes to a halt with the arrival of Trim, who bears Toby's volume of Stevinus, nothing more has to be said. Walter opposes changes to the economy, particularly the introduction of labor-saving devices that would alter the shape of the work force and depreciate if the not the real value of fixed property then certainly its political value, a subject dear to the now retired and insecure Walter Shandy.

It is possible that Walter was not always so determined in his opinions. He lacks the fine sensibility of his brother Toby, who, despite his real hardships, appreciates machines and engines and, by doing so, has also developed the ideal disposition to face the challenges of a more industrialized and anonymous nation-state. Walter himself, as we piece things together, has lived through a critical period in England's economic development, the 1690s, when the published debate about the future of the commercial nation grew heated in light of the recoinage crisis and the development of the Bank of England. Because of his experiences, we can perhaps better appreciate why Walter is so hardened against the idea of change.

That Walter spent the critical decades of his adult life as a Turkey merchant is not without significance for, as we see him, he has retired to the family's paternal estate after his advantageous marriage late in life to Elizabeth Mollineux. Like Crusoe's father, Walter is already an elderly man when he begins to have children. But whether he has enjoyed more success in the Turkey trade than in parenting is difficult to know. From what Sterne tells us, we can determine that he began his business in London in the 1690s. On at least one front this trade was distressed during his period of entry, as can be determined from the petition of 50,000 silk throwers who bitterly complained about the interruption of raw silk from Turkey during the war. "Pray," they implored Parliament, "that liberty may be given to English merchants to import overland all sorts of raw silk, which usually come from Turkey."[17]

The Turkey trade is in this regard the one occupation perfectly suited to vex Walter, given its unpredictabilities and his abiding interest in just the opposite. Why he chooses the Turkey trade is itself a mystery. Apprenticeship premiums for the Levant trade were as much as £860 in 1679 and during the first decade of the eighteenth century 68 percent of London merchants fell to bankruptcy. That Walter has retired from trade suggests that bankruptcy was not his fate, but that he stayed in it for so long might indicate that he was not among the most successful. Of those merchants who remained in trade into their fifties, the highest percentage (31 percent) had fortunes of under £1000. The financial rewards of marriage may have aided Walter greatly when he retired sometime between his fiftieth and sixtieth years; its emotional rewards were, however, another story.[18]

Complicating this matter all the more is the fact that Walter comes from a landed family, though both he and his brother Toby turn to occupations that were generally reserved for younger sons: that is, trade and the military. From this circumstance we may surmise that the Shandy family placed a good deal of promise on the mercantile success of Walter and that Walter himself somehow internalized his sense of obligation to the family. At one point, for example, when he is already retired, he pleads the cause of the country interest, noting chauvinistically that the same cannot be done in France, where interest does not serve the public welfare, only the ruling monarch. Moreover, at an earlier period in his history, he works the Exchange, possibly to discover the northwest passage to wealth, perhaps to bypass the uncertainties of mercantile hard work. We do, however, get a sample of his investing skills when he takes the £1000 left to him by aunt Dinah and puts it into the Mississippi Scheme. Walter intends the dividends of this speculation "mostly for the honour of his family"; unfortunately this project to colonize Louisiana went belly up (4, 31:394). Tristram wryly notes that had his father taken the money and put it into the Ox-moor, land long lying fallow, Walter would have been assured of an abundant harvest and economic gain.

A year before his retirement from the Turkey trade Walter ventures down a different and equally perilous course as a writer, though even here his thoughts are never far removed from the trading life. Describing his father's new enterprise as something on the order of an epic trading voyage, Tristram muses that Walter "set out with so full a sail, and in so swelling a tide of heroic greatness" (5, 12:440). Needless to say, he reconstructs his father's enthusiasm, since Walter's new career occurs years before Tristram's birth, and concludes that the "Life of Socrates," the object of his father's writerly attention, "was the means of hastening him out of [his old one]" (5, 12:440). Like so many other conjectures made throughout, this one also inspires our own. It is evident that, like Toby, Walter lives in a self-contained world only a few steps removed from his brother's bowling green. A life of writing may have served that insulated end. But the other and more striking possibility is that Walter could not be a merchant and writer at the same time. That is, he could not divide his labor, as his son so successfully manages when he writes his own *Life and Opinions*.

The content of the "Life of Socrates" thus sheds light on the character of its author. Although we do not hear much about the "Life," we probably hear enough. The underlying premise of this work is captured in the rough balance between sentimental inevitability and an assertion of defiance: *"That we and our children were born to die, —but neither of us born to be slaves"* (5, 12:440). Walter next worries about the transmission of "that sentiment" and concludes that it made its way to England via "land carriage":

By water the sentiment might easily have come down the *Ganges* into the *Sinus Gangeticus*, or *Bay of Bengal*, and so into the *Indian Sea*; and following the course of trade, (the way from *India* by the *Cape of Good Hope* being then unknown) might be carried with other drugs and spices up the *Red Sea* to *Joddah*, the port of *Mekka*, or else to *Tor* or *Sues*, towns at the bottom of the gulf; and from thence by karrawans to *Coptos*, but three days journey distant, so down the *Nile* directly to *Alexandria*, where the SENTIMENT would be landed at the very foot of the great stair-case of the *Alexandrian* library,— and from that store-house it would be fetched.——Bless me! what a trade was driven by the learned in those days! (5, 12:441)

Walter draws on knowledge derived from the study of maps, an activity not unknown to his brother, and culled from books. But the absurdity of this commercial navigation is one that eludes him. Ideas do not have heft and bulk because, as Locke had already proved, words and things do not necessarily accord. Walter discloses in his "Life" a passionate need for certainty and exactitude, tactile and ordered sentiment, a precision and measure that modern commerce has rendered immaterial and invisible.

The differences between the ancient and modern, the past and present, prick Walter mercilessly. While pontificating to Toby about his theories of the ancient world, Elizabeth Shandy walks into the middle of this modern confabulation to hear her husband, in his assumed persona of Socrates, confess that " 'I have three desolate children.'——Then, cried my mother, opening the door,——you have one more, Mr. *Shandy*, than I know of. By heaven! I have one less,—said my father, getting up and walking out of the room" (5, 13:442). Lost to Walter is the Socratic jest history plays upon him with the unnecessary, though perfectly ironic return of Xanthippe. By popping her head in the door at just the right moment, Elizabeth performs the role of audience, whose misunderstanding depends upon a partial hearing of all the evidence. Yet her role is no better than ours, since we too only hear a fragment of the "Life of Socrates." Whether Walter silently internalizes this lesson and determines that anything he says is subject to misinterpretation is impossible to know. We do learn, however, that he refuses to offer his manuscript for publication and hence preserves the integrity of his work by keeping it out of circulation and fating it to silence.

Though his career as a Turkey merchant has depended upon circulation, Walter has reservations about the practice of that economic mechanism. He never addresses the matter directly, but through his characteristic obliquities he declares just that. Under the premise of keeping his wife from delivering in London, he rejects his contractual obligations as a matter of public virtue, though his motives are purely self-interested. Summarizing the findings of political writers since the time of Queen Elizabeth, he declares "that the current of men and money towards the metropolis . . . [has] become dangerous to our civil rights . . . a *distemper* was here his favourite metaphor, and he would run it down into a perfect allegory, by maintaining it was identically the same in the body national as in the body natural, where blood and spirits were driven up into the head faster than they could find their ways down;———a stoppage of circulation must ensue, which was death in both cases" (1, 18:52–53). Walter's association between the place where his child is born and the economic well-being of his nation, while curious, is significant; from it we see that putative national ills are also domestic ills. In addition, this passage suggests how, with the development of commercial and financial centers, Walter not only opposes economic change but also justifies his position based on the faltering premises of body politic/body natural imagery.

In the wake of his career as a trader, Walter appears intolerant of modern forms of circulation; he prefers, instead, to stay put. His refusal to budge on any points of interest may obliquely fill in the largely unwritten void that surrounds his earlier life in which compromise and negotiation would have been the order of business. In strange ways, then, the fragments of Walter's past history produce his character and hint at the reasons for his lack of fulfillment. If his present has been prefigured by his past, it does so because the past can only predict the present through discontinuity and division—the sudden emergence of Xanthippe, for instance. In the process, we piece together an individual who aches for predictable verities and unshakable precision, as if absolutes and theoretical purity were the only answers for the frustrations of modern life. His unwillingness to publish the "Life of Socrates" becomes, in this light, an act of self-imposed withdrawal. Only with the next generation, curiously incarnated in son Tristram, does this "Life" and the life of its author come to mean anything—by an exchange with readers and through the act of "circulation."

Walter's dated outlook on the economy has its corollary in his outlook on character: he is a typologist. In this respect, he bears a strong resemblance to Crusoe, Pamela, and Joseph Andrews, who are all outfitted in typological garments. Walter, as a disciple of Robert Filmer, author of *Patriarcha*, subscribes to the belief that the greatest monarchies have been "stolen from that admirable pattern and prototype of this household and paternal power" (1, 18:55). Unwittingly he reduces both pattern and prototype merely by acting in his modern world. This "absolute prince" must pull up "his breeches with both hands," before rising from his throne, to wit, his armchair, in order to deliver an oration on the state of England.

For Walter, pontificating comes easily; making his decrees comply with things is much more difficult. By his deeds he offers living proof of the abuse and imperfections of words Locke had espoused, although in doing so he must also reject the same Locke who repudiated Filmer's theory of government. As the typed king of his own household, Walter cannot even exert a borrowed royal prerogative in his own bedroom or in the beds of justice. His lovemaking to his wife deadens whatever spirit she may have felt for her postfigured prince, a husband in the flesh. His exertions make her think instead of clocks not fully wound and their mechanical tick-tock, as if her husband were adrift in Stevinus's sailing chariot, a machine that, by Walter's account, damaged commerce. Indeed, through her association of ideas Elizabeth challenges her husband's masculinity. And by unwittingly injecting Locke into their sexual commerce, she "cuckolds" her absolute husband's most cherished belief, that he is *de jure* the indisputable head of his household.

The beds of justice prove no more accommodating to Walter's ancient prerogative, though paradoxically they pay him the absolute obedience his self-appointed typed character demands. Following the custom of the Goths who debated matters of state twice, once drunk and a second time sober, Walter tries his best to modernize that ancient practice in ways suitable to his condition. We soon discover that the past and present do not easily yoke in his bedroom on Sunday nights, where the precisions of habit command his presence. Because of his affliction with gravel he cannot drink but does exchange desire for intoxication and satiety for sobriety. On one occasion when an important matter of state has arisen—that is, retiring Tristram's vests and tunics for breeches—he submits the matter to Elizabeth's counsel. In the longest exchange between husband and wife to occur in the novel, she does not once disagree with him about the need for the sartorial change or the material out of which the breeches should be made. Nor does she help him out of his quandary about the large size of his young child since, as Walter confesses, "——I am very short myself. . . . You are very short, Mr. *Shandy*,—said my mother. Humph! quoth my father to himself, a second time: in muttering which, he plucked his pillow a little further from my mother's" (6, 18:527). Growing more irritated with his wife's now predictable deference, Walter presses home the matter of the breeches. Elizabeth naturally agrees with him again, adding "if it pleases you, Mr. *Shandy*." With his temper now lost, Walter can only sputter in frustration that his wife cannot distinguish "betwixt a point of pleasure and a point of convenience" (6, 18:529). Acquiescence has been paid the supine Filmerian, but if justice has been served it is of the most paradoxical sort.

These fragments of pillow talk provide at least partial explanations of why Walter types himself according to the Filmerian model. That once authoritative system compensates for the inadequacies and failures that Walter, rightly or wrongly, perceives in himself. As we probe more deeply into his character through the fragments that Tristram scatters throughout, we detect someone for whom certainty, precision, and predictability are more akin to the need for personal assurance rather than absolute ends unto themselves. His psychic economy precludes any explicit awareness of this order since his manner of dealing with practical desires is to sublimate them as theoretical perplexities. Like most practiced typologists, Walter finds that the facts alone always prove disappointing. In his study of noses, which are in themselves a substitution for something else, Walter tortures himself to find their secret meaning in the doctrine "laid down by Erasmus." Tristram reports his father's disappointment "in finding nothing more from so able a pen, but the bare fact itself; without any of that speculative subtilty or ambidexterity of argumentation upon it." Nevertheless, he persists, believing all along that "Learned men . . . don't write dialogues upon long noses for nothing." He tells Toby that he will "study the mystic and the allegoric sense, [because] here is some room to turn a man's self in" (3, 37:271). Or inside out. When he lights upon the mystical sense of Erasmus to within a single letter, he reports his premature findings to Toby, who notes, "But you have marr'd a word. . . . My father put on his spectacles, — bit his lip, — and tore out the leaf in a passion" (3, 37:272), a response that befits the subject.

The same kinds of problems hound Walter with the composition of his *Tristrapaedia*, a treatise designed, in part, to prove the theory "that there is a North west passage to the intellectual world; and that the soul of man has shorter ways of going to work, in furnishing itself with knowledge and instruction, than we generally take with it" (5, 42:484). This imagined shortcut turns out to be just as elusive as the direct route to the commercial wealth of the East. Like most practitioners of a craft in the modern commercial state, Walter undertakes a specialized form of labor, grown doubly difficult, since the intended audience of the *Tristrapaedia* is his wife. A sense of urgency also seizes Walter since few things have gone right for Tristram. From the start his conception was wrong, his birth was botched, and his name got confused. According to Tristram, Walter fractionizes the problem, reserving the last quarter of paternal intercession for the education of his sole surviving son: "he had lost, by his own computation, full three fourths of me — that is, he had been unfortunate in his three first great casts for me — my geniture, nose, and name, — there was but this one left" (5, 16:445). The *Tristrapaedia*, if followed dutifully, would negate the three unpropitious casts with an education that would assure his son's character once and for-ever—something Walter has failed to do up to this point.

Because Walter determines that the *Tristrapaedia* must be compact enough to fit in Elizabeth's hussive, he must take exacting care in its composition. Accordingly, he sweats over each word. In three years' time he manages to finish precisely half his system of education. By that time Elizabeth has already taken over the custody and care of Tristram, while her husband races fruitlessly against the clock for a second time. Forced by circumstances to recover a whole son from the fourth that remains of him, Walter gets neither the whole nor its parts. By the time he finishes the *Tristrapaedia*, his son has outgrown its usefulness.

From the example of his father's authorship Tristram cautions against its imitation: "Matter grows under our hands.—Let no man say,—'Come—I'll write a *duodecimo*' " (5, 16:446). Although Tristram can make a good jest out of his father's writerly misfortunes, he cannot alter those conditions that created them. Walter's speculative and sys-tematical leanings chafe against the division of labor and its perfection in parts. He searches instead after the continuities of tradition and sys-tematical knowledge that the modern age has fragmented. Both the ex-plosion of "icals" and the commercialization of knowledge have done irrevocable damage to teleological models and, in the process, have made Walter their victim. The next generation, embodied in Tristram, can make light of even this idea—and, by doing so, can also transgress the legitimacy of a plenum in his own day and age with a narrative "life" and educational treatise ("to instruct [us] of what passes in a man's own mind" [1, 2:98]) that borders on incoherence.

As a good Shandean author, Tristram's *Life and Opinions* delights in divisions and lives suspended without being confused by them. By capi-talizing on the generational and philosophical divide between himself and his father, Tristram manages to show how he has discovered in his lineage a redemptive victory of difference predicated upon commercial change and development. Filled with apparent fragments and useless parts, not unlike the intellectual endeavors of his father, the *Life and Opinions* recounts its narrator's own beds of justice.[19] When "full" Tris-tram writes heedless of any cares; when "fasting" he pays "the world all possible attention and respect" (6, 17:525). In this composite, some-times this, sometimes that role he is both a supplier and consumer in a commercial world and gives that world its due. Accordingly, the econ-omy of moral realism for Sterne is not a source of unremitting friction, as it is in the novels of Defoe, Richardson, and Fielding.

Character and Productivity in the Manufactured Book

In the best sense of the term, *Tristram Shandy* is a manufactured story—probably the most extreme of its kind in the eighteenth century.

From the standpoint of narrative, parts dominate the novel, yet, in a powerful way, print technology, bound volumes, and the book as consumer good impart to it the coherence it has as a narrative. For Sterne, book as narrative and book as physical object participate equally in the commerce of meaning, though, on another level, they are divisible categories. As a consequence, Sterne does not purport to give us the secret memoirs of x or the recently discovered letters of y, because in these instances narrative dominates the vehicle of its conveyance. *Tristram Shandy*, in short, does not attempt to deceive its readers into believing that the book they read is a factual fiction. Like any other book, Sterne's novel utilizes linear typography, but this form of sequentiality and apparent coherence is routinely disturbed by other kinds of divisions and other suspended forms, all of which underscore the bookishness and artifice of *Tristram Shandy*: the black page suggests a drunken compositor; the marbled page a misguided binder who forgets that marbled papers serve a decorative function. Compounding these anomalies are others, such as missing chapters or pages left unprinted for doodling or sketching—and these are only some of the more egregious. The effect of these elements only amplify the fictionality—the fashioned manufactory—of *Tristram Shandy*.

Yet our impression of this novel is that there is something more lifelike to be gathered from all this fiction-making than from any of those novels whose authors advertise factual reportage. Ian Watt makes a comparable claim when he comments that "many of the scenes in *Tristram Shandy* achieve a living authenticity that combines Defoe's brilliant economy of suggestion with Richardson's more minutely discriminated presentation of the momentary thoughts, feelings and gestures of his characters. So assured, indeed, is this mastery of realistic presentation that, had it been applied to the usual purposes of the novel, Sterne would probably have been the supreme figure among eighteenth-century novelists."[20] Because of Sterne's handling of setting and time—the lack of sequentiality they produce—Watt sees *Tristram Shandy* not so much as a novel, but as a parody, a *reductio ad absurdum*, of the novel. He assumes, however, that fictional time must remain a universal constant and that the methods of Defoe and Richardson adjudicate all subsequent cases.

Sterne can answer for himself. Although his disruptions of sequentiality are too numerous to count, one of the most amusing violates the typical organizational features of a book. Around the middle of book 3, Tristram finally writes the PREFACE to his *Life and Opinions*. There, he complains about his distaste for "set dissertations." While engaged in writing one himself, he singles out for particular censure those that are plagued by "a number of tall, opake words, one before another, in a right line, betwixt your own and your readers conception" (3, 20:235).

Preface writers so inclined, as far as he is concerned, lack the requisite sense of humor to appreciate the way in which he attempts to instill moral authority through perspiration and imagination or to reconceive of wit and judgment as the knobs of a chair. Referring to these worthies not as moralists, but as "great wigs or long beards," Tristram leaves his disagreement pretty much at that, while recognizing that his method and theirs are not reconcilable. Thus he bids them peace, stating, "—☞ mark only,—I write not for them" (3, 20:238). While this exclusion has no bearing on Ian Watt, it does for those who believe that morality speaks a universal truth and can only be packaged in a particular way. The simple truth is that by the middle of the eighteenth century the separation of morality into categorical divisions—the "icals" phenomenon—had already developed a head of steam that could and did power changes in the novel. Watt himself alludes to just this point earlier in *The Rise of the Novel*: "the division of labour has done much to make the novel possible: partly because the more specialised the social and economic structure, the greater the number of significant differences of character, attitude and experience in contemporary life which the novelist can portray, and which are of interest to his readers."[21]

By virtue of its formal properties, *Tristram Shandy* announces a different way of apprehending literary and moral realism that depends upon a heightened consciousness of what this "more specialised . . . social and economic structure" entailed. The needs and wants of readers are forced to change accordingly, though, clearly, some will resist and others will not comply. Yet, as Sterne is aware, readerships are themselves divided entities and will remain so. In this spirit, he deems moral universality untenable and unrealistic, which is contrary to the prevailing ethos of the realistic novel and its exemplary character. Tristram, in the meantime, may claim that his *Life and Opinions* is a moral story, even the most moral of stories, but there is no indication that he expects others to subscribe to this view.

These same principles that apply to readers apply also to the representation of character. We learn of it through incidental acts or remarks—Toby's unwillingness to kill a fly, for example, cues us to his moral character—through hobby horses, or from behind the shroud of "mysteries and riddles"; not from the "set" character made up of tall, opaque words. Thus, Tristram is forever throwing obstacles in the way to block direct apprehension of character. He will not disclose even simple facts: for instance, whether he is married to Jenny. This approach leaves suspense intact, but goes against the grain of Walter, who ardently believes that the *mysteria* can be translated into the common tongue and character rendered predictable. Had Tristram been baptized Trismegistus, rather than saddled with the sad name he goes by, his future would have been preserved from vicissitude.

At least partially in reaction to his father's theorizing and out of deference to his own philosophy of benevolence, Tristram conceives of character as universally suspended. We are apprised of this belief early in the novel when he objects to the "arch-critick" who would have character conform to the theory of the Momus glass.

> [H]ad the said glass been there set up, nothing more would have been wanting, in order to have taken a man's character, but to have taken a chair and gone softly, as you would to a dioptrical bee-hive, and look'd in, — view'd the soul stark naked;—observ'd all her motions,—her machinations;—traced all her maggots from their first engendering to their crawling forth;—watched her loose in her frisks, her gambols, her capricios; and after some notice of her more solemn deportment, consequent upon such frisks, &c.——then taken your pen and ink and set down nothing but what you had seen, and could have sworn to. (1, 23:82–83)

This practice, as Tristram jokes, is one perhaps acceptable on Mercury, where, given its intense heat, all bodies are likely vitrified anyway. But on earth, where moderate temperatures and climatic differences have made easy characterological detection impossible, such practices should never be encouraged.

By figuring character in this way, Tristram takes a calculated risk. He rejects the evidentiary standards of the morally typed character to propose instead that the true character lies scattered in bits and fragments beneath what is immediately apparent. This manner of character conceptualization—the incarnate form of suspense—does not parody the methods of Defoe, Richardson, and Fielding so much as it articulates the contradictions they introduced. In addition, character so depicted enables Sterne to organize a division of labor with his readers so that they can be taught the need for trusting, crediting, and valuing their own opinions, as Tristram does his. Sermonizing is not the legitimate means to this end, as Sterne could well appreciate. He goes out of his way to demonstrate this point when he illustrates the varied responses a literal sermon—one of his own, "The Abuses of Conscience"—elicits.[22] By ordering character in this way, Sterne internalizes the ethos of commercial productivity in order to probe the unwritten causes behind character motivation and to explore the tenuous bonds that keep such a society united. *Tristram Shandy* invites no imitative behavior, yet it prompts a lesson about character. Sterne implicitly asserts that the future of character, only half-realized in earlier novels, must rely upon new ways of understanding outside experience, no matter what its confusions and unpredictabilities.

The critical factor behind Tristram's representation of character is productivity. One of the major virtues of his father and uncle, for instance, is that they remain busy, forever plotting and strategizing to bring endeavors, both large and small, to fruition. That the completion of these projects almost never happens—or happens with a whimper— suggests that productive endeavor becomes an end unto itself in the novel. Tristram is the much more important wheel in this machine, however, since every word he writes serves as a measure of his productivity. It is not surprising, therefore, to discover that when he fixes his attention on others so much of his commentary and narration gravitates toward matters of sexuality and human generation, since both are intimately connected to reproduction. When looking away from his narrative material to himself, he shifts his focus, as it were, from the manufactured goods themselves to the machine that facilitates this production. Interestingly, he divulges little about his own domestic circumstances, which, in its way, parallels the protracted testament of his birth and coming of age. The former creates narrative suspense without relief and the latter a *terminus a quo* without much of a coherent resolution in sight. Both, however, serve the ends of productivity. The evasive Tristram, we think, may become less so in subsequent volumes, while the late-arriving Tristram has created room for other narrative matters, detailed accordingly, and freed up the space for more biographical data. At odd moments, moreover, we are promised chapters that sometimes appear but, more often, do not.

The burdens of productivity are taxing all around—for uncle, father, and son. Tristram complains on a number of occasions about being in debt, with cartloads of books yet to be sold. And at other times we get glimpses of him as he struggles with his thoughts and emotions, frustrated by his waning years and the great unfinished enterprise he imagines for himself. Or the unfinished enterprise before him. His travels to France do not merely parody the methods of travel writers or the memoirists of the Grand Tour. Underwriting this elaborate episode is productivity, since the thing that defines Tristram most personally is Death itself, which knocks at his door at the beginning of book 7. Although Death signals mortality, in Tristram's world it signifies the end of productivity.[23] For the moment, at least, Death itself can be outrun, but its memory hounds Tristram all the way to France. "There is nothing more pleasing to a traveller—or more terrible to travel-writers," he tells us, "than a large rich plain; especially if it is without rivers or bridges; and presents nothing to the eye, but one unvaried picture of plenty; for after they have once told you that 'tis delicious! or delightful! . . . they have then a large plain upon their hands, which they know not what to do with. . . . —This is most terrible work; judge if I don't manage my plains better" (7, 42:646). Whether he does is debatable. But, while on this plain, Tristram diverts his attention to eggs and figs that, by creating a moment of suspense in his travelogue, afford him the time he needs to expand his own productive labors as a writer.

> —How we disposed of our eggs and figs, I defy you, or the Devil himself . . . to form the least probable conjecture: You will read the whole of it—not this year, for I am hastening to the story of my Uncle Toby's amours—but you will read it in the collection of those which have arose out of the journey across this plain—and which, therefore, I call my
>
> PLAIN STORIES
>
> How far my pen has been fatigued like those of other travellers, in this journey of it, over so barren a track—the world must judge— . . . I turned my *plain* into a *city*
>
> (7, 43:647–48).

Although Tristram is initially derisive of the travel writer who uses the plain as an avenue to the next town, he does precisely the same thing himself. While these circumstances allow that his principles may have suffered compromise, the wheels of his productivity continue to turn— and so he lives on, his need and want to survive fulfilled for a time.

By the time he gets to his final book debt, volume 9, his production rate has been cut in half, that is, if we use the measure of two volumes per publication year. This volume is the only instance we have in the publication history of *Tristram Shandy* when Sterne published just the single volume. It is a curious volume in other ways as well. Although we have been held in suspense about the Widow Wadman and Uncle Toby's amours throughout much of the novel, here in volume 9 the goods are delivered. We have sampled the preparations for this amorous undertaking in volume 8 and, in volume 7, we hear about Toby's adventures with a sense of urgency, since Tristram, troubled by his compositional practices while in France, tells us that he hastens, as he has against Death, to move on to a more engaging subject. Although we have long recognized that Toby is wounded, volume 9, in effect, brings about his fall—his submission to the laws of gravity.[24] This volume, significantly, also suspends the beloved uncle beyond the pale of his productivity. King William's Wars have come to an end: the bowling green as a staging ground for the martial exploits of the English nation must succumb to peace. In the process, Tristram complains about writer's block or, alternatively, laments his inability to outpace the various debts he has accumulated. Moreover, there is a surprising element of self-reflection contained in this volume, as if the burden of being the heir apparent has finally caught up with Tristram. He draws a number of strong comparisons between the measure of life as the productive measure of his literary output and even turns to the purple patch, perhaps as a way of combating writer's block.

> Time wastes too fast: every letter I trace tells me with what rapidity Life follows my pen: the days and hours of it, more precious, my dear Jenny! than the rubies about thy neck, are flying over our heads like light clouds of a windy day, never to return more—every thing presses on—whilst thou art twisting that lock,—see! it grows grey; and every time I kiss thy hand to bid adieu, and every absence which follows it, are preludes to that eternal separation which we are shortly to make.—(9, 8:754)

The elegiac tone of this passage is in utter contrast to the machines and production rates we have familiarized ourselves with earlier in the novel. For all the sentiment of this reflection, however, there is a sense in which industrialization even reaches into its plaintiveness. The separation Tristram refers to between him and Jenny is eternal—a division separating them from a heavenly and "perfect" union—yet it is the notion of reunion after death that the Christian faith promotes. Something unspoken is omitted from the elegy.

Nevertheless, the same kind of problem has remained since early in the novel, as Tristram expresses it through his brief history of Yorick, though its manner of delivery and appearance have a much more manufactured look. The story of the eternal jester, Yorick, is one of the first stories Tristram tells (1, 12). He begins his narration, appropriately enough, with a series of terms familiar to the commercial world: mortgager, interest, sums, payments, and credit, which contrast the world at large with the one in which Yorick circulates. This sentimental and good-hearted parson contracts a number of book debts that he disregards as cavalierly as he does the advice of his friend Eugenius, who encourages him to meet his obligations. Believing himself without malignant or invidious intention, Yorick thinks that his "honesty of mind" and "jocundity of humour" will cause his debts to "be cross'd out in course" (1, 12:30), since he imagines all others to be of his kidney. As it turns out, the jokes performed by Yorick at the expense of others backfire on him. Malignant feelings swirl about him, his heart breaks, death follows, and we are left to contemplate the emblematic riddle and mystery of his demise, the black page, the appearance of which, in a printed book, is atypical, uncharacteristic, utterly manufactured, yet highly effective: that is, we cannot help but remember Yorick's death. Tristram, by contrast, is acutely aware of his book debts, as he is of interest, sums, and credit—indeed, the whole matrix of commercial society. As a producer and manufacturer of the arts and sciences, he recognizes that his survival depends on keeping the wheels of his novel-machine turning, of paying his debt to the monochromatic black page by fragmenting and dividing it into discernible characters, if the desired exchange with readers is to continue. Like it or not, the machine makes possible the commerce of the book.

The Contexts of Moral Realism

To propose that *Tristram Shandy* is a paradoxical novel or one that hinges its fate on narrative suspense is to state nothing that I have not indicated or implied throughout. Tristram's elusive presence in his own life history contributes to these conditions, but it also underscores an important lesson about literary property in the commercial book trade. Self-rendering is akin to "self-rending" in Sterne's novel so that the obscurity, effacement, and invisibility of Tristram protect him, in effect, from active participation in his own life history. The black page awaits him, however, as he is only too aware. Only by employing whatever machinery he can think of to hoodwink the inevitable and unknown does he expand his literary property and sustain his commerce. When compared with other characters of the early novel who vainly try to minimize their literary properties for the sake of other values, Tristram locates his principal value in the literary property that he produces. In it and through it the ramifications and operations of commercial society unfold, as the individual life—a part among many others—draws from its capital the resources of productivity. When Death appears to him in volume 7, Tristram can only say: "I care not which way he enter'd, quoth I, provided he be not in such a hurry to take me out with him—for I have forty volumes to write, and forty thousand things to say and do, which no body in the world will say and do for me" (7, 1:576). By his own admission he runs in order to remain productive, fleeing the ultimate definition that makes the rest silence.

But to insist too strenuously that *Tristram Shandy* is a satire or parody, I think, misses the mark. Satire and parody are predicated on human frailty and corruptibility but also tend to draw too much attention to the objects or persons being satirized. Sterne, obviously enough, looked back as he wrote *Tristram Shandy*, but other novels have only a kind of vague, invisible presence in his narrative. The contribution of *Tristram Shandy* to the discourse of the novel, if we care to call it that, is positive and direct, zeroing in on the commercial ethos and the here and now in ways that earlier novelists resist. In the commercial world, however, all is corruptible, calling for new answers and accommodations to old problems. We can, for example, fruitfully compare Walter

Shandy more fully with Crusoe's father. Both had careers in merchandise, both retired to estates, both married advantageously later in life
and had their children as elders, both had problems with their sons,
and both had an interest in determining their conspicuous son's future.
Crusoe, as I have described him, turns back to his father's world,
whereas Tristram turns away from his. *Robinson Crusoe* cannot even
begin to anticipate the directions *Tristram Shandy* takes because, among
other things, it relies upon a historical teleology that is antithetical to
Sterne's narrative, in which the whole is never an antecedent to its
parts.

Sterne rejects the plotted or formal realism of Defoe, Richardson,
and Fielding, in whose works the prescriptive solution so often obtains:
the traveler returns or the virtuous are united.[25] Fittingly, their characters remain generally oblivious to their own motivations, though the acquisition of property tends to be unequivocal. These interests are
thoroughly deranged in *Tristram Shandy*, but not forgotten. In it the way
to morality is through benevolence, sentiment, or the affective response
in general, not prescription, so that, as Sterne admits, in the Shandean
world "the distribution and balance of [the world's] property and
power, may in time depend greatly upon the right understanding of" a
gesture (5, 7:431). In this wholly imperfect world, both words and
things constantly fail but, in doing so, expose the fallen world of needs,
wants, desire, and interest, as these passions are informed by divided
labor and commercial aspiring. As far as we can tell, Tristram does not
feather his desire and interest with a fat bank account, a prosperous
marriage, or a neat estate set apart from the world. For this reason his
life cannot be rounded off as a tidy function of plot, discretely figured
to advance some moral or ideological concern. By avoiding the quick
fixes of narrative realism, in other words, Sterne could sustain his novel
without closure and thereby ensure its unpredictability. Hence Tristram
cautions us to remember that " 'La Vraisemblance (as *Baylet* says in the
affair of *Liceti*) n'est pas toujours du Cotè de la Verité' " (4, 15:347).
In every way *Tristram Shandy* heralds this modern world of deceptive
representation, for at every turn both the novel and its principal character are simultaneously incorporated and alienated—a whole and a fragment—existing within the history of suspense and under the
commercial narrative.

In the end, Sterne seems largely indifferent about whether we read
his book as a novel or romance. At one point he has Tristram recommend to Madame, who worries about the nature of his relationship with
Jenny, that she "study the pure and sentimental parts of the best *French*
Romances" (1, 18:57) to find out for herself. At another, he takes up
the challenge of the "hypercritick," who, in fretting over the two min-

utes thirteen seconds it takes Obadiah to locate Dr. Slop, gladly transforms the *Life and Opinions* from a "book apocryphal" into a "profess'd
ROMANCE." Tristram: "If I am thus pressed—I then put an end to the
whole objection and controversy about it all at once,—by acquainting
him, that . . ."(2, 8:120). Only circumstances, we gather, make such
answers necessary.

Afterword: Market Access
and Economic Relationship

A CULTURE OF NEEDS AND WANTS, AS I HAVE TRIED TO MAKE CLEAR, played a central role in the developing complications associated with the representation of character. Although it is fair to assume that this phenomenon reached shores other than Britain's, I have tried not to speculate beyond the scope of my research and, consistent with what I accept as the distinctiveness of English capitalism in a state of flux, have steadfastly resisted any attempts to "universalize" my findings. Instead, I have attempted to document the context that I believe informs the novels of Defoe, Richardson, Fielding, and Sterne and to evaluate their local achievements accordingly, as each wrestled with "market" circumstances. My design has not been to bestow upon these writers a special place in the history of the novel or to link their writings to the "origins" of the genre. Origins especially invite questions that reach well beyond what the relevant evidence accommodates and lend themselves to the dubious historical claim that the novel is of recent vintage. Among other things, this belief instigates genre discrimination, at least within institutional circles, to the degree that the realistic "novel" must be posterior to the lesser form, the female "romance." The more neutral model I have proposed avoids the inherent ranking and subordination that results from discriminating between romances and novels. It is certainly not my claim, however, that inequalities and a stacked economic deck did not exist in the eighteenth century, but this is a matter that refers to representationality, not to the novel itself. Many battles could be fought in the pages of the period novel and many were—precisely because it was a genre accessible to both women and men.

Although I have treated Defoe and other practitioners of realism as influential players in the history of the English novel, I have also shown how the internal history of the episode they authored introduced significant and enduring interest in character—what I deem their major contribution to the genre. By examining that history in detail, we realize a number of things: 1.) the persistent demand for the regulation of character in the face of commercial change; and 2.) the strength of the material economy (the narrative of commerce) in rewriting the terms of adaptation. Whether a particular novelist resisted or accepted the effects of the commercial economy matters of course but not to the degree that preference, one way or another, alters the state of character. In either case, it becomes suspended amid levels of equivocation—hence my title, "governing consumption," the meaning of which varies according to whether we read "governing" as a gerund or participle. The novels of Defoe, Richardson, Fielding, and Sterne, in this regard, indicate that neither gender could control the effects of the economy; that, in general, was the function of the narrative of commerce itself.

In assigning these developments to male novelists, which, as I concede, suffers from certain limitations, I want to urge that this body of writers simply expanded certain features of earlier narratives and reworked others. The resulting product not only included a good deal of moral larding, circumstantial detailing, romance and sentimental dealings but also capitalized on those changes that the "romance" novel anticipated and the commercial economy demanded. Although my emphasis on the contributions of male novelists to the genre may be unduly strong, I would continue that stress while drawing a distinction between "access" to the market and "relationship" to the economy. The truth is that the formal discourse of what we would call economics was overwhelmingly the intellectual enterprise of males during much of the seventeenth and eighteenth centuries; such was not the case for novels. Access to the market for novels did not suffer the same gender overload, since the proportion of women novelists to men was high, especially in relationship to other types of callings. To illustrate this difference between access and relationship, I want to look briefly at two novels, both by women, that were published within the period in question, Charlotte Lennox's *The Female Quixote* (1751) and Sarah Scott's *Millenium Hall* (1762). In these narratives the incidence of "romance" elements remains high, yet the breadth and texture of character and contextual detailing they exhibit more readily evokes the male-practiced novel than what we are apt to identify as the "amatory" or "romance" novel.

Both of these novels, stunning examples in their own right, filter "romance" through the lens of the novel. Lennox does this in the most literal way possible, for her heroine, Arabella, has defined her life around the predictable, open-book character drawn from the pages of French romances. As we are led to believe, however, this preference is misguided so that most of the novel deals with attempts taken to restore some sense of balance to Arabella not by dispelling her faithfulness to typologies and the predictable character but by realigning her fidelity to these truths. Only reluctantly does Arabella leave her self-enclosed world, never far removed from a library of romances, to venture forth in a public realm dominated by men or infused with their sensibility to discover her authentic and respectable self. Even so, modeled after the dreamer Quixote, Arabella underscores how far removed from the "Pitch of Greatness of Soul" the contemporary age is from the heroic one she imagines to exist; though to trust the modern world, with its ethos of *doux commerce*, over the heroic in this novel is a faith better left for the most determined.[1]

The work of reforming Arabella's character falls to a man, a divine, in the penultimate chapter that has been partially attributed to Dr. Johnson. There Arabella learns that the only reliable testimony of history is the documentable evidence of fact and that the only remedy for the transgressions of romance is a frigid morality and an enforced sublimation of desire. As the novel would have it, it is in Arabella's interest to change. To that end, this divine urges that "we can judge of the Future only by the Past" (372), a position of predictability and fulfillment that Arabella has subscribed to all along. But, he goes on, excluded from this history of fact is love—a meretricious enterprise—"the Business, the sole Business of Ladies in Romances" (381). True to his Johnsonian frame, the cleric states his qualifications for issuing moral sense. "I have lived long in a public Character, and have thought it my Duty to study those whom I have undertaken to admonish or instruct. . . . [Y]our Writers have instituted a World of their own, and that nothing is more different from a human Being, than Heroes or Heroines" (379–80).

Probable facts alone authenticate history for the public character. Arabella's history, by contrast, has been shaped in private at her *father*'s secluded home. Her entrance into the public world of "historical veracity" tests every belief she holds. Foolishly, it seems, she believes in the hero and has defined him as one who "neglect[s] those mean and selfish Considerations, and, loving Virtue in the Persons of his Enemies, can prefer their Glory before his own particular Interest" (229). Although steeped in Christian charity, her ideal moral hero has a far more encumbered journey in eighteenth-century England, a hero who defies the probability of character Johnson upholds in *Rambler* number four. That is to say, Arabella's desires must be replaced by the sterner moral governance dictated by the public character.

The ideal *The Female Quixote* proposes, then, does not depend upon the eradication of types but their restoration as an active moral voice properly applied in the decipherment of character. Once this shift occurs, the conflicts of the novel dissolve; Arabella immediately understands and recants the folly of her past, she marries Glanville, and the novel itself comes rapidly to a halt. Yet the end of Lennox's novel is not at all like its beginning. There Arabella's father falls victim to the self-interested "Plots [that] were continually forming against him," when he effectively governed the kingdom and "disposed of all Places of Profit as he pleased" (5). So injured by these attacks, the marquis retires from the world to a remote castle at once sublime and beautiful. "The most laborious Endeavours of Art had been used to make [the grounds of the castle] appear like . . . wild, uncultivated Nature. . . . [T]he Inside of the Castle was adorned with a Magnificence suitable to the Dignity and immense Riches of the Owner" (6).

Arabella's father creates for himself what would later become the sum and substance of the Gothic novel, a retreat whose reality seems an improbable fiction. But no one criticizes or corrects this erstwhile public character for indulging himself in such a "romantic" manner. And it is from *his* library, a legacy from his now-deceased wife, that his daughter draws her reading material without being reproved for doing so. The cruel lessons of political reality and self-interest that her father experienced never once invade Arabella's conscious consideration of character because the typed character does not look beneath the surface for its answers. Yet in every way she inherits her father's revised legacy. Her obsession with the Christian hero, had it only been true, would have scripted her father's life to fit a different story. In it backstabbers and the ruthlessly appetitive would have been without substantial reality. With her father's death Arabella effectively becomes the orphan of the castle, and the imperatives of an ideal fiction accordingly root themselves even more deeply in her psychic interior.

It is not a woman's prerogative in *The Female Quixote* to wish for more than what already is. This lesson is stressed to Arabella when she is under the tutelage of the Countess in London. As a poor substitute for Arabella's long-dead mother and a prefiguration of Arabella herself, the Countess tries to lead her charge into a life of constriction that determines her fate. The call to realism in her counsel is laced with a desire that has long since been crushed. The customs that change the "Nature of Things" indicate, as the Countess herself prompts, that a millennium ago different social codes organized behavior. Far removed from the customary manners and impulses sanctioned by the French romances that the Countess herself imbibed as a girl, the demands of the contemporary world prove "that 'tis impossible such Adventures should ever happen." A woman's needs and wants, in short, must remain unanswered in that world. Little wonder then that Arabella turns away from this wisdom purchased with experience.

That the emotive and passionate female Quixote would suddenly convert in the face of the rational and evidentiary appeal of the cleric creates improbability in her character and yields a dissatisfying conclusion for the novel. But as a devotee of types she has no other real choice. At her most vulnerable moment she confesses to him the substance of her understanding: "Human Beings cannot penetrate Intentions, nor

regulate their Conduct but by exterior Appearances" (371). By men-
tioning intentions she hints that other ways of divining human behavior
or plumbing the "suspended" character exist—or should exist. For
whatever reason, these methods are not accessible to her. If they were,
then she would be able to see the injustice experienced in her own family through the plottings of public characters and would understand the
inequality that circumscribes her gender. The irony of the novel is that
once her understanding has been corrected, Arabella quickly becomes
the defeated heroine of her own romance as she settles into the wordless
domain of marriage. But as long as she remains resistant and barely
governable she circulates freely in her tale, which simply underscores
how extreme her isolation becomes at the end. The most workable
economy of *The Female Quixote* is to stop, with Arabella's character suspended in the balance.

Had Lennox written fifty years before, her novel would have been
something substantially different from what it turned out to be. The realistic novel comes between her effort and the earlier "romances." It
yields a generic equivocation, suspending both novel and romance in a
manner of speaking. Still, the influence of the "novel" makes more accessible the realm of motivation in Arabella and invites examination of
both the gross and subtle inequalities that affect her, even though Arabella herself sees none of this and attains her most perfect role when
she ceases to circulate among us, left to her isolated domesticity.

Sarah Scott's *Millenium Hall* effectively answers Lennox, though we
cannot consider these two novels as companion pieces. Generic concerns are given ample space in her novel, as the narratives that trace
the history of the individual women who make up the almost exclusively
women's community at Millenium Hall are cut from the cloth of romance. But circumscribing these narratives is another that frames the
novel as a conduct book designed for the education of men. It is the
latter, the novelistic frame, that vests these "romance" tales with properties and a point that they otherwise would have lacked. Millenium
Hall itself is a kind of Paradise Hall or even, perhaps, a Shandy Hall
devoid of bunglers, with its management, if not perfect, then efficient.
All that can be cultivated or utilized is to maximize profitable forms of
benevolence. Indeed, everything that occurs in its pastoral locale demonstrates how well women can participate not just in all stages of the
four stages of history but in the discourse of economic growth as well.[2]
These activities, however, take place beyond the pale of man, though it
is a man, two in fact, who must bear witness to the women's achievement as outsiders yet seem not to understand it at all other than in the
most superficial of ways. In this sense, Millenium Hall is a paradoxical
place, a locale of suspense at once isolated and complete, populated

with women whose romance tales can tell only partial or divided stories that mysteriously fragment into coherence.

Behind their enterprise lies a version of needs and wants so intense that it can only endure in isolation, as if both to mimic and mock the world beyond that is so inclined to type and restrict the offices of acceptable female behavior. In *Female Quixote* and *Millenium Hall* we recognize male tyranny and oppressiveness as operative forces; nevertheless, it is only through a complex exchange mechanism of women novelists appropriating the methods, techniques, and emphases of the male-authored novel that allows us to realize that yet another episode in the capital strategies of novel production was already unfolding in a vital display of narrative writing. In this light, the "progressive" development of the novel did not discriminate in ways that other structural sectors of the economy tolerated. When we hold the male novel up to the female-authored novel that is contemporaneous with it, its generic raw materials introduce new elements into the texture of narrative and the composition of character so that the competition for fuller expression of self, needs, and wants in general becomes accessible in ways that had not existed before. We must not minimize the role of commercial capitalism and the instruments of the marketplace in this process either. For without these elements, though imperfect unto themselves, few could have benefitted, other than, of course, the true hegemonists in the reaches of English history.

Least of all, finally, should we minimize suspense, the chief cultural by-product of commercial capitalism. Without it, the novel would have staggered under its own weight, as one last example from the period narrative archive intimates. In Frances Sheridan's *Memoirs of Miss Sidney Bidulph* (1761), Sidney's descent into fragmentation and oblivion is propelled by the romantic Orlando Faulkland. As the widow who awaits his response to her fateful letter recommending he marry another, she has already made suspense proprietary: "How uneasy has been my suspense these three days!"[3] Yet in a novel in which every fifth page seizes upon this word, it is its omission from an earlier scene that we feel wanting. Here the rusticating and impecunious Sidney, happily reunited with her profoundly destructive husband, writes her friend Cecilia. "But, I suppose, if I were to tell you, that on such a day my white Guiney-hen brought out a fine brood of chickens, you might be as well pleased with it, as I should be to hear from you of the birth of an arch duchess. Indeed, my Cecilia, there is such a sameness in my now tranquil days, that I believe I must have recourse to telling you my dreams, to furnish out matter of variety" (270). Systems of exchange, we gather, have never been entirely fair. But for the sake of the narrative, indeed for its representational complexity of character, Sidney's husband luckily fractures his skull and dies. Were it not so, our commerce with Sheridan's novel might well have been abbreviated long before its conclusion. But as one attentive to the literary marketplace and friend of Samuel Richardson, who encouraged her to write *Memoirs*, as well as a resident of commercial London, a place she dearly loved, Sheridan knew better than to allow her readers to lose interest. The uncertainties, mysteries, and suspense that surround Sidney's character make us eager to read on.

Notes

Chapter 1: Against the Grain: An Essay on "Origins"

1. Hunter, *Before Novels*, 29.
2. Hunter, *Before Novels*, 23–25.
3. Hunter, *Before Novels*, 30.
4. Students of the novel are well aware, for example, of Baker's ten-volume *The History of the English Novel* (1924), which from the outset does not betray any special fondness for the genre but more than amply demonstrates its lengthy transmission, since we must pass through three volumes before arriving, with the fourth, at the eighteenth century. Auerbach's *Mimesis* (1946) presents a different attitude toward narrative fiction, mapping its odyssey through the Western tradition and finding its culmination in realistic representation. Lukács's *The Theory of the Novel* (1920), only later translated into French (1963) and English (1971), offers a third attitude about the novel, one deeply colored by a longing for the simpler ways that preceded novels, as he collapses the childlike totality of the epic world into the inner form of the novel, "the art-form of virile maturity;" see *Lukács, Theory of the Novel*, 71. Collectively, these works have created an aura about the novel, whose mystery we so often have been eager to investigate.
5. Watt, *Rise of the Novel*, 7, 11.
6. Hunter, *Before Novels*, 57.
7. Hunter, *Before Novels*, 58.
8. Heiserman, *Novel Before the Novel*, 4.
9. See Bakhtin, *Dialogic Imagination*, 4–11.
10. Foucault, "What is an Author?" 149.
11. Stewart, *Crimes of Writing*, 9.
12. Warburton, *Literary Property*, B1r; see also 15–37 for the history of literary property.
13. On the role of the "knowing subject" under the division of labor, see Barrell, *Birth of Pandora*, 90–91. On the trials of introducing English literature into the university curriculum (at the University of London), see Court, "First English Literature Professorship in England."
14. Douglas and Isherwood, *World of Goods*, 17, 65.
15. Marx, "Theses on Feuerbach," 145.
16. Davis, *Factual Fictions*, 214–16, alludes precisely to this point.
17. Davis, *Factual Fictions*, 42.
18. Davis, *Factual Fictions*, 222.
19. See, e.g., Brown, "Title to Things Real," also his *Institutions of the English Novel* esp. 176–77; and Folkenflik, "Heirs of Ian Watt."
20. McKeon, *Origins of the English Novel*, 20.
21. It is difficult to universalize either stability or instability during the period. We should not automatically assume, for instance, that all change is instability. For the

breadth of the issues involved, see, e.g., Plumb, *Growth of Political Stability in England*, especially 1–30; Holmes, "Achievement of Stability," and Stallybrass and White, *Politics and Poetics of Transgression*, 27–31, 84–100.

22. McKeon, *Origins of the English Novel*, 22.

23. McKeon, *Origins of the English Novel*, 418.

24. The "aristocracy" is another loaded term that probably means more for the paradigm than it does in fact. According to Cannon's numbers (*Aristocratic Century*, 32–33), the social elite, made up of English, Irish, and Scottish peers, baronets, and knights, declined from 1546 in 1700 to 1363 in 1800. English population, however, increased dramatically over the same interval from about 9½ million to 16 million, which means that at the turn of the eighteenth century the social elite made up 0.000164% of the total population and by the end of the century it fell to 0.0000857%.

25. Marx, *Capital*, 989, 562, 614.

26. McKeon, *Origins of the English Novel*, 164.

27. Marx, *Capital*, 247

28. *Present State of Europe*, 2–11; Mortimer, *Elements of Commerce, Politics and Finances*, 222–23. Collini, Winch, and Burrow (*That Noble Science of Politics*, 28) offer that political science arises under the terms of the jurisprudential model, whereby people found "security by means of the regular administration of justice."

29. Wood, *Pristine Culture of Capitalism*, 3.

30. Wood, *Pristine Culture of Capitalism*, 22.

31. Wood, *Pristine Culture of Capitalism*, 3–4.

32. Wood, *Pristine Culture of Capitalism*, 4.

33. Wood, *Pristine Culture of Capitalism*, 17.

34. Wood, *Pristine Culture of Capitalism*, 18.

35. Wood, *Pristine Culture of Capitalism*, 33.

36. Wood, *Pristine Culture of Capitalism*, 34.

37. Wood, *Pristine Culture of Capitalism*, 39.

38. McKeon, *Origins of the English Novel*, 163.

39. McKeon, *Origins of the English Novel*, 164.

40. *Address to Britons of all Ranks* (1793), 6.

41. McKeon, *Origins of the English Novel*, 164

42. Jameson, *Political Unconscious*, 79.

43. Jameson, *Political Unconscious*, 18–19.

44. Tomlinson, *Cultural Imperialism*, 25–26.

45. Brown, "Title to Things Real," 927.

46. Armstrong, *Desire and Domestic Fiction*, 64.

47. Brown, "Title to Things Real," 947.

48. Folkenflik, "Heirs of Ian Watt," 203.

49. Armstrong and Tennenhouse, *Imaginary Puritan*, 201–202, 204, 208. While transatlantic migrations occurred, so did national migrations, from outlying regions to London and other urban centers, in numbers that were significant. Clark has estimated that as many as one in six citizens between 1650–1750 made this type of journey and notes of the phenomenon that it "probably contributed to the communication of new ideas and attitudes, particularly those generated in the forcing-ground of the metropolis, as well as encouraging changes in the status and importance of women. . . . [It] continued to serve as a powerful adhesive force in the provincial society, integrating towns with the villages of their hinterlands . . . [and] was also a sensitive barometer of economic, social and political change." Although periodic abatements in migration occurred, these fluctuations demonstrate how well-attuned potential migrants were to meeting their needs in a given locale. What remains indisputable over the long-term,

however, is the extent of migration, which "ensured a steady but flexible labour response to economic change [that, in turn,] played an important role in the orderly progress towards early industrialization;" see Clark, "Migration in England," 57, 90. As students of the period literature are aware, migratory behavior is amply represented in the period fiction and is not restricted to the materially blessed.

50. Armstrong and Tennenhouse, *Imaginary Puritan*, 41, 102.

51. Armstrong and Tennenhouse, *Imaginary Puritan*, 138–39, 158.

52. Armstrong and Tennenhouse, *Imaginary Puritan*, 201.

53. Character is not identical with subjectivity, the preferred term in criticism. Both Armstrong (*Desire and Domestic Fiction*) and Nussbaum (*Autobiographical Subject*) identify the latter in terms of repressive structures. Armstrong contends that, within the frame of sexual relationships as power relationships, "such a structure . . . makes it possible to see the female as representative of all subjections and to use her subjectivity as if it were a form of resistance" (24). In a like vein, Nussbaum remarks that "one consequence of the subject's entering into the culture's language and symbol system is a subjectivity placed in contradiction among dominant ideologies while those ideologies simultaneously work to produce and hold in place a unified subject" (33). These descriptions, while useful and insightful, are based on a privation model; one wonders how empowerment could take place in the absence of a more positive model. Character is the older term, but I do not use it to signify the older character. Even the traditional understanding of character was undergoing change, as Korshin observes. See *Typologies in England*, 242–43.

54. Although Doody's *True Story of the Novel* appeared after I wrote this chapter, her positions on such matters as the longevity of the novel in the Western tradition; the unwelcome segregation of romance and novel that has occurred among English and American commentators; and the dubious historical merits of any theory advancing the late origins of the novel are basic to my study. One unavoidable effect of her magisterial work, whether intended or not, is that she has simply pushed the origins of the novel further back in time. If, moreover, these origins are not Western, then they are Eastern. She admits a strong affiliation with Northrop Frye, this century's great systematic critic, but she also cites Jacques Derrida, who cautions against origins as dangerously "fictitious" and implicates them in "a plot of power," though Derrida is too black for her to embrace fully (307). She also finds inspiration in Bishop Huet, whose *Traité de l'origine des romans* (1670) locates the "first origin [of the novel] in the nature and spirit of man" (17). Doody, in addition, classifies novels consistent with an extensive series of tropes, "the 'deep rhetoric' of the Novel rather than its 'form'. . . figures not of phrasing but of narrative" (304). My view, by contrast, does not rely upon system and is fixed essentially upon two things: needs and wants, as a function of the commercial economy, and character. Whereas Doody is concerned with the "set" of novels, (xvii), I am concerned with a particular "subset," one in fact that she characterizes unfavorably as "Prescriptive Realism" (287–91).

Chapter 2: From Anthropology to Economy: Needs and Wants and the Narrative of Commerce

1. Nedham, *Excellencie of a Free State*, 129.

2. On politeness/mannered behavior as socially empowering vehicle in relationship to commercialization, see Klein, "Third Earl of Shaftesbury," 186–214. Klein also

draws a distinction between politeness and virtue, the principal term of civic republicanism (esp. 187–91), which will bear upon observations later in this chapter.

3. Douglas and Isherwood, *World of Goods*, 137, 89.

4. Douglas and Isherwood, *World of Goods*, 15.

5. Douglas and Isherwood, *World of Goods*, 31.

6. McKendrick, "Consumer Revolution of Eighteenth-Century England," 28–29.

7. Warburton, *The Divine Legation of Moses Demonstrated*, 1:155. On the role of secrecy in its relationship to narrative and interpretation, see Kermode, *The Genesis of Secrecy*, esp. 23–47.

8. Varey, *Space and the Eighteenth-Century English Novel*, 202.

9. Varey, *Space and the Eighteenth-Century English Novel*, 91.

10. Anstey, "Letter XIII. A Public Breakfast," in *New Bath Guide*, 96.

11. Douglas and Isherwood, *World of Goods*, 72.

12. Stewart, *On Longing*, 23.

13. On the social difficulties emulation caused, see Raven, *Judging New Wealth*, 239–43. By way of contrast, see Perkin (*The Origins of Modern English Society*) who comments that "if consumer demand . . . was the key to the Industrial Revolution, social emulation was the key to consumer demand" (96).

14. Wheeler, *Treatise of Commerce*, 5–6; and Barbon, *Apologie for the Builder*, 5. On the variety of goods available during the seventeenth century, see Thirsk, *Economic Policy and Projects*, 106–109, 113–17, 178–79, 182–85.

15. Sommerville, *Secularization of Early Modern England*, 149.

16. Spadafora, *Idea of Progress*, 6–7, 3–4.

17. When Goodman turns from the universal decline of man to its particular signs, he complains that "the incroaching Hollander . . . desires to vnite seas . . . and to make himselfe the greate Lord of the Ocean for as in ancient times their golden fleece was made of our English Wooll, so now their great Fleete must incroach vpon our seas" (*The Fall of Man*, 365). Hakewill responds that if these signs predict universal corruption, why has not each nation been so affected—why not the Dutch too? The answer lies not in Scripture, but in the practices of a national citizenry. Visitors to less civilized countries, which subsist "according to *nature*," report that natives, veritable antediluvians, "exceed vs in *stature*, first retaining as it seemes the vigorous Constitution of their Predecessours, which should argue, that if any decay be, it is not *vniverall*, and consequently not *naturall*, but rather *adventitious* and *accidentall*" (*Apologie of the Power and Providence of God*, 176). Hakewill, in effect, suggests that the consumption habits of a nation explain what biblical prophecy cannot. Harris (*All Coherence Gone*, 149) contends that after 1635 "the popularity of the belief in natural decay suffers an immediate, considerable, and permanent drop," which is not the least bit true.

18. Spadafora, *Idea of Progress*, 23–24.

19. Spadafora, *Idea of Progress*, 317–18.

20. Spadafora, *Idea of Progress*, 219, 218.

21. Burnett, *Origin and Progress of Language*, 23–24. Subsequent citations will appear parenthetically.

22. Pocock, *Machiavellian Moment*, 484.

23. That temper may best be described in the following passage, which, though written after the *Estimate*, reflects the opinion Brown struggled against: "if Society is a Means of procuring a Supply for our *Animal* Wants, it creates a Multitude of others, which may be called *Social*; because their Rise and Progress must be ascribed to Society, and the Figure which Men make in it"; see *Discourse on the Natural Disposition of Mankind in respect to Commerce*, 6.

24. Brown, *Estimate of the Manners and Principles of the Times*, 152–53. Subsequent citations will appear parenthetically.

25. Pocock, *Machiavellian Moment*, 484.

26. Pocock, "Modes of Political and Historical Time in Early Eighteenth-Century England," in *Virtue, Commerce, and History*, 92–93.

27. Davenant, *Ballance of Trade*, 154.

28. Davenant, "An Essay upon Universal Monarchy," in *Essays*, 267. Subsequent citations will appear parenthetically.

29. Pocock, "Mobility of Property and the Rise of Eighteenth-Century Sociology," in *Virtue, Commerce, and History*, 123.

30. Trenchard, *An Argument, Shewing, that a Standing Army is Inconsistent with a Free Government*, 7.

31. Robertson, "Scottish Enlightenment at the Limits of the Civic Tradition," 138; also Burtt (*Virtue Transformed*, 9) who has proposed that "the case for publicly oriented virtue faltered in eighteenth-century English political argument, [at which time] the idea of a civic virtue more privately oriented emerged."

32. Davenant, "Essay upon the Ballance of Power," in *Essays*, 48.

33. Davenant, *Ballance of Trade*, 154–55.

34. Pocock, *Machiavellian Moment*, 499.

35. Ferguson, *History of Civil Society*, 19

36. Dr. Johnson intimates similar processes in the mutability of language and the "progress of its meaning." The only languages spared the traumatizing change would be those used in precommercial countries, "raised a little, and but a little above barbarity, secluded from strangers, and totally employed in procuring the conveniencies of life." Under these conditions, as Johnson imagines, everything would be familiar, close to the "original"—or in my terminology devoid of "suspense"; see Johnson, "Preface to the English Dictionary," in *Johnson*, 320.

37. Ignatieff, *Needs of Strangers*, 93.

38. Trusler, *Luxury No Political Evil*, 72–73. Cf. *Reflections on Various Subjects Relating to Arts and Commerce*, in which the anonymous author writes: "Civil Societies are properly concerned only in our social Principles; religious ones in their Purity are private, and affect not the State but to strengthen the Obligations to Morality" (79).

39. Berkeley, *Essay Towards Preventing the Ruine of Great Britain*, 11. Subsequent citations will appear parenthetically.

40. Berkeley, *The Querist* in *Works of George Berkeley*, 2:240.

41. Paley, *Works of William Paley*, 2:55. Subsequent citations will appear parenthetically.

42. Boswell, *Life of Johnson*, 2:357.

43. Johnson, *Journey to the Western Islands* in *Johnson*, 789.

44. On a related matter, in the *Life of Johnson*, (2:177) Boswell reports talking "of the little attachment which subsisted between near relations in London," to which Johnson replies: "Sir, . . . in a country so commercial as ours, where every man can do for himself, there is not so much occasion for that attachment"; see *Life of Johnson*. Ignatieff makes a similar point: "only a society of strangers, of mediated and indirect social relations, has the dynamism to achieve progress. Only by delegation, specialization, the narrow enclosing of the self in one task, could societies effect the transition from barbarism to civilization"; see *Needs of Strangers*, 119.

45. Barrell, *Birth of Pandora*, 92.

46. Barrell, *Birth of Pandora*, 89, 110.

47. Agnew, *Worlds Apart*, 53, 56, 60.

48. Even though his aim is to disclose the literary nature of economic theory, McCloskey's *Rhetoric of Economics*, by virtue of its existence alone, tends to reinforce our prejudice against such linkages. When he proposes, for instance, that economists' "uses

of metaphor—are not very different from Cicero's speeches or Hardy's novels," we find ourselves wondering how practicing economists would greet this revelation (83).

49. In a related matter, Feather has commented that "[r]eading for pleasure was widespread among all classes," a phenomenon recognized by both Johnson and Voltaire; and that by the end of the century in excess of one thousand "[c]irculating libraries, as commercial enterprises, were stocked with books which met a popular demand"; see *Provincial Book Trade in Eighteenth-Century England*, 40–41.

50. Povey, *Unhappiness of England*, 85.

51. *Character of the True Publick Spirit*, 64.

52. Addison and Steele, *Spectator*, 1:261. Subsequent citations will appear parenthetically.

53. On the feudal divide, another commonly cited landmark used to distinguish the past from the present, see writers such as: Fielding, "Preface" to *Inquiry into the Causes of the Late Increase of Robbers* in *Complete Works of Henry Fielding*, 13:12–13; Hume, "Of Refinement in the Arts," in *Essays*, 277; Millar, *Origin of the Distinction of Ranks*, 224, 234; Millar, *Historical View of English Government*, 192; M'Farlan, *Tracts on Subjects of National Importance*, 9–13; Wilson, *Letter, Commercial and Political*, 33.

54. Anderson, *Imagined Communities*, 5–7.

55. Pocock, *Machiavellian Moment*, 452–56.

56. Goldsmith, *Deserted Village* in *Poems of Thomas Gray, William Collins and Oliver Goldsmith*, lines 63–64. Subsequent line numbers will be from this edition and appear parenthetically.

57. The simple fact is that agriculture had become more efficient over the century. Jones, following Deane and Cole, observes that statistics for 1811–12 indicate that almost a third of the population was still engaged in occupations that helped supply domestic tables; nearly two-thirds of the nation's capital derived from land, including agricultural lands; and that over a third of national income depended upon agriculture (*Agriculture and the Industrial Revolution*, 85.)

58. The agricultural system had made significant advances in the second half of the eighteenth century, as it had to, supporting an ever expanding body of expert thought and innovative practice; employing technical innovation; and maintaining its superiority through the expansion of arable lands—while stocking the larders of an increasing population, the majority of which did not flee to Georgia, as Goldsmith would have it, to face "crouching tigers"; see Deane, *First Industrial Revolution*, 37–52. In addition, a network of provincial shops existed to supply the provisions that those living in outlying regions either needed or wanted. Davis's *History of Shopping*, which is devoted to London, does not provide a very good guide to shops in the hinterlands. Shammas's more recent research in *Pre-Industrial Consumer in England and America* offers a much more comprehensive analysis (225–60) of the proliferation of country shops and builds upon the Muis' *Shops and Shopkeeping in Eighteenth-Century England*.

59. Goldsmith, *Deserted Village*, line 265.

60. Anderson, *Observations on the Means of Exciting a Spirit of National Industry*, 27.

61. Temple, *Vindication of Commerce and the Arts*, 99, 104.

62. Wallace, *Characteristics of the Present Political State of Great Britain*, 40. Subsequent citations will appear parenthetically.

63. Wallace, *Various Prospects of Mankind, Nature, and Providence*, 89–97, 72–74.

64. Massie, *Representation Concerning the Knowledge of Commerce as a National Concern*, 9. Subsequent citations will appear parenthetically.

65. It should be noted that Steuart saw the foundations of political economy in the needs and wants of the citizenry. "The principal object of this science is to secure a certain fund of subsistence for all the inhabitants, to obviate every circumstance which

may render it precarious; [and] to provide every thing necessary for supplying the wants of the society"; see Steuart, *Inquiry into the Principles of Political Œconomy*, 1:3.

66. Hutchinson contends that political economy was a largely mid eighteenth-century phenomenon, which took form when "a critical intellectual state had been reached regarding a nexus of basic theoretical issues concerned with values and prices, money, the circular flow of payments, and the nature and extent of self-adjusting processes in the economy or in this or that sector or market"; see *Before Adam Smith*, 187. I do not want to claim that the term "political economy" was not used prior to mid century, but its incidence has not burned itself into my memory. Whiston, e.g., uses the term, but in the context of the ancient Jews: "All Ages afford innumerable Instances of this undoubted Truth; the Tenour of the Holy Scripture is direct in this point, not one Revolution that happened in the Jewish Political Oeconomy but what was for the Punishment of their Crimes, and neglect of the Regular Means"; see *England's State-Distempers*, 3.

67. Teichgraeber, *'Free Trade' and Moral Philosophy*, 8–9.

68. The language of secrecy appears in a variety of ways beginning in the middle decades of the seventeenth century, but the gist was that some dimension of the commercial network had to be unlocked, solved, exposed, or discovered; in a similar vein, monopolies were represented to function in the manner of a cabal. See, e.g., Potter, *Key of Wealth*; Violet, *Mysteries and Secrets of Trade and Mint-affairs*; Cradocke, *Wealth Discovered*; or the prefatory matter in Johnson, *Plea for Free-Mens Liberties*.

69. Hazeland, *View of the Manner in which Trade and Civil Liberty Support Each Other*, 14.

70. Weston, *Dissertation on the Following Question*, 11.

71. See, e.g., Napier, *Plaine Discovery of the Whole Revelation of S. Iohn*, A1r-A2v.

72. See, e.g., Bates (*Harmony of Divine Attributes*, 329–30) who proposes that "the Knowledge of the *Jews* was obscure and imperfect, and the *external* part of their Religion was ordered in such a manner, that the Senses were much affected. . . . Add further, the Dispensation of the Law was *typical* and *mysterious*, represented by *material* Objects, and their Power to ravish the Senses, Spiritual Things, and their efficacy to work upon the Soul. But our Redeemer hath rent the Veil, and brought forth Heavenly things into a full Day, and the clearest Evidence."

73. Spencer, *Discourse Concerning Prodigies*, 27. Harvey maintains that "division emerged as the central social problem" during this period, whether it pertained to political myths, economic realities, or the distance between church and chapel; see "Problem of Social-Political Obligation for the Church of England in the Seventeenth Century," 158. Kroll sees the divide in terms of the "knowledge explosion": "the Restoration marks a multiple discursive reorientation, responding to a series of pressures that focuses and encourages a new constellation of discursive activities"; Kroll finds that "'commerce' offers an excellent example of semantic, and by implication paradigmatic, migration"; see *Material World*, 39, 57.

74. Glanvill, *Plus Ultra*, 129–30

75. Zimmerman, *Boundaries of Fiction*, 62; also Frei, *Eclipse of Biblical Narrative*, esp. 142–50.

76. Boyle, *Some Considerations Touching the Style of the Holy Scriptures*, 14.

77. Collins, *Scheme of Literal Prophecy Considered*, 112.

78. Toland, "The Origin of Idolatry, and Reasons of Heathenism," in *Letters to Serena*, 98.

79. South, "An Account of the Nature and Measures of Conscience," (Christ Church, Oxford, 1 Nov. 1691), in Simon, *Three Restoration Divines*, 2:189.

80. See, e.g., South: "since [the ministry] is made a Labour of the Mind; as to inform Mens Judgments, and more their Affections, to resolve difficult Places of Scripture, to decide and clear off Controversies; I cannot see how to be a Butcher,

Scavenger, or any other such Trade, does at all qualify, or prepare Men for this work";
from his sermon "Ecclesiastical Policy the Best Policy" in Simon, *Three Restoration Divines*, 2:73.

81. See, e.g., Richardson, *Canon of the New Testament Vindicated*, 9.

82. I make this characterization of mercantilism reluctantly since it is only partially accurate. See, e.g., Wiles ("Mercantilism and the Idea of Progress," 62–66) on "mutual gain" theory. One also needs to be careful not to lump the English economy with continental economies, particularly in light of the "pristine culture of [English] capitalism." Wilson, for one, notes that the "constant mingling of blood, class and occupation was of supreme importance to the economic and social evolution of England. . . . [This] social intermixture . . . gave assurance and influence to trade, it reinforced the declining fortunes of hundreds of landed families, and it brought intelligence and social influence to bear on economic policies of governments which might otherwise have been swayed, as rulers in Continental Europe often were, simply by considerations of royal income and dynastic interest"; see *England's Apprenticeship, 1603–1763*, 11.

83. Hakewill demonstrates the antagonism toward authority and impulse toward freedom that commerce aroused, when he wrote: "I think the king cannot restrain the passage of Merchants, but for some speciall cause," in *Liberty of the Subject*, 130. The issue of redefining authority via commercial mechanisms, however, was already at the root of the debate between de Malynes and Misselden early in the seventeenth century. Thus questions concerning what is exchanged in commercial transactions, what has priority in these exchanges, and so forth stood as primal issues in need of reconciliation. Misselden, on these matters, disputed Malynes's claims about the intrinsic value of money and the political symbolism that it bore. In Misselden, *Circle of Commerce* he writes that "the finenes of monies, is the *Cynosure* or *Center*, whereunto all *Exchanges* haue their naturall propension. But if you should so limit or restraine *Exchanges*, that no man should take or deliuer any mony, but according to the iust finenes: then the vse of *Exchanges* in all places would bee taken away" (97).

84. We get a good sense of the closed order of the economy in Malynes, *Maintenance of Free Trade*: "*Natvrall Mother wit*, did teach man, before Arts and Sciences were inuented; that of all things and in all humane actions: the *Beginning, Progresse, Continuance* and *Termination* or *End* is to be obserued; whereupon *Politicians* or *Statesmen* haue noted, that the often comparing of a thing vnto [t]his *Principle or Originall* produceth the longer continuance, shewing . . . how the same is decayed and may bee reduced to the first integrity and goodnesse. For there was neuer any thing by the wit of man so well deuised, or so sure established; which in continuance of time hath not bin corrupted" (1–2). Appleby is especially insightful about the conceptual disagreements of Malynes and Misselden, noting how their argument broke "with the past" and propelled commercial discourse in a new direction; see *Economic Thought and Ideology*, 42–49

85. Mead, *Key of the Revelation*, A3r.

86. Ascham, *Confusions and Revolutions of Government*, 25. Subsequent citations will appear parenthetically.

87. Stillingfleet, *Origines Sacrae*, 424. Subsequent citations will appear parenthetically.

88. Wolseley, *Reasonableness of Scripture-Belief*, 181. Subsequent citations will appear parenthetically.

89. Parker, *Demonstration of the Divine Authority*, 38. Subsequent citations will appear parenthetically.

90. Burnet, *[Sacred] Theory of the Earth*, 247–48.

91. Mortimer, *Elements of Commerce, Politics and Finances*, 17.

92. Bolingbroke, "Letter 14" from *Remarks on the History of England* in *Works of Lord*

Bolingbroke, 1:376. Also other notables such as Tucker, *Elements of Commerce*, 136; Defoe, *Plan of the English Commerce*, 131; and a seventeenth-century example: Philopatris [Child] (*A Treatise*, 30) who gives higher praise to "those wise and worthy Counsellors that assisted Queen *Elizabeth* in those infant time of our Reformation and Trade."

93. *Ancient and Modern Constitution of Government*, 16, 7, 4.

94. See Dickinson, "Eighteenth Century Debate on the 'Glorious Revolution,'" 42.

95. Hooke, *National Debt, and National Capital*, 33.

96. For these common distinctions, see Gee, *Trade and Navigation of Great Britain*, 1–5.

97. Wood, *Survey of Trade*, 28–29. Subsequent references will appear parenthetically.

98. Roberts, *Treasure of Traffike*, 1.

99. Smith, *Wealth of Nations*, 1, 4:477.

100. *Discourse Consisting of Motives for the Enlargement and Freedome of Trade*, 1–2. For an early eighteenth-century example of providential commerce set forth in some detail, see Baston, *Thoughts on Trade, and a Publick Spirit*, 1–2; Baston, however, goes on essentially to prophesy heavenly doom (190–203). A new edition of this work appeared in 1728, enlisted obviously to counteract Mandeville's thesis. Providential commerce actually retains a footing in the discourse into the nineteenth century; see Viner, *Role of Providence in the Social Order*, 40–45.

101. Tucker (*Elements of Commerce*) remarks that "this System of *Commercial Industry* is equally the Plan of Providence with the System of *Morals*, we may rest assured, That both are consistent with each other" (41); Mortimer (*Elements of Commerce*) prefaces his providential excursus that we "for a moment, suspend our enquiries" (3–4).

102. Whately, *Principles of Trade*, A3r.

103. Appleby, *Economic Thought and Ideology*, 52–72; and Letwin, *Origins of Scientific Economics*, 81–82.

Chapter 3: The "Suspended" Character

1. Hundert ("The Making of *Homo Faber*," 3–22) reads the modern history of labor beginning with Locke: his "divorce of labor from social obligation and his establishment of human activity as a possessive entity guided the discussion of work and workers in a new direction; one which understood human activity as a commodity and human relationships on the model of commodity relationships" (20). After 1750, wages increased because economic writers started to appreciate "that high money wages did not necessarily mean high labour costs" and that labor-saving mechanical devices reduced "production costs in both agriculture and manufacturing, and thereby increased employment and sales, both at home and abroad"; see respectively, Coats, "Changing Attitudes to Labour in the Mid-Eighteenth Century," 46–48; and Wiles, "Theory of Wages in Later English Mercantilism," 113–26.

2. Anderson, *Observations on the Means of Exciting a Spirit of National Industry*, 27.

3. Hutcheson, *Essay on the Nature and Conduct of the Passions and Affections*, 9–10; Hutcheson goes on to comment that "The *Desire of Wealth* must be as necessary as any other Desires of our Nature, as soon as we apprehend the usefulness of Wealth to gratify all other Desires" (111).

4. De Bolla, *Discourse of the Sublime*, esp. 6, 102, 111–12.

5. Korshin, *Typologies in England*, 226–45; also Korshin, "Probability and Character in the Eighteenth Century."

6. Lynch, "Overloaded Portraits," 143.

7. Bakhtin, *The Dialogic Imagination*, 39.

8. Hunter, *Before Novels*, 167–92.

9. Warner ("Elevation of the Novel in England," 577–92) characterizes the relationship between the male novelists and their female precursors as hegemonic.

10. See Watt, *Rise of the Novel*, 30; and Hunter, *Before Novels*, 54.

11. Richetti, *Popular Fiction Before Richardson*, 121.

12. Behn, *Love Letters Between a Nobleman and His Sister*, 49.

13. Manley, *Secret History of Queen Zarah* 1:A3v. Subsequent citations will appear parenthetically.

14. Haywood (?), *Mercenary Lover*, A2r. Subsequent citations will appear parenthetically.

15. Manley, *Secret History of Queen Zarah*, A3r-A4v.

16. Ballaster, *Seductive Forms*, 19–24

17. Warner ("Elevation of the Novel") establishes the important point of "overwriting": "the elevation of the novel is grounded in an antagonistic, but never acknowledged or conscious intertextual exchange with the earlier novel" (584).

18. In Haywood, *Lasselia* (1723), there exists something akin to an analytical or discursive breach; on repeated occasions the narrator says the equivalent of: "Lasselia being such, and infinitely more agreeable than I have power to represent her, 'tis easy to believe she was not without a very great Number of Adorers" (9). In *Betsy Thoughtless*, by contrast, this reluctance to detail has evaporated: "The reader, if he has patience to go through the following pages, will see into the secret springs which set this fair machine in motion, and produced many actions which were ascribed, by the ill-judging and malicious world, to causes very different from the real ones" (Haywood, *Betsy Thoughtless*, 8). Nearly six hundred pages later, and after experiencing the wide compass of London life, Betsy ceases to be thoughtless.

19. Coventry, *History of Pompey the Little*, xliii.

20. "Sure, such was the condition of the grand apostate when first he lost his purity," cries Barnwell; see Lillo, *London Merchant*, 25 (2, 1:11–12).

21. De Bolla (*Discourse of the Sublime*) recognizes the long history of the analogy (112); on "natural-unnatural" dichotomy in classical thought, see Shell, *Economy of Literature*, 91–96.

22. Appleby, *Economic Thought and Ideology*, 52–72; cf. Letwin, *Origins of Scientific Economics*, 81–82. Toward the close of *Economic Thought and Ideology*, Appleby comments, "The disappearance of religious references in the writings on trade after 1660 indicates that economic virtues could be defended on purely economic grounds" (276). By way of a contradictory example, however, I would refer readers to Evelyn, *Navigation and Commerce*, 3–4.

23. Nedham, *Interest Will Not Lie*, 3.

24. Gunn, "'Interest Will Not Lie,'" 560.

25. Gunn, "'Interest Will Not Lie,'" 564. Hirschman argues, I believe wrongly, that interest ensures predictable behavior; see *Passions and the Interests*, 48–56.

26. Steuart, *Inquiry into the Principles of Political Œconomy*, 2:165.

27. Coke, *Church and State of England*, A2r.

28. Coke, *Discourse of Trade*, B2v. Subsequent citations will appear parenthetically.

29. *Essay, or, Modest Proposal*, 2. Subsequent citations will appear parenthetically.

30. Briscoe, *Discourse of Money*, 23. Subsequent citations will appear parenthetically.

31. Abercromby, *Moral Discourse of the Power of Interest*, 8. Subsequent citations will appear parenthetically.

32. Appleby, *Economic Thought and Ideology*, 264.

33. Appleby, *Economic Thought and Ideology*, 251.

34. At the turn of the century, the Dutch model of "interested" economy appears in England in a work that purports to come from the pen of the illustrious "John de Witt (and other great men in Holland)," entitled *The True Interest and Political Maxims of the Republick of Holland and West-Friesland*. From it we learn about the dangers of one-sided interest: the "true Interest of all Countrys consists in the joint Welfare of the Governors and Governed; . . . but . . . where the well or ill-being of the Rulers necessarily follows or depends on the well or ill-being of the Subjects . . . true Interest cannot be compassed by a Government, unless the generality of the People partake thereof" (2).

35. Barbon, *Discourse of Trade*, 72. Subsequent citations will appear parenthetically.

36. North, *Discourses upon Trade*, 14. Subsequent citations will appear parenthetically.

37. Locke, e.g., contended that although mankind has "put an imaginary Value upon Gold and Silver . . . Men [must be] assured, in Exchange for them to receive equally valuable things to those they parted with for any *quantity* of these Metals. By which means it comes to pass, that the intrinsick Value regarded in these Metals made the common Barter." The other way of ascertaining value was through the "Stamp and Denomination," as indicated on the coin itself; see Locke, *Locke on Money*, 1:231–32.

38. Vanderlint, *Money Answers all Things*, 21. See also Philips (*The State of the Nation*) who notes that "All Commodities have their Value from the Demand for them. A Scarcity of any one Commodity and a Demand for it will raise the Value even where there is a Scarcity of Gold and Silver. But though Gold and Silver be the Measure of Goods, yet they have often varied according to their Quantity" (40). On the variable meanings of luxury over the period, see Sekora, *Luxury*, 47–51, 77–100.

39. Harris, *Essay upon Money and Coins*, 26. Subsequent citations will appear parenthetically. Thompson properly notes that Harris's conception of money is "systematic and functional" and that it serves as a "representation of value rather than as value itself"; see *Models of Value*, 77. Cf. Cole, *Discourses on Luxury, Infidelity, and Enthusiasm*, 14, 18, 23; Fawconer, *Essay on Modern Luxury*, esp. 43; and de Pinto, *Essay on Luxury*, 54–64; de Pinto's viewpoint and approach especially underscore luxury in the context of public and private interest.

40. Philemerus, *Of Luxury, More Particularly with Respect to Apparel*, 5, 8, 10, 1. Subsequent citations will appear parenthetically.

41. See Jones, *Luxury, Pride and Vanity*, 2. Subsequent citations will appear parenthetically. Around the turn of the century, the author of *The Naked Truth* remarks that "The K. of *France* made a Market of us by the prohibition of his Alamodes and Lutestrings, they are always plenty and the Custom saved; and Fashion is truly termed a Witch, the dearer and scarcer any Commodity, the more the Mode" (Blanch, 11). A few years later, the author of *A Brief History of Trade in England* (1702) notes the disproportion of people living in cities and by trade, forsaking "rural Affairs." Now "every Hundred Boys and Girls that are gleaned from the remote parts of the Kingdom, and come yearly into Trade, do in an average consume in Meats, Drinks and Cloathing, five times as much as they did when they were scatter'd in their several Countries, more especially, those in *London* and other great Cities; for whilst they remained under the Conduct of their own Parents, they did not spend a Shilling in a Week a piece, for if they had, how could a Father maintain three, four, or five Children with his Wages" (82–83).

42. *London, What It Is, Not What It Was*, ii–iii.

43. Hume, *Treatise of Human Nature*, 492.

44. Weatherill, *Consumer Behaviour*, 82–83

45. Weatherill, *Consumer Behaviour*, 9, 11, 28.

46. Given patterns of emulation and the documented reciprocity between town and country during the century, domiciles in outlying regions almost certainly followed similar organizational schemes.

47. See, e.g., Tucker (*Elements of Commerce*) who proposes a similar split, albeit one

on the universal scale: "*the* Circulation of *Commerce* may be conceived to proceed from the *Impulse* of two distinct Principles of Action in Society, analogous to the *centrifugal* and *centripetal* Powers in the Planetary System. But unerring Wisdom being the Guide and Director of these Powers in the heavenly Bodies, causes that *Constancy* and *Regularity* in their Motions, which is never observable in the Affairs of Commerce. And why is that? — It is because the Circulation of Commerce being only directed by the Reason or Wisdom of Man, is therefore subject to all those Impediments, Obstructions and Irregularities, which result from the Vices and Extravagancies, the partial Interests, the false Conceptions, and mistaken Policy of Mankind" (7).

48. Teichgraeber, *'Free Trade' and Moral Philosophy*, xiii–xiv; also Winch, *Adam Smith's Politics*, 10–11, 92–93, 167–68.

49. Pocock, "Cambridge Paradigms and Scotch Philosophers," 242.

50. Marshall, *Figure of Theater*, 167.

51. Smith, *Moral Sentiments*, 129–30. Subsequent citations will appear parenthetically.

52. Smith, *Wealth of Nations*, 1, 1:14.

53. Smith, *Wealth of Nations*, 1, 4:477.

54. Smith, *Moral Sentiments*, 184.

55. Smith, "Principles which Lead and Direct Philosophical Enquiries," 49.

56. Smith, *Moral Sentiments*, 50.

57. Smith suggests this state by the unintended effects of the invisible hand. On the role of interest as a tamer of passion, see Hirschman, *Passions and Interests*, 31–42.

58. Smith, *Lectures on Rhetoric and Belles Lettres*, 9. Subsequent citations will appear parenthetically.

59. Walpole, *Castle of Otranto*, 17.

60. Gallagher, *Nobody's Story*, xvi.

61. Gallagher, *Nobody's Story*, 173.

62. Hume, *A Treatise of Human Nature*, 494.

63. Spacks, *Desire and Truth*, 81.

64. Fielding, *Tom Jones*, 445. Subsequent citations will appear parenthetically.

65. Bunn, "Aesthetics of British Mercantilism," 311, 315.

66. Millar, *Origin of the Distinction of Ranks*, 3–4. On Millar's role in dissipating the moral critique of commercialism, see Ignatieff, "John Millar and Individualism," Ignatieff comments that "in a society in which individuals measured their obligations only in terms of personal advantage, family life risked becoming as brittle a human engagement as a business deal" (339).

67. Watt, *Rise of the Novel*, 43–47; Hunter, *Before Novels*, 76–78.

68. Lovell's *(Consuming Fiction)* is helpful on matters of institutionalization. She characterizes the early novel, those produced between 1770 and 1820, as commodity fiction, pricey items with small press runs, acting upon and challenging some of the assumptions of the "bourgeois consciousness" (47–48). Afterward, between 1840 and 1894, as she observes, the novel assumed its elevated position, once it gained "literary and class respectability" (73–75).

69. Wallace, *Characteristics of the Present Political State*, 245.

Chapter 4: Primitive Evidence versus Commercial Civilization: The Case of *Crusoe*

1. Backscheider, *Daniel Defoe*, 533–34.

2. Backscheider, *Daniel Defoe*, pp. 417–18.

3. Richetti, *Defoe's Narratives*, 192.

4. On the completeness of *Roxana*, see, e.g., Dijkstra, *Defoe and Economics*, 70–85.

5. Zimmerman, "Defoe and Crusoe," 387.

6. Braudy, "Anxieties of Autobiography," 76. Sim ("Interrogating an Ideology," 168) argues that "Defoe brings to the surface all the latent tensions in his ideology between radical individualism and authoritarian collectivism, free-will, and predeterminism."

7. Braudy, "Anxieties of Autobiography," 78.

8. Braudy, "Anxieties of Autobiography," 84.

9. Backscheider, *Daniel Defoe*, 511.

10. On the power-plenty model of mercantilism, see, e.g., Viner, "Power Versus Plenty," 61–68, 71–76.

11. Backscheider *Daniel Defoe*, 511.

12. Defoe, *Advantages of Peace and Commerce*, 6–7. Thompson (*Models of Value*) rejects the idea of harmonizing Defoe the novelist and Defoe the economic theoretician (87–88), but I do not see the value or utility of this argument when it is clear that there are connections.

13. Evelyn, *Trade and Navigation*, 14.

14. Defoe, *Plan of the English Commerce*, 109–10. Subsequent citations will appear parenthetically. Novak (*Economics and the Fiction of Daniel Defoe*) correctly maintains that Defoe advanced "few theories ahead of his time and many ideas that were more typical of the early seventeenth century" (5). He goes on to refer to his affiliation with the providential tradition: "six years before *Robinson Crusoe*, in his *General History of Trade*, Defoe argued that although God had created the world in such a way as to make commerce essential, he might have done it so that 'every Man should have been his own Labourer, or his own Manufacturer.' But whereas God assured each country its share of the necessities of life, he spread the articles needed for comfort and convenience all over the earth" (49).

15. Like other proponents, before and after, Defoe spoke favorably of the division of labor. Yet the mechanics of commercial productivity alone did not satisfy his aesthetic need for systematic harmony, through which parts and divisions contributed to the whole of what he called "This Beautiful Scheme of Trade." No clock, he remarks, could be brought to perfection by a single hand, just as "the least Pin contribute[s] its nameless Proportion to the Maintenance, Profit, and Support of every Head, and every Family concerned in those Operations, from the Copper Mine in *Africa* to the Retailer's Shop in the Country Village, however remote." See Defoe, *Brief State of the Inland or Home Trade of England*, 13. On the aesthetics of trade, see McVeagh, "Defoe and the Romance of Trade," though McVeagh tends to stress only the celebratory side of commerce in Defoe, not its dark side.

16. Defoe, *Complete English Tradesman*, 1, 1:85. Subsequent citations will appear parenthetically.

17. I do not want to create the impression that Defoe's stories lack emotion, though displays of it are rare. See, e.g., Boyce, "Question of Emotion in Defoe."

18. In *Advantages of Peace and Commerce*, Defoe comments that "trading nations" are superior to "fighting nations"; and the "want of Trade" signals lands left desolate and unimproved: "no settled Government . . . whole Provinces left wild, and like a *Terra deserta*, remaining in a meer State of Nature" (11).

19. Patey, *Probability and Literary Form*, 31–32.

20. Paulson, "Life as Journey and as Theater," 44–45.

21. Damrosch, *God's Plot & Man's Stories*, 187.

22. Defoe, *Robinson Crusoe*, 1; Defoe, *Serious Reflections*, ix. Subsequent citations of these works will be from these editions and appear parenthetically.

23. Defoe, *Serious Reflections*, ix.

24. For a thorough examination of Crusoe's possible motives for and psychology of hiding himself, see Brown, "Displaced Self in the Novels of Daniel Defoe," 563–90.

25. See, e.g., Butler, "Effect of the Narrator's Rhetorical Uncertainty on the Fiction of *Robinson Crusoe*," 77–90; Merrett, "Narrative Contraries in Defoe's Fiction," 171–85; and Kavanaugh, "Unraveling Robinson," 416–32.

26. Foster, "*Robinson Crusoe* and the Uses of the Imagination," 186.

27. Kavanaugh, "Unraveling Robinson," 420.

28. Defoe, *Farther Adventures*, 8.

29. Defoe, *Serious Reflections*, xvi.

30. Noteworthy among the many fine studies in the area of exegesis are Starr, *Defoe and Spiritual Autobiography*, and Hunter, *Reluctant Pilgrim*. On matters dealing with the role of interpretation, see Maddox, "Interpreter Crusoe."

31. Spacks, "Soul's Imaginings," 422.

32. See, e.g., Zelnick, "Ideology as Narrative," 97.

33. Cottom, "*Robinson Crusoe*," 273.

34. Locke, *Human Understanding*, 2, 4:367.

35. Shapiro, *Probability and Certainty*, 177.

36. See Daston, *Classical Probability in the Enlightenment*, 43–45, 62–63.

37. Glanvill, *Plus Ultra*, 14.

38. Glanvill, *Some Discourses, Sermons and Remains*, 288.

39. Hume, *Treatise of Human Nature*, 404, 406.

40. "Of the Imperfections of the Jewish Religion," in Barrow's *Theological Works*, 5:435.

41. Defoe, *Robinson Crusoe*, 35. Subsequent citations will appear parenthetically.

42. Locke, *Human Understanding*, 2, 4:366.

43. Locke, *Human Understanding*, 2, 4:366.

44. McKeon (*Origins of the English Novel*) proposes that "the dilemma of quantitative completeness arises within the plot of *Robinson Crusoe*, as a function of that impulse toward materialistic quantification which is so characteristic of empirical epistemology." With the Journal, however, "quantitative completeness is dwarfed by the apparent problem that the journal violates both the substance and the sequence of the narrative's historicity" (326).

45. We can be certain that Crusoe writes his memoirs and reflections after 1705 because of the final paragraph he writes in *Robinson Crusoe*: "All these things, with some very surprising Incidents in some new Adventures of my own, for ten Years more, I may perhaps give a farther Account of hereafter" (306). The "farther adventures" are already a *fait accompli*.

46. Spacks ("Soul's Imaginings"), e.g., believes that "Almost after a year after his shipwreck, [Crusoe] draws up" his affairs in the Journal (421).

47. Gaskell (*New Introduction to Bibliography*, 125) provides the ingredients.

48. Shapiro, *Probability and Certainty*, 173.

49. There is of course a world of difference between what Crusoe knows and what Defoe knows. Seidel ("Crusoe in Exile," esp. 367–70) shows the relevance of political allegory for the novel.

50. Braverman, "Crusoe's Legacy," 3.

51. Richetti (*Defoe's Narratives*, 21–62) exploits this theme, which I believe has greater relevance for volume 1 than for the subsequent volumes.

52. Braverman, "Crusoe's Legacy," 21.

53. Hunter, *Reluctant Pilgrim*, 197.

54. Zomchick, *Family and the Law in Eighteenth-Century Fiction*, 9.

55. Zimmerman, "Defoe and Crusoe," 397, 387.

56. Maddox, "Interpreter Crusoe," 50.

57. Defoe, *Farther Adventures*, 3.

58. Defoe, *Robinson Crusoe*, 159.

59. On the relevance of circumstantial evidence to *Crusoe*, see Welsh, *Strong Representations*, 2–8.

60. Locke, *Human Understanding*, 2, 4:463.

61. Although I am hesitant about seeing too much of a Scriptural template in *Farther Adventures*, at least as an overt structuring device, Schonhorn emphasizes this point, while also stressing "the continued dramatic rendering of the evolution of society"; see "Defoe," 38–42. Sill also maintains that "[f]or Defoe, the historical evolution of man and society did not end with the attainment of monarchy; there was still a further level of social and moral order for Crusoe to discover"; see *Defoe and the Idea of Fiction*, 166.

62. Defoe, *Serious Reflections*, 217. Subsequent citations will be noted parenthetically.

63. On the divisions and reversals that *Serious Reflections* effects, see Hopes, "Real and Imaginary Stories."

64. Defoe, *Farther Adventures*, 9.

65. Pursuing the religious dimensions of retirement, Blewett ("The Retirement Myth in *Robinson Crusoe*," 37–50) holds that retreat from the world is inconsistent with Christian retirement and is "profoundly un-Puritan" (39); he draws particularly on Crusoe's experience with the Muscovite Prince toward the end of *Farther Adventures* in making this determination.

66. Flint ("Role of Kinship in *Robinson Crusoe*,") comments usefully and insightfully about the division in the novel that occurs at this point: "The break between the island episode in the first half of the *Farther Adventures* and the continuation of the adventure narrative in the concluding half is startling, dramatically signifying the separation of Crusoe from his earlier attachments. . . . Neither wife and family nor island community reassert themselves in Crusoe's thoughts once he renews his adventures" (405).

67. See Beattie (*Crime and the Courts in England*, 363–76) for these and other relevant issues.

Chapter 5: Domestic Exchange: Richardson versus Fielding

1. Richardson, *Pamela*, 9. Subsequent citations will appear parenthetically.

2. Fielding, *Joseph Andrews*, 10.

3. McKeon, *Origins of the English Novel*, 410.

4. Campbell, *Romantic Ethic*, 39.

5. Campbell, *Romantic Ethic*, 215, also 69–76, 88–95.

6. Campbell, *Romantic Ethic*, 215, also 154–59, 193–95.

7. Barker-Benfield (*Culture of Sensibility*) plots the association of benevolence and consumerism over the period, paying special attention to this connection for women. He comments, in brief, on the broad history of change from the seventeenth through the eighteenth centuries, so that by the time it reached Mary Wollstonecraft it was "a central theme in [her] *Rights of Woman*, one she placed in her vision of historical change." By contrast, "Richardson testifies to women's appetite for public consumer pleasures at the same [time] he tried to direct women to the pursuit of private virtue at home" (203, 200).

8. Armstrong, *Desire and Domestic Fiction*, 96–97.

9. Armstrong, *Desire and Domestic Fiction*, 121.

10. Armstrong, *Desire and Domestic Fiction*, 60.

11. On the question of readability, see Schellenberg ("Enclosing the Immovable") who persuasively contends that "Richardson's ideal social and literary structure is modelled on the moral perfection and stasis of heaven" in the sequel (37); in effect, Schellenberg reads the sequel as Richardson's attempt at governing part 1. Bowers ("'Point of Conscience'") proposes that the novel is "a strategically assembled conduct-book" (263).

12. Castle, *Masquerade and Civilization*, 169. Obviously there is disagreement about the relationship between the two parts of the novel. Castle is of the "dynamic" school, finding the sequel eventually repeating the "saturnalian fantasia of Part I"—its original. What is interesting is that although Castle notes that the "reunion of Pamela and B. in Part 2 is achieved relatively swiftly, with little in the way of intervening narrative suspense" (169), it is the rare occasion of this suspense that suddenly enlivens the novel for Castle.

13. Richardson, *Pamela* (Part 2), 4:295–96. Subsequent citations will appear parenthetically.

14. About this passage, Castle comments that "like a true ideologue Pamela objects to repetition even in the nebulous form of public memory" (*Masquerade and Civilization*, 147).

15. Schellenberg ("Enclosing the Immovable") reads Prudentia as Pamela (31).

16. Richardson, *Pamela*, 201.

17. Korshin (*Typologies in England*) comments that "Richardson discovered, to his embarrassment, that Pamela's chastity which made her, in the eyes of some readers, a postfiguration of that Christian saintliness which could convert the ungodly, simply made her a huge joke to many others" (228).

18. *Pamela Censured*, 24, 8.

19. Foucault, *Order of Things*, 140, 145.

20. Gwilliam (*Samuel Richardson's Fictions of Gender*) writes about the "duplicity"of Pamela (cf. Watt, *Rise of the Novel*, 168–73), though in a way to complicate our apprehension of what the term means as applied to the character herself; thus, she writes, "in my view *Pamela*, as well as the reactions it provoked, illuminates instead a complex interaction and confusion between surface and depths, and evidences the persistent attractions of the body under the purportedly new ideology of femininity" (17).

21. Gooding ("*Pamela, Shamela*, and the Politics of the *Pamela* Vogue," 109–30) sees "strident egalitarianism" in the first part that is "all but absent from . . . Part II"; he goes on to observe from his survey of anti-*Pamela* works that they all originate with *Shamela*, noting that these "attacks invariably dehumanize Pamela by stripping away the complex, authentic self that she attributes to the influence of Lady B., her parents, and Mrs Jervis" (113, 125).

22. Fielding, *Shamela*, 320.

23. Straub advances the idea of gendered voyeurism in *Pamela* and notes in particular about the passage I discuss that Pamela "further endangers her[self] since [her mirror image] blinds her to the social controls that create and define her"; see "Reconstructing the Gaze," 427. Dussinger considers the idea of reflection and mirroring in a more neutral manner in "What Pamela Knew." There he explores objectification (characters who serve as "reflectors") through which Pamela measures her subjective growth as a woman who takes command of B. in "a superior role as his creator" (303). The first mirror scene, I should add, prefigures Pamela's "investiture" as the new Lady B., when later, with her marriage but a few days off, she clothes herself in garments formerly belonging to her now-dead employer and, in looking in a glass, sees herself as "a little proud Hussy" who is thankful she can dress "with so much Comfort" (256).

24. Ribeiro, *Dress in Eighteenth Century Europe 1715–1789*, 42.

25. Richardson, *Pamela*, 60.

26. Larson ("'Naming the Writer,'" 140), by contrast, maintains that because of her ability to externalize herself as a role player, Pamela as a writer desublimates herself and escapes the "mechanisms of repression and sublimation."

27. Watt (*Rise of the Novel*, 135) contrasts Richardson's handling of formal problems with Defoe's, indicating that the former's "solution was remarkably simple: he avoided the episodic plot by basing his novels on a single action, a courtship."

28. Pierce ("Pamela's Textual Authority," 145) in fact demonstrates how Pamela appropriates and adapts sacred stories and fables to add to her textual authority. These are piecemeal appropriations that evidence an "autonomous creative personality."

29. Flynn (*Samuel Richardson*, 239) has observed that "Pamela's own personality, ambiguous, self-conscious, and calculated, transcends her rather limited moral pattern."

30. Larson ("'Naming the Writer,'" 130) observes that "the more vehemently [B.] enforces his authority, the more that authority is crippled by a 'rageful recognition' of its own desperate foundations."

31. Donovan has maintained that the focus of *Pamela* is the impact of the middle classes upon the aristocracy; see "The Problem of Pamela."

32. For a brief, though cogent discussion of embarrassments from the past, see Dussinger, "What Pamela Knew," 389–91.

33. In an essay on fabrication in *Pamela*, Conboy notes how B. falls in love with the way that Pamela works the "completion of his character," as she herself departs the traditional labor of needlecraft for the work of weaving words; see "Fabric and Fabrication in Richardson's *Pamela*," 94.

34. Mueck ("Beauty and Mr. B") points out *Pamela*'s resemblance to the fairy tale.

35. Not unrelated, Kearney ("Richardson's 'Pamela,'") comments on how Richardson masters Pamela by objectifying or making socially fit the contents of her sometimes erotically charged mind.

36. Doody (*A Natural Passion*, chap. 3) sees *Pamela* as a novel always on the verge of disintegration, but which is spared that fate through the unifying force of its pastoralism.

37. McKeon, *Origins of the English Novel*, 378.

38. Bond, "Representing Reality," 127, 133.

39. *Joseph Andrews* frustrates Watt a bit—or at least the investment he has made in formal realism. As he argues, this novel has less to do with "social change" than with the "neo-classical literary tradition" and the "epic's false code of honour," at once "masculine, bellicose, aristocratic, and pagan" (*Rise of the Novel*, 239, 244). Spilka ("Fielding and the Epic Impulse," 73) works with Watt's "pagan" model to advance that "in adopting the role of the omniscient narrator, Fielding takes an overall view—objective, social, public—of a potentially definable world. . . . His role is godlike or perhaps muse-like; it allows for a control of scale and variety which approximates the epic view" but which does not have a significant impact on subsequent novelists (73). McKeon abandons these categorical differences but uses others to suggest the ways in which Fielding's narrative attacks the progressivism and historicity of *Pamela* as inadequate or incomplete (*Origins of the English Novel*, 398–409).

40. The issue of theory versus practice is most apparent through the character of Parson Adams, which has received appreciable commentary; see, e.g., Osland, "Tied Back to Back," 194–95. Another sense of the "divided" world Fielding inhabits is apparent in Plank's essay, "Narrative Forms of *Joseph Andrews*" in which he comments on Fielding's attempt to draw literary and social conventions into a useful harmony. Fielding himself believed that the dissemination and subsequent weakening of authority

quickened once the Augustan Age lost its champion: with "the demise of King Alexander" the state lapsed into "democracy" or "down-right anarchy" (*Covent-Garden Journal* in *Complete Works*, 14:145. As a consequence, the self-interested mode of history prevailed, in which "Fashion," not authority, became "the great governor of this world" (*True Patriot* in *Complete Works*, 14:7).

41. The concept of the good-natured man is one linked to latitudinarian Christianity, which Battestin (*Moral Basis of Fielding's Art*) has detailed; see, esp., 26–43.

42. One cannot dispute Fielding's intention to impose a typological design upon the novel and all that implies about teleology and historical continuity. Succeeding in doing so was another matter entirely. Braudy (*Narrative Form in History and Fiction*, 91) goes so far as to attribute to Fielding the belief that "public history was bankrupt as a source for moral values or even informative analogies." Davis alludes to this paradoxical effect of Fielding's narrative when he urges that he does not even pretend to write a factual fiction with *Joseph Andrews*, other than through his "more or less direct [reaction] to contemporary events" (*Factual Fictions*, 195).

43. Fielding, "Essay on the Knowledge of the Characters of Men," in *Complete Works*, 14:303. Subsequent citations will appear parenthetically.

44. Fielding, *Amelia*, 17. Subsequent citations will appear parenthetically.

45. Interestingly, Donaldson ("Fielding, Richardson, and the Ends of the Novel") draws attention to what appears a patent reversal of roles when he contends that Richardson sought to integrate art with life, whereas Fielding preferred stressing the "palpably fictitious." In *God's Plot & Man's Stories*, Damrosch fleshes out this notion through his distinction of the Puritan and Augustan character: that is, between the inward-dwelling Richardsonian character and the outward-directed Fieldingesque character. He comments that Fielding uses "types," consistent with the "neoclassical conception of character." In this framework, "sentiment or feeling becomes a guide to conduct," the morality of which "attaches to choices rather than personality" (Damrosch, 267–269).

46. See, e.g., Barrell, *Birth of Pandora*, 89–95.

47. Fielding, "Characters of Men," in *Complete Works*, 14:303.

48. Fielding, *Inquiry into the Causes of the Late Increase of Robbers*, in *Complete Works*, 13:14.

49. Fielding, *True Patriot*, in *Complete Works*, 14:21.

50. Fielding, *Proposal for Making an Effectual Provision for the Poor*, in *Complete Works*, 13:138.

51. Fielding, *Increase of Robbers*, in *Complete Works*, 13:16.

52. Fielding, *The Champion*, in *Complete Works*, 15:153.

53. Fielding, *Proposal for Making an Effectual Provision for the Poor*, in *Complete Works*, 13:142.

54. Fielding, *True Patriot*, in *Complete Works*, 14: 18. Subsequent citations will appear parenthetically.

55. Knight ("*Joseph Andrews* and the Failure of Authority") provides an excellent example of how Fielding bungled his enterprise. He argues that generic instability ensues from Fielding's division of plot into two incompatible components, the romantic and Cervantic. This awkward juxtaposition accounts for the demonstrable inconsistencies and shifts that trouble the narrator and compromise his authority. Tandrup supplies another way of looking at this same phenomenon, though on the micronarrative level. She points to Fielding's "technique of qualification" as a habitual practice that "has the effect of constantly surprising the reader into an awareness of diversity and ambiguity"—in other words, shifting the burden of coherence to the reader, as if conceding that the parts do not form a perfect whole; see "Technique of Qualification in

Fielding's *Joseph Andrews* and *Tom Jones*," 234. Raymond Stephanson ("Education of the Reader in Fielding's *Joseph Andrews*," 246) puts a more favorable spin on these matters when he comments that "our sense of privilege [as readers] is completely dependent on a superior and omniscient authorial-narrative plan that deliberately withholds and discloses information not for *our* comfort . . . but for narrative purposes."

56. Fielding, *Joseph Andrews*, 4. Subsequent citations will appear parenthetically.

57. For this characterization see Fielding, *Joseph Andrews* (Houghton Mifflin xx). Frank ("Comic Novel and the Poor") demonstrates, on the other hand, how Fielding has encrypted economic discrimination within the preface, a position that is not consistent with Sherburn's view that Fielding's outlook is that "of all classes working together for the good of the whole"; see "Fielding's Social Outlook," 255. In this vein, see also McCrea ("Rewriting *Pamela*") who examines the absence of the democratic spirit in Fielding's novel.

58. For a more extended examination of the theory versus practice issue in the novel, see Cruise, "Precept, Property, and 'Bourgeois' Practice in *Joseph Andrews*."

59. Reed (*Exemplary History of the Novel*, 134) comments that 2, 1 "ends with a figurative displacement of literary authority into the realm of commercial enterprise." Stevick (*Chapter in Fiction*, 25) contends that the irony of 2, 1 is so baffling "that it leaves quite unclear what Fielding meant to assert."

60. Perl ("Anagogic Surfaces," 260) comments that "with *Joseph Andrews*, Fielding hoped to make classicism modern and modernity classical." To effect this end, however, he proposes that we must read this paradoxical circumstance anagogically.

61. Bartolomeo, e.g., ("Interpolated Tales as Allegories of Reading," 410) remarks that, in particular, the interpolated "tales help to deconstruct the notion of a single, normative implied reader by illustrating diverse responses determined by character, circumstances, and acuity." Warner ("Interpolated Narratives in the Fiction of Fielding and Smollett," 272–76) urges that Fielding uses these interpolations to underscore the epistemological uncertainty of the times.

62. Weinstein, in *Fictions of the Self*, by contrast, argues that Joseph and Fanny embody a fecund code of nature (114–28).

63. On the competitive nature of the narrator, see Cruise, "Fielding, Authority, and the New Commercialism in *Joseph Andrews*," 263–64.

64. The abrupt changes in Joseph's character have been a source of interest among scholars of the period novel for some time. Needless to say, although these changes are readily conceded, they signify different things, based in part on the willingness of the individual critic to work within the social program that *Joseph Andrews* implies. Taylor ("Joseph as Hero in *Joseph Andrews*") proposes that Joseph separates himself ethically from Adams, though the measure of this change is registered largely through action and appearance. Hunter (*Occasional Form*, 100) indicates that "Professor Battestin is ultimately right that Joseph is a type of chastity who responsibly and admirably upholds a strict sexual ethic and extends his moral conclusions to social responsibility, but Fielding does not begin by assuming his reader's concurrence with such attitudes, and he sends Joseph on a circuitous route to moral heroism." Ruml ("Joseph Andrews as Exemplary Gentleman") associates the bumpy evolution and elevation of Joseph's character with Fielding himself and proposes that the novel does not offer a model of upward mobility because Joseph is endowed only once his pedigree becomes certain.

Chapter 6: Sterne and the Industrial Novel

1. Sterne, *Tristram Shandy*, 1, 19:60. Subsequent citations will appear parenthetically.

2. Berg, *Age of Manufactures*, 289.

3. Berg, *Age of Manufactures*, 288.

4. *Reflections on Various Subjects Relating to Arts and Commerce*, 27. Subsequent citations will appear parenthetically.

5. Steuart, *Inquiry into Principles of Political Œconomy*, 1, 19:66. Subsequent citations will appear parenthetically.

6. Young, *Conjectures on Original Composition*, 7. Subsequent citations will appear parenthetically.

7. Lamb, *Sterne's Fiction and the Double Principle*, 50.

8. New, "Sterne and the Narrative of Determinateness," 329.

9. Steuart, *Inquiry into Principles of Political Œconomy*, 1, 19:163.

10. On the intellectual tradition in general behind *Tristram Shandy*, see D. W. Jefferson, " 'Tristram Shandy' and Its Traditions," 333–45. On Sterne's borrowings from contemporaneous sources, see Golden, "Periodical Contexts in the Imagined World of *Tristram Shandy*."

11. Paulson, *Satire and the Novel in Eighteenth-Century England*, 249, 250.

12. Fielding's narrators, by contrast, never act in the novels; they only direct.

13. Ferguson, *History of Civil Society*, 181. Subsequent citations will appear parenthetically.

14. Hume, "Rise and Progress of the Arts and Sciences," in *Essays Moral, Political, and Literary*, 119.

15. Dowling, by contrast, argues that a fundamental tension exists in the novel between Tristram, who is in the vanguard of the imagination, and those opposed to the imagination, the forces of church and state; see "Tristram Shandy's Phantom Audience."

16. Hume, "Rise and Progress of the Arts and Sciences," in *Essays Moral, Political, and Literary*, 136–37.

17. *Lords' Manuscripts* cited in Cherry, "Development of the English Free-Trade Movement in Parliament," 110–11.

18. My figures on premiums and fortunes at retirement are from Earle, "Age and Accumulation in the London Business Community," 52, 55; the bankruptcy percentage is from Hoppit, *Risk and Failure in English Business*, 97.

19. Harries ("Sterne's Novels") argues the side of a religious disposition to account for the fragmentation in the novel, which, she maintains, alludes to biblical fragments of bread and fishes.

20. Watt, *Rise of the Novel*, 291.

21. Watt, *Rise of the Novel*, 71.

22. By contrast, Hunter ("Response as Reformation") distrusts the priority of the ideological approach in favor of the methodological. In focusing on the "Abuses of Conscience" sermon, from which he reads outward, he dismisses the hobby-horsical version of interpretive authority as unacceptable to the didactic aims of the novel.

23. In this light, Tristram bears comparison with Yorick who also travels to France in *A Sentimental Journey*. During his journey to Bourbonnois, he complains that he has insufficient room in his journal to detail this adventure: "Just heaven!—it will fill up twenty volumes—and alas! I have but a few small pages left of this to croud into—and half of these must be taken up with the poor Maria my friend, Mr. Shandy, met with near Moulines"; see Sterne, *Sentimental Journey*, 113. Likewise, when Tristram prepares to write about and represent others, he faces no encumbrances and has ample volumes to fill. One such example dominates the opening of volume 2: "I might have begun a new book, on purpose that I might have room enough to explain the nature of the perplexities in which my Uncle *Toby* was involved, from the many discourses and interrogations about the siege of *Namur*, where he received his wound" (2, 1:93).

24. On this subject, see Burckhardt, "*Tristram Shandy*'s Law of Gravity."

25. Politi (*Novel and Its Presuppositions*, 161) notes that "Tristram's fractured narrative . . . [is] a reflection of the ideological crisis that was beginning to be felt and articulated in fiction." According to Politi, this crisis was effected from the loss of teleological structure, assisted in good part by Hume. See also, Cruise, "Reinvesting the Novel," 217–218.

Afterword: Market Access and Economic Relationship

1. Lennox, *Female Quixote*, 229. Subsequent citations will appear parenthetically.

2. Cruise, "House Divided," 566.

3. Sheridan, *Memoirs of Miss Sidney Bidulph*, 318. Subsequent citations will appear parenthetically.

Bibliography

I have divided my research materials into four categories: two that deal with primary sources and two that address matters of commentary and criticism. Because my argument depends heavily upon period economic history, I have, in the first section, attempted to provide a substantial, though not exhaustive, bibliography of published works that I found relevant to my understanding of how the economy worked during the period. I hope that others interested in the period economy may find something useful from this list. The second and fourth sections are less exhaustive than the first. They do, however, manage to identify those works that have figured most prominently in the ways in which I conceive the nexus of commerce and the novel. The third section provides a list of primary literary works.

Primary Sources: Economic, Political, Religious

Abercromby, David. *A Moral Discourse of the Power of Interest*. London, 1690.

An Abstract of Several Cases Relating to the Trade to Africa. N.p., n.d.

In the Act for Raising Two Millions. London, 1698.

[Adair, James]. *Observations on the Power of Alienation in the Crown before the First of Queen Anne*. London, 1768.

An Address to Britons of All Ranks. Durham, 1792.

Address to Parents Earnestly Recommending them to Promote the Happiness of Their Children, by a Due Regard to Their Virtuous Education. Uxbridge, 1787.

The Allegations of the Turkey Company and Others against the East-India Company. N.p., n.d.

The Ancient and Modern Constitution of Government Stated and Compared. London, 1774.

Anderson, Adam. *An Historical and Chronological Deduction of the Origin of Commerce*. 2 vols. London, 1764.

Anderson, James. *An Inquiry into the Causes that have hitherto retarded the Advancement of Agriculture in Europe*. Edinburgh, 1779.

———. *Observations on the Means of Exciting a Spirit of National Industry*. Edinburgh, 1777.

An Answer to a Paper call'd Particulars against the Bill for an Open Trade to Africa. N.p., n.d.

An Appeal to Facts, Regarding the Home Trade and Inland Manufactures of Great Britain and Ireland. London, 1751.

Ascham, Antony. *Of the Confusions and Revolutions of Governments*. London, 1649.

Asgill, J. *Several Assertions Proved, In Order to Create another Species of Money than Gold and Silver*. London, 1696.

The Assiento Contract Consider'd. London, 1714.

Barbon, Nicholas. *An Apologie for the Builder*. London, 1685.

————. *A Discourse concerning Coining the New Money Lighter.* London, 1696.

————. *A Discourse of Trade.* London, 1690.

Barnard, John. *A Present for an Apprentice: or, a Sure Guide to Gain both Esteem and Estate.* Edinburgh, 1787.

Barrow, Isaac. *The Theological Works of Isaac Barrow, D.D.* Edited by Alexander Napier. 9 vols. Cambridge: At the University Press, 1859.

Baston, Thomas. *Thoughts on Trade, and a Publick Spirit.* London, 1716.

Bates, William. *Harmony of Divine Attributes.* 4th ed. London, 1697.

Bell, William. *A Dissertation on the Following Subject: What Causes Principally Contribute to Render a Nation Populous?* Cambridge, 1756.

Belsham, Thomas. *A Review of Mr Wilberforce's Treatise.* London, 1798.

[Bentley, Thomas]. *The Poor Man's Answer to the Rich Associates.* N.p., n.d.

————. *To the Tradesmen of this Kingdom in General.* London, 1760.

Berkeley, George. *An Essay Towards Preventing the Ruine of Great Britain.* London, 1721.

————. *The Works of George Berkeley, D.D.* Edited by G. N. Wright. 2 vols. London, 1843.

Bethel, Slingsby. *The Present Interest of England Stated.* London, 1671.

A Bill for Continuing the Trade and Corporation Capacity of the United East-India Company. N.p., n.d.

Bindon, David. *A Letter from a Merchant Who has left off Trade to a Member of Parliament.* London, 1738.

————. *A Political Essay upon Commerce.* London, 1738.

Black, David. *Essay upon Industry and Trade.* Edinburgh, 1706.

Blanch, John. *The Naked Truth, in an Essay upon Trade.* London, 1696.

Bolingbroke [Henry St. John]. *The Works of Lord Bolingbroke.* 4 vols. Philadelphia: Carey and Hart, 1841.

Boyle, Robert. *Reflections upon a Theological Distinction.* London, 1690.

————. *Some Considerations Touching the Style of the H. Scriptures.* London, 1663.

Brewster, Francis. *New Essays on Trade.* London, 1700.

A Brief Essay on the Advantages and Disadvantages, which respectively attend France and Great Britain, with Regard to Trade. London, 1749.

A Brief History of Trade in England. London, 1702.

Brief State of the East India Trade. N.p., n.d.

Briscoe, John. *A Discourse of Money.* London, 1696.

————. *A Discourse on the Late Funds of the Million Act, Lottery Act, and Bank of England.* London, 1694.

Brittaine, William de. *Human Prudence.* 1710. 10th ed. Aberdeen, 1784.

Britannia in Mourning: or, a Review of the Politicks and Conduct of the Court of Great Britain with regard to France, the Ballance of Power, and the True Interest of these Nations, from the Restoration to the Present Times. London, 1742.

Britannia Languens, or A Discourse of Trade. London, 1680.

Brown, John. *An Estimate of the Manners and Principles of the Times.* 2d ed. London, 1757.

Brown, William Lawrence. *An Essay on the Natural Equality of Men.* 2d ed. London, 1794.

Browne, John. *A Collection of Tracts.* London, 1729.

[Budgell, Eustace]. *A Short History of Prime Ministers.* London, 1733.

Burnet, Thomas. *The [Sacred] Theory of the Earth*. 2d ed. London, 1691.

Burnett, James [Lord Monboddo]. *Of the Origin and Progress of Language*. 6 vols. Edinburgh, 1773–92. Vol. 1. 2d ed. 1774.

C., W. *Trades Destruction is Englands Ruine: or Excise Decryed*. London, 1659.

Campbell, Alexander. *An Enquiry into the Original of Moral Virtue*. Edinburgh, 1733.

Campbell, John. *A Political Survey of Britain*. 2 vols. London, 1774.

Cantillon, Philip. *The Analysis of Trade, Commerce, Coin, Bullion, Banks, and Foreign Exchanges*. London, 1759.

Cary, John. *An Essay on the State of England, in Relation to its Trade*. Bristol, 1695.

Chamberlain, Hugh. *A Collection of Some Papers*. London, 1696.

―――. *A Safe and Easy Method for Supplying the Want of Coin*. London, 1695.

Champion, Richard. *Comparative Reflections on the Past and Present Political, Commercial, and Civil State of Great Britain*. London, 1787.

The Character of the True Publick Spirit. N.p., 1702.

Child, Josiah. *Brief Observations Concerning Trade and Interest of Money*. London, 1668.

―――. *A Discourse about Trade*. London, 1690.

―――. *A Discourse concerning Plantations*. London, 1692.

―――. *A Discourse of the Nature, Use and Advantages of Trade*. London, 1694.

―――. *The Great Honour and Advantage of the East-India Trade to the Kingdom*. London, 1697.

―――. *A New Discourse of Trade*. London, 1693.

―――. *A Treatise Wherein is Demonstrated* . . . London, 1681.

Chubb, Thomas. *Two Enquiries*. London, 1717.

Clare, M. *Youth's Introduction to Trade and Business*. 1719. 2d ed. London, 1727.

Clayton, David. *A Short System of Trade*. London, 1719.

Clement, Simon. *A Discourse of the General Notions of Money, Trade, and Exchanges*. London, 1695.

Coke, Roger. *A Discourse of Trade*. London, 1670.

―――. *England's Improvements*. London, 1675.

―――. *A Treatise wherein is demonstrated, that the Church and State of England, are in Equal Danger with the Trade of It*. London, 1671.

Cole, Thomas. *Discourses on Luxury, Infidelity, and Enthusiasm*. London, 1761.

Collins, Anthony. *The Scheme of Literal Prophecy Considered*. London, 1727.

Comparison between the Proposals of the Bank and the South-Sea Company. London, 1720.

The Compleat Tradesman. London, 1720.

A Compleat View of the Present Politicks of Great Britain. London, 1743.

A Complete Investigation of Mr. Eden's Treaty, as it may affect the Commerce, Revenue, and the General Policy of Great Britain. London, 1787.

Considerations on the Present State of the Nation, as to Publick Credit, Stocks, the Landed and Trading Interests. London, 1720

Coole, B. *Miscellanies, or, Sunday Discourses concerning Trade, Conversation, and Religion*. London, 1712.

A Copy of Captain le Wright's Warrant. London, 1706.

Coulthurst, H. W. *The Evils of Disobedience and Luxury*. Cambridge, 1796.

Cradocke, Francis. *An Expedient for taking away all Impositions*. London, 1660.

————. *Wealth Discovered*. London, 1661.

Crosfeild, Robert. *England's Glory Reviv'd*. London, 1693.

————. *Truth Brought to Light*. London, 1694.

Davenant, Charles. *An Account of the Trade Between Great-Britain, France, Holland, Spain, Portugal, Italy, Newfoundland*. London, 1715.

————. *An Essay upon the Probable Methods of Making a People Gainers in the Ballance of Trade*. London, 1699.

————. *An Essay upon Ways and Means of Supplying the War*. London, 1695.

————. *Essays*. London, 1701.

————. *The Political and Commercial Works*. 5 vols. London, 1774.

————. *Two Manuscripts*. Introduced by Abbott Payson Usher. Baltimore: Johns Hopkins University Press, 1942.

Defoe, Daniel. *The Advantages of Peace and Commerce*. London, 1729.

————. *A Brief State of the Inland or Home Trade of England*. London, 1730.

————. *The Complete English Tradesman*. 2d ed. 2 vols. London, 1727.

————. *An Essay upon Publick Credit*. London, 1710.

————. *The Family Instructor*. 2d ed. 2 vols. London, 1715–18.

————. *The Original Power of the Collective Body of the People of England*. London, 1702.

————. *A Plan of the English Commerce*. 2d ed. London, 1730.

————. *Some Further Observations on the Treaty of Navigation and Commerce between Great-Britain and France*. 2d ed. London, 1713.

Dekker, Matthew. *An Essay on the Causes of the Decline of Foreign Trade*. London, 1744.

Dennis, John. *Vice and Luxury, Public Mischiefs: or, Remarks on a Book Intituled, The Fable of the Bees*. London, 1724.

A Discourse Consisting of Motives for the Enlargement and Freedome of Trade. London, 1645.

A Discourse on the Natural Disposition of Mankind in respect to Commerce. London, 1768.

A Discourse on Trade, Liberty, and Taxes. Lincoln, 1733.

Donaldson, James. *The Undoubted Art of Thriving*. Edinburgh, 1700.

Downing, George. *A Short Vindication of the French Treaty*. London, 1787.

[Eden, William]. *A View of the Treaty of Commerce with France: Signed at Versailles, Sept. 20, 1786, by Mr Eden*. 2d ed. London, 1787.

[Egleton, John]. *A Vindication of the Late House of Commons, in rejecting the Eight and Nine of the Treaty of Navigation and Commerce*. London, 1714.

England's Interest or the Great Benefit to Trade by Banks or Offices of Credit in London. London, 1682.

An Enquiry &c.. [London, 1795].

An Enquiry into the Melancholy Circumstances of Great Britain. London, 1743.

An Enquiry into the Nature, Foundation, and Present State of Publick Credit. [London, 1748].

An Enquiry into the Reasons for and against Inclosing the Open Fields. Coventry, 1767.

An Enquiry Whether A General Practice of Virtue Tends to the Wealth or Poverty, Benefit or Disadvantages of a People? London, 1795.

An Enquiry Whether the Christian Religion is of any Benefit, or only a Useless Commodity to a Trading Nation. London, 1732.

Erskine, K., Lord Dun. *Lord Dun's Friendly and Familiar Advices, Adapted to the Various Stations and Conditions of Life*. Edinburgh, 1754.

An Essay for Discharging the Debts of the Nation, by Equivalents. London, 1720.

An Essay on Publick Industry. London, 1724.

An Essay on Tea, Sugar, White Bread and Butter, Country Alehouses, Strong Beer and Geneva, and other Modern Luxuries. Salisbury, 1777.

An Essay on the Causes of the Present High Price of Provisions. London, 1773.

An Essay on the Increase and Decline of Trade, in London and the Out-Ports. London, 1749.

Essay on Ways and Means for the Advancement of Trade. London, 1726.

An Essay, or, Modest Proposal, of the Way to Encrease the Number of People, and Consequently the Strength of this Kingdom. N.p., 1693.

Evelyn, John. *Navigation and Commerce.* London, 1674.

Extract out of the Act for Raising Two Millions. N.p., n.d.

Fatal Effects of Luxury and Indolence, Exemplified in the History of Hacho, King of Lapland. Chesterfield, 1778.

A Father's Advice to his Daughters. Sherborne, 1776.

Fawconer, Samuel. *An Essay on Modern Luxury.* London, 1765.

The Fears of the Nation Quieted. London, 1714.

Ferguson, Adam. *An Essay on the History of Civil Society.* 1767. Introduction by Louis Schneider. New Brunswick, N.J.: Transaction Books, 1980.

Fletcher, Andrew, of Saltoun. *An Account of a Conversation concerning A Right Regulation of Governments for the Common Good of Mankind.* London, 1704.

Fortrey, Samuel. *Englands Interest and Improvement.* London, 1673.

Free Thoughts on Despotic and Free Governments. London, 1781.

Fricx, Eugene Henry. *The Freedom of Commerce of the Subjects of the Austrian Nether-lands.* N.p., n.d.

G., S. *The Father's Legacy to his Children.* London, 1711.

Gee, Joshua. *The Trade and Navigation of Great Britain.* London, 1729.

A General Collection of Treatys. 2d ed. Vol. 1. London, 1732.

General View of England. 1762. London, 1766.

Gervase, Isaac. *The System or Theory of Trade of the World.* London, 1720.

Glanvill, Joseph. *Plus Ultra: or, the Progress and Advancement of Knowledge.* London, 1668.

———. *Some Discourses, Sermons and Remains of the Reverend Mr Jos. Glanvil.* London, 1681.

Goodman, Godfrey. *The Fall of Man, or the Corruption of Nature, proved by the Light of Our Naturall Reason.* London, 1616.

Graunt, John. *Natural and Political Observations.* London, 1662.

[Gray, Charles]. *Considerations on Several Prospects lately made for the Better Maintenance of the Poor.* London, 1751.

The Groans of Britons at the Gloomy Prospect of the Present Precarious State of their Liberties and Properties. London, 1743.

The Guide to Domestic Happiness. 3d ed. London, 1781.

Hakewill, George. *An Apologie of the Power and Providence of God in the Government of the World.* Oxford, 1627.

Hakewill, William. *The Liberty of the Subject.* London, 1641.

Hanway, Jonas. *Virtue in Humble Life.* London, 1774.

Harrington, James. *The Oceana of James Harrington, Esq.; and His Other Works*. Dublin, 1737.

[Harris, Joseph]. *An Essay upon Money and Coins*. London, 1757.

Hay, William. *An Essay on Civil Government*. London, 1728.

Haynes, John. *Proposals Offered to the Honourable House of Commons, for the more effectual preventing the Exportation of Wool*. N.p., n.d.

Hazeland, William. *A View of the Manner in which Trade and Civil Liberty Support Each Other*. London, 1756.

Helps to a Right Decision upon the Merits of the Late Treaty of Commerce with France. London, 1787.

[Hervey, John]. *Ancient and Modern Liberty Stated and Compared*. London, 1734.

Historical and Political Remarks upon the Tariff of the Commercial Treaty. London, 1787.

The History of the Norfolk Stewart, in Two Parts. London, 1728.

History of the Rise, Progress, and Tendency of Patriotism. London, 1747.

Hoadly, Benjamin. *The Fears and Sentiments of All True Britains*. London, 1710.

Hodges, James. *Considerations and Proposals*. Edinburgh, 1705.

Hodson, Septimus. *An Address to the Different Classes of Persons in Great Britain*. London, 1795.

Homer, Henry. *An Enquiry into the Means of Preserving and Improving the Publick Roads of this Kingdom*. Oxford, 1767.

————. *An Essay on the Nature and Method of Ascertaining the Specifick Shares of Proprietors, upon the Inclosure of Common Fields*. Oxford, 1766

Hooke, Andrew. *An Essay on the National Debt, and National Capital*. London, 1750.

The Humble Representation of the Clothiers of Great Britain, For the Improving and Encouraging our Home Trade and Manufactures. N.p., n.d.

Hume, David. *A Treatise of Human Nature*. Edited by L. A. Selby-Bigge and P. H. Nidditch. 2d ed. Oxford: Clarendon Press, 1978.

Hutcheson, Francis. *An Essay on the Nature and Conduct of the Passions and Affections*. 3d ed. London, 1742.

Impartial View of English Agriculture from Permitting the Exportation of Corn. 2d ed. London, 1766.

Increase of Manufactures, Commerce, and Finance, with the Extension of Civil Liberty. London, 1785.

Ingram, Robert Acklom. *An Inquiry into the Present Condition of the Lower Classes*. London, 1797.

The Interest of England. London, 1731.

Interest of Scotland Considered. Edinburgh, 1733.

The Interest of these United Provinces. Middelburg, 1677.

The Interests of Man in Opposition to the Rights of Man. Edinburgh, 1793.

[Jenyns, Soame]. *Thoughts on the Causes and Consequences of the Present High Price of Provisions*. London, 1767.

Johnson, Thomas. *A Plea for Free-Mens Liberties*. London, 1646.

[Jones, Erasmus]. *Luxury, Pride and Vanity, The Base of the British Nation*. 3d ed. London, 1735.

The Judgment of Whole Kingdoms and Nations. 3d ed. London, 1710.

Justice and Policy. An Essay on the Increasing Growth and Enormities of Our Great Cities. London, 1774.

Key to the Present Politicks of the Principal Powers of Europe. London, 1743.

Kames, Lord [Henry Home]. *Sketches of the History of Man*. 3d ed. 2 vols. Dublin, 1774.

The Landed Interest Consider'd. London, 1733.

Law, John. *Money and Trade*. Edinburgh, 1705.

Law, William. *Remarks upon a Late Book, Entituled, "The Fable of the Bees."* 3d ed. London, 1726.

A Letter from an English Merchant at Amsterdam, to His Friend at Amsterdam. London, 1695.

A Letter to a Member of Parliament, in the Setting a Trade to the South-Sea of America. N.p., n.d.

A Letter to the Honourable the Lords Commissioners of Trade and Plantations. London, 1747.

Letter to William Paley, M.A., Archdeacon of Carlisle, from a Poor Labourer, in Answer to His Reason for Contentment. London, 1793.

Lewis, W. *Commercium Philosophico-Technicum*. 1763.

Liberty and Property, preserved against Republicans and Levellers. A Collection of Tracts. London, 1792.

Literary Liberty Considered; in a Letter to Henry Sampson Woodfall. London, 1774.

Locke, John. *An Essay Concerning Human Understanding*. Edited by Alexander Campbell Fraser. 2 vols. New York: Dover, 1959.

—————. *Further Considerations Concerning Raising the Value of Money*. London, 1695.

—————. *Locke on Money*. Edited by Patrick Hyde Kelly. 2 vols. Oxford: Clarendon Press, 1991.

London, What It Is, Not What It Was: or, the Citizen's Complaint against Publick Nuisances. London, [1725?].

Lowndes, William. *A Report Containing an Essay for the Amendment of the Silver Coins*. London, 1695.

Mackworth, Humphrey. *England's Glory; or, the Great Improvement of Trade in General, by a Royal Bank*. London, 1694.

Malthus, Thomas Robert. *An Essay on the Principle of Population [1798]; A Summary View of the Principle of Population [1800]*. Edited by Antony Flew. Reprint, Harmondsworth, England: Penguin Books, 1976.

Malynes, Gerald. *The Center of the Circle of Commerce*. London, 1623.

—————. *The Maintenance of Free Trade*. London, 1622.

The Management of the Four Last Years Vindicated. London, 1714.

Mandeville, Bernard. *The Fable of the Bees*. Edited by Philip Harth. Harmondsworth, England: Penguin Books, 1970.

Martyn, Joseph. *Englands Wants*. London, 1667.

Marx, Karl. *Capital: A Critique of Political Economy*. Edited by Ernest Mandel. Vol. 1. Reprint, London: Penguin, 1990.

—————. "Theses on Feuerbach." In *The Marx-Engels Reader*, edited by Robert C. Tucker. 2d ed. New York: Norton, 1978.

Massie, Joseph. *An Essay on the Governing Causes of the Natural Rate of Interest*. London, 1750.

—————. *A Representation Concerning Commercial Knowledge*. London, 1760.

Matter of Fact; or, the Arraignment and Tryal of the DI——RS of the S—— S—— Company. London, 1720.

McCulloch, J. R., ed. *Early English Tracts on Commerce.* Cambridge: At the University Press, 1954.

McKinnon, Charles. *Observations on the Wealth and Force of Nations.* Edinburgh, 1781.

Mead, Joseph. *The Key of the Revelation.* Translated by William Twisse. 2d ed. London, 1650.

Merchant, A. *Family-Prayers, and Moral Essays in Prose and Verse.* London, 1769.

M'Farlan, John. *Tracts on Subjects of National Importance.* London, 1786.

Millar, John. *An Historical View of the English Government.* Dublin, 1790.

——. *The Origins of the Distinction of Ranks.* 1771. Introduction by John Craig. 4th ed. Edinburgh and London, 1806

Misselden, Edward. *The Circle of Commerce.* London, 1623.

——. *Free Trade, or, the Means to Make Trade Florish.* London, 1622.

Mortimer, Thomas. *The Elements of Commerce, Politics and Finances.* London, 1772.

Moss, Robert. *Sermons and Discourses on Several Subjects.* Vol. 8. London, 1738.

Mun, Thomas. *A Discovrse of Trade from England vnto the East Indies.* London, 1621.

——. *England's Treasure by Foreign Trade.* 1664. London, 1713.

Nalson, John. *The Common Interest of King and People.* London, 1677.

——. *The Complaint of Liberty and Property against Arbitrary Government.* London, 1681.

Nap[ie]r, Iohn. *A Plaine Discovery of the Whole Revelation of S. Iohn.* Rev. ed. London, 1611.

National Oeconomy Recommended, As the only Means of retrieving our Trade and securing our Liberties. London, 1746.

Nedham, Marchamont. *The Case of the Kingdom.* London, 1647.

——. *The Excellencie of a Free State.* London, 1656.

——. *Interest Will Not Lie.* London, 1659

Newball, John. *A Concern for Trade.* London, n.d.

[Newton, Benjamin]. *Another Dissertation on Mutual Support of Trade and Civil Liberty.* London, 1756.

North, Dudley. *Discourses upon Trade.* London, 1691.

Observations on the Agricultural and Political Tendency of the Commercial Treaty. London, 1787.

The Oeconomical Table. London, 1766.

The Oeconomist, or, Englishman's Magazine for 1798. Newcastle upon Tyne, 1798.

[Ogilvie, William]. *An Essay on the Right of Property in Land.* London, 1781.

[Paget, Thomas Catesby]. *Some Reflections upon the Administration of Government.* London, 1740.

Paley, William. *The Works of William Paley, D.D.* Edited by D. S. Wayland. London: George Cowie, 1837.

Parker, Henry. *Of a Free Trade.* London, 1648.

Parker, Samuel. *A Demonstration of the Divine Authority of the Law of Nature and the Christian Religion.* London, 1681.

[Parnell, Thomas]. *Live and Let Live: A Treatise on the Hostile Rivalship between the Manufacturer and Land-Worker.* London, [1787].

Patton, Robert. *The Effects of Property upon Society and Government Investigated*. London, 1797.

Petty, William. *Political Arithmetick, or A Discourse*. London, 1690.

Philemerus, J. *Of Luxury, more particularly with Respect to Apparel*. London, 1736.

Phil[l]ips, Erasmus. *An Appeal to Common Sense*. London, 1721.

———. *The State of the Nation, in respect to her Commerce, Debts and Money*. 2d ed. London, 1731.

Philopatris [Josiah Child]. *A Treatise*. London, 1681.

Philopatris [Benjamin Worsley]. *The Advocate*. London, 1652.

Pigs' Meat; or, Lessons for the Swinish Multitude. 2d ed. 2 vols. London, 1793.

Pinto, Isaac de. *An Essay on Circulation and Credit*. Translated by S. Baggs. London, 1774.

———. *An Essay on Luxury*. London, 1766.

Pleasant Art of Money-Catching. 4th ed. London, 1737.

P[ollexfen], J[ohn]. *Of Trade*. London, 1700.

The Poor Child's Friend; or Familiar Lessons Adapted to the Capacities of All Ranks of Children. 2d ed. York, 1790.

The Poor Man's Friend: An Address to the Industrious and Manufacturing Part of Great Britain. Edinburgh, 1793.

The Poor Vicar's Complaint. London, 1705.

Postlethwayt, Malachy. *Britain's Commercial Interest Explained and Improved*. 2 vols. London, 1757.

———. *Great-Britain's True System*. London, 1757.

———. *The Merchant's Public Counting-House*. London, 1751.

Potter, William. *The Key of Wealth*. London, 1650.

———. *The Trade-Man's Jewel*. London, 1650.

Povey, Charles. *The Unhappiness of England as to its Trade by Sea and Land*. London, 1701.

The Present Condition of Great-Britain. London, 1746.

The Present State of Europe. London, 1750.

Price, Richard. *Observations on the Expectations of Lives, The Increase of Mankind, The Influence of Great Towns on Population, and particularly the State of London, with respect to Healthfulness and Number of Inhabitants*. London, 1769.

Private Worth the Basis of Public Decency. London, 1789.

Proposals for the Increase of Trade. London, 1693.

Raleigh, Walter. *Observations Touching Trade and Commerce*. London, 1653.

Ray, John. *Three Physico-Theological Discourses*. London, 1693.

Reasons for Encouraging the Linnen Manufacture of Scotland. London, 1735.

Reasons for Making void and Annulling those Fraudulent and Usurious Contracts (submitted to Parliament). N.p., n.d.

Reasons for Settlement of the Trade to Africa, in a Joynt-Stock. N.p., n.d.

Reasons Humbly Offer'd by the Merchants Trading to Spain and Portugal. N.p., n.d.

Reasons Humbly Offer'd by the Portugal, Spanish, and Italian Merchants. N.p., n.d.

Reflections on the Repeal of the Marriage-Act. London, 1765.

Reflections on Various Subjects Relating to Arts and Commerce: Particularly, the Consequences of admitting Foreign Artisans on Easier Terms. London, 1752.

Reflections upon Naturalization, Corporations, and Companies; Supported by the Authorities of both Ancient and Modern Writers. London, 1753

A Regulated Company more Natural than a Joint-Stock in the East-India-Trade. N.p., n.d.

Remarks upon the Bank of England. London, 1705.

Rennell, Thomas. *A Sermon Preached before the University of Oxford, May 6, 1705*. Oxford, 1705.

Reynel, Carew. *The True English Interest*. London, 1674.

Ricardo, David. *The Principles of Political Economy and Taxation*. 1817. Introduction by Michael P. Fogarty. Reprint, London: J. M. Dent and Sons, 1955.

Richardson, John. *The Canon of the New Testament Vindicated*. London, 1719.

Roberts, Lewes. *The Merchants Map of Commerce*. 4th ed. London, 1700.

———. *The Treasure of Traffike or A Discourse of Forrayne Trade*. London, 1641.

Shebbeare, J. *Essay on the Origin, Progress and Establishment of National Society*. London, 1776.

Sheridan, Thomas. *A Discourse of the Rise and Power of Parliaments*. N.p., 1677.

Simon, Irène, ed. *Three Restoration Divines: Barrow, South, Tillotson*. Vol. 2, *Selected Sermons*. Paris: Société d'Editions, 1976.

Single Life Discouraged, For the Publick Utility. London, 1761.

Smalbroke, Richard. *Our Obligation to Promote the Publick Interest*. London, 1724.

Smith, Adam. "The Principles which Lead and Direct Philosophical Enquiries; Illustrated by the History of Astronomy." In *Essays on Philosophical Subjects*, edited by W. P. D. Wightman and J. C. Bryce. Oxford: Clarendon Press, 1980.

———. *The Theory of the Moral Sentiments*. Edited by D. D. Raphael and A. L. Macfie. Reprint, Oxford: Clarendon Press, 1979.

———. *The Wealth of Nations*. Edited by Edwin Canaan. 2 vols. Chicago: University of Chicago Press, 1976.

Some Remarks relating to the African Trade. London, 1711.

Some Serious Reflections on the Melancholy Consequences which too naturally attend the Neglect of Parents, in the Education of their Children. London, 1752.

Some Thoughts of the Interest of England. London, 1697.

[Somers, John?]. *A Letter Ballancing the Necessity of Keeping a Land-Force in Times of Peace*. London, 1697

The South Sea Scheme Examin'd. 3d ed. London, 1720.

Spencer, John. *A Discourse concerning Prodigies*. 2d ed. London, 1665.

———. *A Discourse concerning Vulgar Prophecies*. London, 1665.

Sprat, Thomas. *The History of the Royal Society of London, for the Improving of Natural Knowledge*. 1667. 3d ed., London, 1722.

Steele, Richard. *The Trades-man's Calling*. London, 1684.

Steuart, James. *An Inquiry into the Principles of Political Œconomy*. 1767. 6 vols. London, 1805.

Stillingfleet, Edward. *Origines Sacrae*. 1662. 3d ed. London, 1666.

Stockdale, Percival. *Three Discourses*. London, 1773.

Temple, William, of Trowbridge. *A Vindication of Commerce and the Arts*. London, 1758.

Thirsk, Joan, and J. P. Cooper, eds. *Seventeenth-Century Economic Documents*. Oxford: Clarendon Press, 1972.

Thorold, John. *A Short Examination of the Notions Advanc'd in a (late) Book, intituled, The Fable of the Bees*. London, 1726.

To the Worthy Electors of Exeter. London, 1784.

Toland, John. *Letters to Serena*. London, 1704.

Towers, Joseph. *A Vindication of the Political Principles of Mr Locke: in Answer to the Objections of the Rev. Dr. Tucker*. London, 1782.

The Trade of England Revived: and the Abuses thereof Rectified. London, 1681.

The Trade with France, Italy, Spain, and Portugal, Considered. London, 1713.

Tradesman's Looking Glass: or, a Hue-and-Cry after Mrs. Money and her Sister Trade. London, N.d.

Translation of the Treaty of Commerce. London, 1715.

A Treatise on Trade: or, The Antiquity and Honour of Commerce. London, 1750.

Treaty of Commerce betwixt Anne Queen of Great Britain and Peter King of Portugal. In *General Collection of Treatys of Peace and Commerce*. 2d ed. Vol. 4. London, 1732.

[Trenchard, John and Walter Moyle]. *An Argument Shewing, that a Standing Army is Inconsistent with a Free Government*. 1697.

———. "The True Picture of a Modern Tory." 1722. In *A Collection of Tracts by the late John Trenchard and Thomas Gordon*. London, 1751.

Trevors, Joseph. *An Essay to the Restoring of Our Decayed Trade*. London, 1675.

A True Account of the Design, and Advantages of the South-Sea Trade. London, 1711.

[Trusler, John]. *Luxury No Political Evil*. London, [1780].

———. *The Way to be Rich and Respectable. Addressed to Men of Small Fortune*. 3d ed. London, N.d.

Tryon, Thomas, *England's Grandeur, and Way to Get Wealth: or, Promotion of Trade*. N.p., 1699.

Tucker, Josiah. *A Brief Essay on the Advantages and Disadvantages which respectively attend France and Great-Britain with regard to Trade*. London, 1787.

———. *The Case of Going to War, for the Sake of Procuring, Enlarging, or Securing of Trade*. London, 1763.

———. *The Elements of Commerce and the Theory of Taxes*. London, 1755.

Vanderlint, Jacob. *Money Answers All Things: or, an Essay to make Money sufficiently plentiful amongst all Ranks of People*. London, 1734.

Verney, Robert. *England's Interest*. London, 1682.

Violet, Thomas. *The Advancement of Merchandize*. London, 1651.

———. *Mysteries and Secrets of Trade and Mint-Affairs*. London, 1653.

Wallace, Robert. *Characteristics of the Present Political State of Great Britain*. London, 1758.

———. *Various Prospects of Mankind, Nature, and Providence*. London, 1761.

Warburton, William. *An Enquiry into the Nature and Origin of Literary Property*. London, 1762.

———. *The Divine Legation of Moses Demonstrated*. Vols. 1–6 in *Works*. 12 vols. London: T. Cadell and W. Davies, 1811.

A Warning to Britons of All Ranks. London, n.d.

Watson, J. *The Experienced Market Man and Woman*. Edinburgh, 1699.

Wealth and Commerce of Great-Britain Consider'd. N.p., 1728.

[Weston, W.?]. *A Dissertation on the Following Question: In what manner do Trade and Civil Liberty support and assist each other?* London, 1756.

What has been, May be. London, 1721.

Whately, George. *Principles of Trade.* 2d ed. London, 1774.

Wheeler, John. *A Treatise of Commerce.* London, 1601.

Whilst we Live let us Live. A Short View of the Competition between the Manufacturer and Land Worker. Norwich, 1788.

Whiston, James. *A Discourse of the Decay of Trade.* London, 1693.

―――. *England's Calamities Discover'd: with the Proper Remedy to Restore Her Ancient Grandeur and Policy.* London, 1696.

―――. *England's State-Distempers, Trac'd from their Originals.* N.p., 1704.

―――. *The Mismanagements in Trade Discover'd.* London, 1704.

Whitworth, Charles. *State of the Trade of Great Britain in its Imports and Exports.* London, 1776.

Wilberforce, William. *A Practical View of the Prevailing Religious System of Professed Christians, in the Higher and Middle Classes in this Country.* London, 1797.

Wilkins, John. *An Essay Towards a Real Character and a Philosophical Language.* London, 1668.

Wilson, Jasper [Dr. James Currie?]. *A Letter, Commercial and Political.* London, 1793.

Witt, John de (and other great men in Holland). *The True Interest and Political Maxims of the Republick of Holland and West Friesland.* London, 1702.

Wolseley, Charles. *The Reasonableness of Scripture-Bel[ie]f.* London, 1672.

Wood, William. *A Survey of Trade.* 1718. 2d ed. London, 1722.

Wotton, William. *A Discourse concerning the Confusion of Languages at Babel.* 1713. London, 1730.

―――. *Reflections upon Ancient and Modern Learning.* 1694. 2d ed. London, 1697.

Yarranton, Andrew. *England's Improvement by Sea and Land.* London, 1677.

Young, Arthur. *An Enquiry into the State of the Public Mind amongst the Lower Classes.* London, 1798.

―――. *Political Essays concerning the Present State of the British Empire.* London, 1772.

―――[?]. *Questions of Wool Truly Stated.* London, 1788.

―――. *A Six Months Tour through the North of England.* 4 vols. London, 1770.

―――. *A Six Weeks Tour, through the Southern Counties of England and Wales.* London, 1768.

Secondary Sources: Economic, Social, Political, and Intellectual History

Anderson, Benedict. *Imagined Communities: Reflections on the Origin and Spread of Nationalism.* Rev. ed. Reprint, London: Verso, 1995.

Appleby, Joyce Oldham. *Economic Thought and Ideology in Seventeenth-Century England.* Princeton: Princeton University Press, 1980.

Beattie, J. M. *Crime and the Courts in England, 1660–1800.* Princeton: Princeton University Press, 1986.

Berg, Maxine. *The Age of Manufactures: Industry, Innovation and Work in Britain, 1700-1820.* London: Fontana Press, 1985.

Borsay, Peter. *The English Urban Renaissance: Culture and Society in the Provincial Town, 1660–1700*. Oxford: Clarendon Press, 1989.

Bowles, Paul. "The Origin of Prosperity and the Development of Scottish Historical Science." *Journal of the History of Ideas* 46 (1985): 197–209.

Brewer, John. *The Sinews of Power: War, Money and the English State, 1688–1783*. Cambridge: Harvard University Press, 1990.

Burnett, John. *A History of the Cost of Living*. Harmondsworth, England: Penguin Books, 1969.

Burtt, Shelley. *Virtue Transformed: Political Argument in England, 1688–1740*. Cambridge: Cambridge University Press, 1992.

Cain, Louis P. and Paul J. Uselding, eds. *Business Enterprise and Economic Change: Essays in Honor of Harold F. Wilkinson*. Kent, Ohio: Kent State University Press, 1973.

Campbell, Colin. *The Romantic Ethic and the Spirit of Modern Consumerism*. Reprint, Oxford: Blackwell, 1993.

Cannon, John. *Aristocratic Century: The Peerage of Eighteenth-Century England*. Cambridge: Cambridge University Press, 1984.

Cherry, George L. "The Development of the English Free-Trade Movement in Parliament, 1689–1702." *Journal of Modern History* 25 (1953): 103–19.

Clark, Peter. "Migration in England During the Late Seventeenth and Early Eighteenth Centuries." *Past & Present*, no. 83 (1979): 57–90.

Coats, A. W. "Changing Attitudes to Labour in the Mid-Eighteenth Century." *Economic History Review*, 2d ser., 11 (1958): 35–51.

Cohen, Murray. *Sensible Words: Linguistic Practice in England, 1640–1785*. Baltimore: Johns Hopkins University Press, 1977.

Cole, W. A. "Eighteenth-Century Economic Growth Revisited." *Explorations in Economic History* 10, no. 4 (1973): 327–48.

———. "Trends in Eighteenth-Century Smuggling." *Economic History Review*, 2d ser., 10 (1958): 395–410.

Coleman, D. C. "Labour in the English Economy of the Seventeenth Century." *Economic History Review*, 2d ser., 8 (1956): 280–95.

Coleman, D. C. and A. H. John, eds. *Trade, Government and Economy in Pre-Industrial England: Essays Presented to F. J. Fisher*. London: Weidenfeld and Nicolson, 1976.

Collini, Stefan, Donald Winch, and John Burrow. *That Noble Science of Politics: A Study in Nineteenth-Century Intellectual History*. Cambridge: Cambridge University Press, 1983.

Collins, Stephen L. *From Divine Cosmos to Sovereign State: An Intellectual History of Consciousness and the Idea of Order in Renaissance England*. New York: Oxford University Press, 1989.

Cornfield, P. J. *The Impact of English Towns, 1700–1800*. Oxford: Oxford University Press, 1982.

Daston, Lorraine. *Classical Probability in the Enlightenment*. Princeton: Princeton University Press, 1988.

Davis, Dorothy. *A History of Shopping*. London: Routledge & Kegan Paul, 1966.

Davis, Ralph. "English Foreign Trade, 1700–1774." *Economic History Review*, 2d ser., 15 (1962): 285–303.

———. "The Rise of Protection in England, 1689–1786." *Economic History Review*, 2d ser., 19 (1966): 306–17.

Deane, Phyllis. *The First Industrial Revolution*. 2d ed. Cambridge: Cambridge University Press, 1979.

————. "The Output of the British Woolen Industry in the Eighteenth Century." *Journal of Economic History* 17 (1957): 207–23.

Deane, Phyllis and W. A. Cole. *British Economic Growth, 1688–1959*. Cambridge: Cambridge University Press, 1964.

De Grazia, Margreta. "The Secularization of Language in the Seventeenth Century." *Journal of the History of Ideas* 41 (1980): 319–29.

Dickinson, H. T. "The Eighteenth Century Debate on the 'Glorious Revolution.'" *History* 61 (1976): 28–45.

————. *Liberty and Property: Political Ideology in Eighteenth-Century Britain*. New York: Holmes and Meier, 1977.

Dickson, P. G. M. *The Financial Revolution in England: A Study of the Development of Public Credit, 1688–1756*. London: Macmillan, 1967.

Douglas, Mary and Baron Isherwood. *The World of Goods: Towards an Anthropology of Consumption*. New York: Norton, 1979.

Earle, Peter. "Age and Accumulation in the London Business Community, 1665–1720." In *Business Life and Public Policy: Essays in Honour of D. C. Coleman*, edited by Neil McKendrick and R. G. Outhwaite. Cambridge: Cambridge University Press, 1986.

Feather, John. *The Provincial Book Trade in Eighteenth-Century England*. Cambridge: Cambridge University Press, 1985.

Fisher, M. J. "The Development of London as a Centre of Conspicuous Consumption in the Sixteenth and Seventeenth Centuries." *Transactions of the Royal Historical Society* 30 (1948): 37–50.

Foucault, Michel. *The Order of Things: An Archaeology of the Human Sciences*. New York: Vintage Books, 1973.

————. "What is an Author?" In *Textual Strategies: Perspectives in Post-Structuralist Criticism*, edited by Josué V. Harari. Ithaca: Cornell University Press, 1979.

Frei, Hans W. *The Eclipse of Biblical Narrative: A Study in Eighteenth and Nineteenth Century Hermeneutics*. New Haven: Yale University Press, 1974.

Gaskell, Philip. *A New Introduction to Bibliography*. New York: Oxford University Press, 1972.

Goldsmith, M. M. *Private Vices, Public Benefits: Bernard Mandeville's Social and Political Thought*. Cambridge: Cambridge University Press, 1985.

Gould, J. D. "Agricultural Fluctuations and the English Economy in the Eighteenth Century." *Journal of Economic History* 22 (1963): 313–33.

Grassby, Richard. "English Merchant Capitalism in the Late Seventeenth Century: The Composition of Business Fortunes." *Past & Present*, no. 46 (1970): 87–107.

Gunn, J. A. W. "'Interest Will Not Lie:' A Seventeenth-Century Political Maxim." *Journal of the History of Ideas* 29 (1968): 551–64.

Harris, Victor. *All Coherence Gone*. Chicago: University of Chicago Press, 1949.

Harvey, Richard. "The Problem of Social-Political Obligation for the Church of England in the Seventeenth Century." *Church History* 40 (1971): 156–69.

Heckscher, Eli. *Mercantilism*. 1931. 2d ed. 2 vols. Edited by E. F. Söderlund. Translated by Mendel Shapiro. London: George Allen and Unwin, 1962.

Hirschman, Albert O. *The Passions and the Interests: Political Arguments for Capitalism before Its Triumph*. Princeton: Princeton University Press, 1977.

Holmes, Geoffrey. "The Achievement of Stability: The Social Context of Politics from the 1680s to the Age of Walpole." In *Politics, Religion and Society in England, 1679–1742*. London: Hambledon Press, 1986.

Hoppit, Julian. *Risk and Failure in English Business, 1700–1800*. Cambridge: Cambridge University Press, 1987.

Horne, Thomas A. *The Social Thought of Bernard Mandeville: Virtue and Commerce in Early Eighteenth-Century England*. New York: Columbia University Press, 1978.

Hundert, E. J. "The Making of *Homo Faber*: John Locke Between Ideology and History." *Journal of the History of Ideas* 33 (1972): 3–22.

Hutchinson, Terence. *Before Adam Smith: The Emergence of Political Economy, 1662–1776*. Oxford: Basil Blackwell, 1988.

Ignatieff, Michael. "John Millar and Individualism." In *Wealth and Virtue: The Shaping of Political Economy in the Scottish Enlightenment*, edited by Istvan Hont and Michael Ignatieff. Cambridge: Cambridge University Press, 1983.

―――. *The Needs of Strangers*. New York: Viking, 1985.

Ippolito, Richard A. "The Effect of the 'Agricultural Depression' on Industrial Demand in England: 1730–1750." *Economica*, n.s., 42 (1975): 298–312.

Jacob, M. C. "The Church and the Formulation of the Newtonian World-view." *Journal of European Studies* 1 (1971): 128–48.

John, A. H. "Aspects of English Economic Growth in the First Half of the Eighteenth Century." *Economica*, n.s., 28 (1961): 176–90.

Jones, E. L. *Agriculture and the Industrial Revolution*. Foreword by R. M. Hartwell. Oxford: Basil Blackwell, 1974.

Jones, Richard Foster. *Ancients and Moderns: A Study of the Rise of the Scientific Movement in Seventeenth-Century England*. 2d ed. St. Louis: Washington University Studies, 1961.

Klein, Lawrence. "The Third Earl of Shaftesbury and the Progress of Politeness." *Eighteenth-Century Studies* 18 (1984–85): 186–214.

Land, Stephen K. "Lord Monboddo and the Theory of Syntax in the Late Eighteenth Century." *Journal of the History of Ideas* 37 (1976): 423–40.

Langford, Paul. *A Polite and Commercial People: England, 1727–1783*. Oxford: Clarendon Press, 1989.

Lenman, Bruce P. "The English and Dutch East India Companies and the Birth of Consumerism in the Augustan World." *Eighteenth-Century Life*, n.s., 14, no. 1 (1990): 47–65.

Letwin, William. *The Origins of Scientific Economics: English Economic Thought, 1660–1776*. Reprint, Westport, Conn.: Greenwood Press, 1975.

Lindert, Peter H. "English Occupations, 1670–1811." *Journal of Economic History* 40 (1980): 685–712.

Little, Anthony J. *Deceleration in the Eighteenth-Century British Economy*. London: Croom Helm, 1976.

Mathias, Peter. *The Transformation of England: Essays in the Economic and Social History of England in the Eighteenth Century*. New York: Columbia University Press, 1979.

McCloskey, Donald N. *The Rhetoric of Economics*. Madison: University of Wisconsin Press, 1985.

McKendrick, Neil. "The Consumer Revolution in Eighteenth-Century England." In Neil McKendrick, John Brewer, and J. H. Plumb, *The Birth of a Consumer Society:*

The Commercialization of Eighteenth-Century England (1982). Bloomington: Indiana University Press, 1985.

Meek, Ronald L. *Social Science and the Ignoble Savage*. Cambridge: Cambridge University Press, 1976.

Mingay, G. E. "The Agricultural Depression." *Economic History Review*, 2d ser., 8 (1956): 323–38.

Mui, Hoh-Cheung and Lorna H. *Shops and Shopkeeping in Eighteenth-Century England*. Kingston: McGill-Queen's University Press, 1989.

Pagden, Anthony, ed. *The Languages of Political Theory in Early Modern Europe*. Cambridge: Cambridge University Press, 1987.

Perkin, Harold. *The Origins of Modern English Society*. Reprint, London: Routledge & Kegan Paul, 1971.

————. "The Social Causes of the British Industrial Revolution." *Transactions of the Royal Historical Society*, 5th ser., 18 (1968): 123–43.

Plumb, J. H. *The Growth of Political Stability in England, 1675–1725*. London: Methuen, 1967.

————. "The New World of Children in Eighteenth-Century England." *Past & Present*, no. 67 (1976): 64–93.

Pocock, J. G. A. "Cambridge Paradigms and Scotch Philosophers: A Study of the Relations Between the Civic Humanist and the Civil Jurisprudential Interpretation of Eighteenth-Century Social Thought." In *Wealth and Virtue: The Shaping of Political Economy in the Scottish Enlightenment*, edited by Istvan Hont and Michael Ignatieff. Cambridge: Cambridge University Press, 1983.

————. *The Machiavellian Moment: Florentine Political Thought and the Atlantic Republican Tradition*. Princeton: Princeton University Press, 1975.

————. *Virtue, Commerce, and History: Essays on Political Thought and History, Chiefly in the Eighteenth Century*. Reprint, Cambridge: Cambridge University Press, 1986.

Purver, Margery. *The Royal Society: Concept and Creation*. Introduction by H. R. Trevor-Roper. Cambridge: MIT Press, 1967.

Reedy, Gerard, S.J. *The Bible and Reason: Anglicans and Scripture in Late Seventeenth-Century England*. Philadelphia: University of Pennsylvania Press, 1985.

Ribeiro, Aileen. *Dress in Eighteenth Century Europe, 1715–1789*. New York: Holmes and Meier, 1985.

Robertson, John. "The Scottish Enlightenment at the Limits of the Civic Tradition." In *Wealth and Virtue: The Shaping of Political Economy in the Scottish Enlightenment*, edited by Istvan Hont and Michael Ignatieff. Cambridge: Cambridge University Press, 1983.

Robinson, E. "Eighteenth-Century Commerce and Fashion: Matthew Bolton's Marketing Techniques." *Economic History Review*, 2d ser., 16 (1963): 39–60.

Rogers, Nicholas. "Popular Protest in Early Hanoverian London." *Past & Present*, no. 79 (1978): 70–100.

Rusche, Harry. "Prophecies and Propaganda, 1641 to 1651." *English Historical Review* 84 (1969): 752–70.

Sekora, John. *Luxury: The Concept in Western Thought, Eden to Smollett*. Baltimore: Johns Hopkins University Press, 1977.

Shammas, Carole. *The Pre-Industrial Consumer in England and America*. Oxford: Clarendon Press, 1990.

Shapiro, Barbara J. *Probability and Certainty in Seventeenth-Century England: A Study of the Relationships Between Natural Science, Religion, History, Law, and Literature*. Princeton: Princeton University Press, 1983.

Smith, Steven R. "The London Apprentices as Seventeenth-Century Adolescents." *Past & Present*, no. 61 (1973): 149–61.

Sommerville, C. John. *The Secularization of Early Modern England: From Religious Culture to Religious Faith*. New York: Oxford University Press, 1992.

Spadafora, David. *The Idea of Progress in Eighteenth-Century Britain*. New Haven: Yale University Press, 1990.

Stone, Lawrence. *The Family, Sex and Marriage in England, 1500–1800*. Abridged ed. New York: Harper Colophon Books, 1979.

Teichgraeber, Richard F., III. *'Free Trade' and Moral Philosophy: Rethinking the Sources of Adam Smith's Wealth of Nations*. Durham, N.C.: Duke University Press, 1986.

Thirsk, Joan. *Economic Policy and Projects: The Development of a Consumer Society in Early Modern England*. Reprint, Oxford: Clarendon Press, 1988.

———. "Younger Sons in the Seventeenth Century." *History* 54 (1969): 358–77.

Thompson, E. P. "The Moral Economy of the English Crowd in the Eighteenth Century." In *Customs in Common*. New York: The New Press, 1993.

Tomlinson, John. *Cultural Imperialism: A Critical Introduction*. Baltimore: Johns Hopkins University Press, 1991.

Viner, Jacob. "Power Versus Plenty as Objectives of Foreign Policy in the Seventeenth and Eighteenth Centuries." In *Revisions in Mercantilism*, edited by D. C. Coleman. London: Methuen, 1969.

———. *The Role of Providence in the Social Order: An Essay in Intellectual History*. Princeton: Princeton University Press, 1972.

Weatherill, Lorna. *Consumer Behaviour and Material Culture in Britain, 1660–1760*. London: Routledge, 1988.

Wiles, Richard C. "Mercantilism and the Idea of Progress." *Eighteenth-Century Studies* 8 (1974): 56–74.

———. "The Theory of Wages in Later English Mercantilism." *Economic History Review*, 2d ser., 21 (1968): 113–26.

Wilson, Charles. *England's Apprenticeship, 1603–1763*. 2d ed. London: Longman, 1984.

———. "Treasure and Trade Balances: The Mercantilist Problem." *Economic History Review*, 2d ser., 2 (1949): 152–61.

Wilson, John F. *Pulpit in Parliament: Puritanism during the English Civil Wars, 1640–1648*. Princeton: Princeton University Press, 1969.

Winch, Donald. *Adam Smith's Politics: An Essay in Historiographic Revision*. Cambridge: Cambridge University Press, 1978.

Wood, Ellen Meiksins. *The Pristine Culture of Capitalism: A Historical Essay on Old Regimes and Modern States*. London: Verso, 1991.

Wrigley, E. A. "A Simple Model of London's Importance in Changing English Society and Economy, 1650–1750." *Past & Present*, no. 37 (1967): 44–70.

Primary Sources: "Literary" Works

Addison, Joseph and Richard Steele. *The Spectator*. Edited by G. Gregory Smith. 4 vols. Reprint, London: J. M. Dent, 1911.

Anstey, Christopher. *The New Bath Guide: or, Memoirs of the B——r——d Family*. 3d ed. London, 1766.

Behn, Aphra. *Love Letters Between a Nobleman and His Sister*. Introduction by Maureen Duffy. Harmondsworth, England: Penguin Books, 1987.

———. *Oroonoko and Other Writings*. Edited by Paul Salzman. Oxford: Oxford University Press, 1994.

Boswell, James. *Boswell's Life of Johnson*. Edited by George Birkbeck Hill. 6 vols. Oxford: Clarendon Press, 1887.

Breues, John. *The Fortune Hunters*. London, 1754.

Burney, Fanny. *Evelina*. Edited by Edward A. and Lillian D. Bloom. Reprint, Oxford: Oxford University Press, 1987.

Cockings, George. *Arts, Manufactures, and Commerce: A Poem*. London, n.d.

Coventry, Francis. *The History of Pompey the Little: or, the Life and Adventures of a Lap-Dog*. Edited by Robert Adams Day. Oxford: Oxford University Press, 1974.

Defoe, Daniel. *Farther Adventures*. In *The Novels and Miscellaneous Works of Daniel De Foe*. Vol. 2. Reprint, New York: AMS Press, 1971.

———. *The Life and Strange Surprizing Adventures of Robinson Crusoe*. Edited by J. Donald Crowley. Oxford: Oxford University Press, 1981.

———. *Roxana, The Fortunate Mistress*. Edited by Jane Jack. Reprint, Oxford: Oxford University Press, 1988.

———. *Serious Reflections*. Edited by George A. Aiken. Reprint, New York: AMS Press, 1974.

Faustina: or the Roman Songstress, A Satyr, on the Luxury and Effeminacy of the Age. London, n.d.

Fielding, Henry. *Amelia*. Edited by Martin C. Battestin. Middletown, Conn.: Wesleyan University Press, 1984.

———. *The Complete Works of Henry Fielding, Esq*. Edited by William Ernest Henley. 16 vols. New York: Croscup and Sterling, 1903.

———. *The History of the Adventures of Joseph Andrews*. Edited by Martin C. Battestin. Middletown, Conn.: Wesleyan University Press, 1984.

———. *The History of Tom Jones, A Foundling*. Edited by Martin C. Battestin. Middletown, Conn.: Wesleyan University Press, 1975.

———. *Shamela*. In *Joseph Andrews and Shamela*, edited by Martin C. Battestin. Boston: Houghton Mifflin, 1961.

Fielding, Sarah. *The Adventures of David Simple*. Edited by Malcolm Kelsall. Oxford: Oxford University Press, 1987.

———. *The Governess, or, Little Female Academy*. Introduction by Mary Cardogan. London: Pandora, 1987.

Glover, [Richard]. *London: or, the Progress of Commerce. A Poem*. London, 1739.

Goldsmith, Oliver. "The Deserted Village." In *The Poems of Thomas Gray, William Collins and Oliver Goldsmith*, edited by Roger Lonsdale. London: Longman, 1976.

The Happy Bride, or Virtuous Country Maid Rewarded. London, n.d.

Haywood, Eliza. *The History of Miss Betsy Thoughtless*. Introduction by Dale Spender. London: Pandora, 1986.

———. *Lasselia*. In *Four Novels of Eliza Haywood*, introduction by Mary Anne Schofield. Delmar, N.Y.: Scholars' Facsimiles & Reprints, 1983.

——— [?]. *The Mercenary Lover: or, the Unfortunate Heiresses*. London, 1726.

Hume, David. *Essays: Moral, Political, and Literary*. Rev. ed. Edited by Eugene F. Miller. Indianapolis, Ind.: Liberty Classics, 1987.

Johnson, Samuel. *A Journey to the Western Islands* and "Preface to the English Dictionary. In *Johnson, Prose and Poetry*, edited by Mona Wilson. Cambridge: Harvard University Press, 1967.

Lennox, Charlotte. *The Female Quixote*. Edited by Margaret Dalziel. Reprint, Oxford: Oxford University Press, 1989.

Lewis, Matthew. *The Monk*. Edited by Howard Anderson. Reprint, Oxford: Oxford University Press, 1986.

Lillo, George. *The London Merchant*. Edited by William H. McBurney. Lincoln: University of Nebraska Press, 1965.

Manley, Mary Delariviere. *The Secret History of Queen Zarah*. In *The Novels of Mary Delariviere Manley*, edited by Patricia Köster. 2 vols. Vol. 1. Gainesville, Fla.: Scholars' Facsimiles & Reprints, 1971.

Paltock, Robert. *The Life and Adventures of Peter Wilkins*. Edited by Christopher Bentley. Introduction by James Grantham Turner. Oxford: Oxford University Press, 1990.

Pamela Censured. London, 1741.

Richardson, Samuel. *Pamela*. Edited by T. C. Duncan Eaves and Ben D. Kimpel. Boston: Houghton Mifflin, 1971.

————. *Pamela* (Part 2). In *The Shakespeare Head Edition of the Novels of Samuel Richardson*. Vols. 3 and 4. Oxford: Basil Blackwell, 1929.

Richardson, William. *Ambition and Luxury, A Poetical Epistle*. Edinburgh, 1778.

Scott, Sarah. *A Description of Millenium Hall and the Country Adjacent*. Introduction by Jane Spencer. London: Virago, 1986.

Sheridan, Frances. *Memoirs of Miss Sidney Bidulph*. Edited by Patricia Köster and Jean Coates Cleary. Oxford: Oxford University Press, 1995.

Smith, Adam. *Lectures on Rhetoric and Belles Lettres*. Edited by J. C. Bryce. Oxford: Clarendon Press, 1983.

Sterne, Lawrence. *The Life and Opinions of Tristram Shandy*. Edited by Melvyn New, Joan New, Richard A. Davies, and W. G. Day. 3 vols. Gainesville: University Presses of Florida, 1978–84.

————. *A Sentimental Journey*. Edited by Ian Jack. Reprint, Oxford: Oxford University Press, 1988.

Swift, Jonathan. *Gulliver's Travels*. Edited by Louis A. Landa. Boston: Houghton Mifflin, 1960.

Walpole, Horace. *The Castle of Otranto*. Edited by W. S. Lewis and Joseph W. Read, Jr. Reprint, Oxford: Oxford University Press, 1990.

Young, Edward. *Conjectures on Original Composition*. Edited by Edith J. Morley. Reprint, n.p.: Norwood Editions, 1979.

Secondary Sources: Criticism

Agnew, Jean-Christophe. *Worlds Apart: The Market and the Theater in Anglo-American Thought, 1550–1750*. Cambridge: Cambridge University Press, 1986.

Armstrong, Nancy. *Desire and Domestic Fiction: A Political History of the Novel*. New York: Oxford University Press, 1987.

Armstrong, Nancy and Leonard Tennenhouse. *The Imaginary Puritan: Literature, Intellectual Labor, and the Origins of Personal Life*. Berkeley and Los Angeles: University of California Press, 1992.

Auerbach, Erich. *Mimesis: The Representation of Reality in Western Literature*. 1946. Translated by Willard R. Trask. Princeton: Princeton University Press, 1968.

Backscheider, Paula R. *Daniel Defoe: His Life*. Baltimore: Johns Hopkins University Press, 1989.

Baker, Ernest A. *The History of the English Novel*. 1924. 10 vols. Reprint, New York: Barnes and Noble, 1964.

Bakhtin, M. M. *The Dialogic Imagination: Four Essays by M. M. Bakhtin*. Edited by Michael Holquist. Translated by Caryl Emerson and Michael Holquist. Austin: University of Texas Press, 1981.

Ballaster, Ros. *Seductive Forms: Women's Amatory Fiction from 1684 to 1740*. Oxford: Clarendon Press, 1992.

Barker-Benfield, G. J. *The Culture of Sensibility: Sex and Society in Eighteenth-Century Britain*. Chicago: University of Chicago Press, 1992.

Barrell, John. *The Birth of Pandora and the Division of Knowledge*. Philadelphia: University of Pennsylvania Press, 1992.

———. *English Literature in History, 1730–80: An Equal, Wide Survey*. New York: St. Martin's Press, 1983.

Bartolomeo, Joseph F. "Interpolated Tales as Allegories of Reading: *Joseph Andrews*." *Studies in the Novel, North Texas State* 23 (1991): 405–15.

Battestin, Martin C. "Introduction." In Henry Fielding, *Joseph Andrews*, edited by Martin C. Battestin. Boston: Houghton Mifflin, 1961.

———. *The Moral Basis of Fielding's Art: A Study of Joseph Andrews*. 1959. Reprint, Middletown, Conn.: Wesleyan University Press, 1975.

Bender, John. *Imagining the Penitentiary: Fiction and the Architecture of Mind in Eighteenth-Century England*. Chicago: University of Chicago Press, 1987.

Blewett, David. "The Retirement Myth in *Robinson Crusoe*." *Studies in the Literary Imagination* (1982): 37–50.

Bond, Clinton. "Representing Reality: Strategies of Realism in the Early English Novel." *Eighteenth-Century Fiction* 6 (1994): 121–40.

Bowers, Toni. " 'A Point of Conscience:' Breastfeeding and Maternal Authority in *Pamela 2*." *Eighteenth-Century Fiction* 7 (1995): 259–78.

Boyce, Benjamin. "The Question of Emotion in Defoe." *Studies in Philology* 50 (1953): 45–58.

Braudy, Leo. "Daniel Defoe and the Anxieties of Autobiography." *Genre* 6 (1973): 76–97.

———. *Narrative Form in History and Fiction: Hume, Fielding, and Gibbon*. Princeton: Princeton University Press, 1970.

Braverman, Richard. "Crusoe's Legacy." *Studies in the Novel, North Texas State* 18 (1986): 1–26.

Brown, Homer Obed. "The Displaced Self in the Novels of Daniel Defoe." *ELH* 38 (1971): 563–90.

———. *Institutions of the English Novel: From Defoe to Scott*. Philadelphia: University of Pennsylvania Press, 1997.

———. "Of the Title to Things Real: Conflicting Stories." *ELH* 55 (1988): 917–54.

Bunn, James H. "The Aesthetics of British Mercantilism." *New Literary History* 11 (1980): 303–21.

Burckhardt, Sigurd. "*Tristram Shandy*'s Law of Gravity." *ELH* 28 (1961): 70–88.

Butler, Mary E. "The Effect of the Narrator's Rhetorical Uncertainty in the Fiction of *Robinson Crusoe*." *Studies in the Novel, North Texas State* 15 (1983): 77–90.

Campbell, Jill. " 'The exact picture of his mother': Recognizing Joseph Andrews." *ELH* 55 (1988): 643–64.

Castle, Terry. *Masquerade and Civilization: The Carnivalesque in Eighteenth-Century English Culture and Fiction*. Stanford: Stanford University Press, 1986.

Conboy, Sheila. "Fabric and Fabrication in Richardson's *Pamela*." *ELH* 54 (1987): 81–96.

Cottom, Daniel. "*Robinson Crusoe*: The Empire's New Clothes." *Eighteenth Century: Theory and Interpretation* 22 (1981): 271–86.

Court, Franklin E. "The Social and Historical Significance of the First English Literature Professorship in England." *Publication of the Modern Language Association* 103 (1988): 796–807.

Cruise, James. "Fielding, Authority, and the New Commercialism in *Joseph Andrews*." *ELH* 54 (1987): 253–76.

———. "A House Divided: Sarah Scott's *Millenium Hall*." *Studies in English Literature* 35 (1995): 555–73.

———. "Precept, Property, and 'Bourgeois' Practice in *Joseph Andrews*." *Studies in English Literature* 37 (1997): 535–52.

———. "Reinvesting the Novel: *Tristram Shandy* and Authority." *Age of Johnson* 1 (1987): 215–35.

Damrosch, Leopold, Jr. *God's Plot & Man's Stories: Studies in the Fictional Imagination from Milton to Fielding*. Chicago: University of Chicago Press, 1985.

Davis, Lennard J. *Factual Fictions: The Origins of the English Novel*. New York: Columbia University Press, 1983.

de Bolla, Peter. *The Discourse of the Sublime: Readings in History, Aesthetics and the Subject*. Oxford: Basil Blackwood, 1989.

Dijkstra, Bram. *Defoe and Economics: The Fortunes of Roxana in the History of Interpretations*. London: Macmillan Press, 1987.

Donaldson, Ian. "Fielding, Richardson, and the Ends of the Novel." *Essays in Criticism* 32 (1982): 26–47.

Donovan, Robert A. "The Problem of Pamela, or, Virtue Unrewarded." *Studies in English Literature* 3 (1963): 377–95.

Doody, Margaret. *A Natural Passion: A Study of the Novels of Samuel Richardson*. London: Oxford University Press, 1974.

———. *The True Story of the Novel*. New Brunswick, N.J.: Rutgers University Press, 1996.

Dowling, William C. "Tristram Shandy's Phantom Audience." *Novel* 13 (1980): 284–95.

Dussinger, John A. "What Pamela Knew: An Interpretation." *Journal of English and Germanic Philology* 69 (1970): 377–93.

Flint, Christopher. "The Role of Kinship in *Robinson Crusoe*." *ELH* 55 (1988): 381–419.

Flynn, Carol Houlihan. *Samuel Richardson: A Man of Letters*. Princeton: Princeton University Press, 1982.

Folkenflik, Robert. "The Heirs of Ian Watt." *Eighteenth-Century Studies* 25 (1991–92): 203–17.

Foster, James O. "*Robinson Crusoe* and the Uses of the Imagination." *Journal of English and Germanic Philology* 91 (1992): 179–202.

Frank, Judith. "The Comic Novel and the Poor: Fielding's Preface to *Joseph Andrews*." *Eighteenth-Century Studies* 27 (1993–94): 217–34.

Gallagher, Catherine. *Nobody's Story: The Vanishing Acts of Women Writers in the Marketplace, 1670–1820*. Berkeley and Los Angeles: University of California Press, 1994.

Golden, Morris. "Periodical Contexts in the Imagined World of *Tristram Shandy*." *Age of Johnson* 1 (1987): 237–60.

Gooding, Richard. "*Pamela, Shamela*, and the Politics of the *Pamela* Vogue." *Eighteenth-Century Fiction* 7 (1995): 109–30.

Gwilliam, Tassie. *Samuel Richardson's Fictions of Gender*. Stanford: Stanford University Press, 1993.

Harries, Elizabeth W. "Sterne's Novels: Gathering Up the Fragments." *ELH* 49 (1982): 35–49.

Heiserman, Arthur. *The Novel Before the Novel: Essays and Discussions about the Beginnings of Prose Fiction in the West*. Chicago: University of Chicago Press, 1977.

Hopes, Jeffrey. "Real and Imaginary Stories: *Robinson Crusoe* and the *Serious Reflections*." *Eighteenth-Century Fiction* 8 (1996): 313–28.

Hunter, J. Paul. *Before Novels: The Cultural Contexts of Eighteenth-Century English Fiction*. New York: Norton, 1990.

———. *Occasional Form: Henry Fielding and the Chains of Circumstances*. Baltimore: Johns Hopkins University Press, 1975.

———. *The Reluctant Pilgrim: Defoe's Emblematic Method and Quest for Form in Robinson Crusoe*. Baltimore: Johns Hopkins University Press, 1966.

———. "Response as Reformation: *Tristram Shandy* and the Art of Interpretation." *Novel* 4 (1971): 132–46.

Jameson, Frederic. *The Political Unconscious: Narrative as a Socially Symbolic Act*. Ithaca: Cornell University Press, 1981.

Jefferson, D. W. "'Tristram Shandy' and Its Traditions." In *From Dryden to Johnson*. Vol. 4 of The Pelican Guide to English Literature. Reprint, Baltimore: Penguin Books, 1966.

Jones, Richard Foster. *The Seventeenth Century: Studies in the History of English Thought and Literature from Bacon to Pope*. Stanford: University of California Press, 1951.

Kaufmann, David. *The Business of Common Life: Novels and Classical Economics between Revolution and Reform*. Baltimore: Johns Hopkins University Press, 1995.

Kavanaugh, Thomas M. "Unraveling Robinson: The Divided Self in Defoe's *Robinson Crusoe*." *Texas Studies in Language and Literature* 20 (1978): 416–32.

Kearney, A. M. "Richardson's 'Pamela:' The Aesthetic Case." *Review of English Literature* 7 (1966): 78–90.

Kermode, Frank. *The Genesis of Secrecy: On the Interpretation of Narrative*. Cambridge: Harvard University Press, 1979.

Knight, Charles A. "*Joseph Andrews* and the Failure of Authority." *Eighteenth-Century Fiction* 4 (1992): 109–24.

Korshin, Paul J. "Probability and Character in the Eighteenth Century." In *Probability, Time, and Space in Eighteenth-Century Literature*, edited by Paula J. Backscheider. New York: AMS Press, 1979.

————. *Typologies in England, 1650–1820*. Princeton: Princeton University Press, 1982.

Kroll, Richard. *The Material World: Literate Culture in the Restoration and Early Eighteenth Century*, Baltimore: Johns Hopkins University Press, 1991.

Lamb, Jonathan. *Sterne's Fiction and the Double Principle*. Cambridge: Cambridge University Press, 1989.

Larson, Kerry. "'Naming the Writer': Exposure, Authority, and Desire in 'Pamela.'" *Criticism* 23 (1981): 126–40.

Lovell, Terry. *Consuming Fiction*. London: Verso, 1987.

Lukács, Georg. *The Theory of the Novel: A Historico-Philosophical Essay on the Forms of Great Epic Literature* (1920). Translated by Anna Bostock. Cambridge: MIT Press, 1971.

Lynch, Deirdre. "Overloaded Portraits: The Excesses of Character and Countenance." In *Body & Text in the Eighteenth Century*, edited by Veronica Kelly and Dorothea von Mücke. Stanford: Stanford University Press, 1994.

Maddox, James H., Jr. "Interpreter Crusoe." *ELH* 51 (1984): 33–52.

Marshall, David. *The Figure of Theater: Shaftesbury, Defoe, Adam Smith, and George Eliot*. New York: Columbia University Press, 1986.

McCrea, Brian. "Rewriting *Pamela*: Social Change and Religious Faith in *Joseph Andrews*." *Studies in the Novel, North Texas State* 16 (1984): 137–49.

McKeon, Michael. *The Origins of the English Novel, 1600–1740*. Baltimore: Johns Hopkins University Press, 1987.

McVeagh, John. "Defoe and the Romance of Trade." *Durham University Journal* 70 (1978): 141–47.

————. *Tradefull Merchants: The Portrayal of the Capitalist in Literature*. London: Routledge & Kegan Paul, 1981.

Merrett, Robert James. "Narrative Contraries in Defoe's Fiction." *Eighteenth-Century Fiction* 1 (1989): 171–85.

Mueck, D. C. "Beauty and Mr. B." *Studies in English Literature* 7 (1967): 467–74.

Mullan, John. *Sentiment and Sociability: The Language of Feeling in the Eighteenth Century*. Oxford: Clarendon Press, 1988.

New, Melvyn. "'The Grease of God': The Form of Eighteenth-Century English Fiction." *Publication of the Modern Language Association* 91 (1976): 235–44.

————. "Sterne and the Narrative of Determinateness." *Eighteenth-Century Fiction* 4 (1992): 315–29.

Nicholson, Colin. *Writing and the Rise of Finance: Capital Satires of the Early Eighteenth Century*. Cambridge: Cambridge University Press, 1994.

Novak, Maximillian E. *Economics and the Fiction of Daniel Defoe*. Berkeley and Los Angeles: University of California Press, 1962.

Nussbaum, Felicity. *The Autobiographical Subject: Gender and Ideology in Eighteenth-Century England*. Baltimore: Johns Hopkins University Press, 1989.

Osland, Diane. "Tied Back to Back: The Discourse Between the Poet and Player and the Exhortations of Parson Adams in *Joseph Andrews*." *Journal of Narrative Technique* 12 (1982): 191–200.

Park, William. "What was New About the 'New Species of Writing'?" *Studies in the Novel, North Texas State* 2 (1970): 112–30.

Patey, Douglas Lane. *Probability and Literary Form: Philosophical Theory and Literary Practice in the Augustan Age*. Cambridge: Cambridge University Press, 1984.

Paulson, Ronald. "Life as Journey and as Theater: Two Eighteenth-Century Narrative Structures." *New Literary History* 8 (1976): 43–58.

———. *Satire and the Novel in Eighteenth-Century England.* New Haven: Yale University Press, 1967.

Perl, Jeffrey M. "Anagogic Surfaces: How to Read *Joseph Andrews.*" *Eighteenth Century: Theory and Interpretation* 22 (1981): 249–70.

Pierce, John B. "Pamela's Textual Authority." *Eighteenth-Century Fiction* 7 (1995): 131–46.

Plank, Jeffrey. "The Narrative Forms of *Joseph Andrews.*" *Papers on Language and Literature* 24 (1988): 142–48.

Politi, Jina. *The Novel and Its Presuppositions: Changes in Conceptual Structures in the 18th and 19th Centuries.* Amsterdam: Adolf M. Hakkert, 1976.

Raven, James. *Judging New Wealth: Popular Publishing and Responses to Commerce in England, 1750–1800.* Oxford: Clarendon Press, 1992.

Reed, Walter L. *An Exemplary History of the Novel: The Quixotic versus the Picaresque.* Chicago: University of Chicago Press, 1981.

Richetti, John J. *Defoe's Narratives: Situations and Structures.* Oxford: Clarendon Press, 1975.

———. *Popular Fiction Before Richardson, Narrative Patterns: 1700–1739.* Oxford: Clarendon Press, 1969.

Ruml, Treadwell, III. "Joseph Andrews as Exemplary Gentleman." *Studies in Eighteenth-Century Culture* 22 (1992): 195–207.

Schellenberg, Betty A. "Enclosing the Immovable: Structuring Social Authority in *Pamela* Part II." *Eighteenth-Century Fiction* 4 (1991): 27–42.

Schonhorn, Manuel. "Defoe: The Literature of Politics and the Politics of Some Fictions." In *English Literature in the Age of Disguise*, edited by Maximillian E. Novak. Berkeley and Los Angeles: University of California Press, 1977.

Seidel, Michael. "Crusoe in Exile." *Publication of the Modern Language Association* 96 (1981): 363–74.

Shell, Marc. *The Economy of Literature.* Baltimore: Johns Hopkins University Press, 1978.

Sherburn, George. "Fielding's Social Outlook." In *Eighteenth-Century English Literature: Modern Essays in Criticism*, edited by James L. Clifford. New York: Oxford University Press, 1959.

Sill, Geoffrey M. *Defoe and the Idea of Fiction: 1713–1719.* Newark: University of Delaware Press, 1983.

Sim, Stuart. "Interrogating an Ideology: Defoe's *Robinson Crusoe.*" *British Journal for Eighteenth-Century Studies* 10 (1987): 163–75.

Spacks, Patricia Meyer. *Desire and Truth: Functions of Plot in Eighteenth-Century Novels.* Chicago: University of Chicago Press, 1990.

———. "The Soul's Imaginings: Daniel Defoe, William Cowper." *Publication of the Modern Language Association* 91 (1976): 420–35.

Spencer, Jane. *The Rise of the Woman Novelist: From Aphra Behn to Jane Austen.* Reprint, Oxford: Basil Blackwell, 1987.

Spilka, Mark. "Fielding and the Epic Impulse." *Criticism* 11 (1969): 68–77.

Stallybrass, Peter and Allon White. *The Politics and Poetics of Transgression.* Ithaca: Cornell University Press, 1986.

Starr, G. A. *Defoe and Spiritual Autobiography*. Princeton: Princeton University Press, 1965.

Stephanson, Raymond. "The Education of the Reader in Fielding's *Joseph Andrews*." *Philological Quarterly* 61 (1982): 243–58.

Stevick, Philip. *The Chapter in Fiction: Theories of Narrative Division*. Syracuse: Syracuse University Press, 1970.

Stewart, Susan. *Crimes of Writing: Problems in the Containment of Representation*. Durham, N.C.: Duke University Press, 1994.

———. *On Longing: Narratives of the Miniature, the Gigantic, the Souvenir, the Collection*. Durham, N.C.: Duke University Press, 1993.

Straub, Kristina. "Reconstructing the Gaze: Voyeurism in Richardson's *Pamela*." *Studies in Eighteenth-Century Culture* 18 (1988): 419–31.

Tandrup, Birthe. "The Technique of Qualification in Fielding's *Joseph Andrews* and *Tom Jones*." *Orbis Litterarum* 37 (1982): 227–40.

Taylor, Dick, Jr. "Joseph as Hero in *Joseph Andrews*." *Tulane Studies in English* 7 (1957): 91–109.

Thompson, James. *Models of Value: Eighteenth-Century Political Economy and the Novel*. Durham, N.C.: Duke University Press, 1996.

Trotter, David. *Circulation: Defoe, Dickens, and the Economies of the Novel*. New York: St. Martin's Press, 1988.

Varey, Simon. *Space and the Eighteenth-Century English Novel*. Cambridge: Cambridge University Press, 1990.

Warner, John M. "The Interpolated Narratives in the Fiction of Fielding and Smollett: An Epistemological View." *Studies in the Novel, North Texas State* 5 (1973): 271–83.

Warner, William B. "The Elevation of the Novel in England: Hegemony and Literary History." *ELH* 59 (1992): 577–92.

Watt, Ian. *The Rise of the Novel: Studies in Defoe, Richardson and Fielding*. Berkeley and Los Angeles: University of California Press, 1957.

Weinstein, Arnold. *Fictions of the Self: 1500–1800*. Princeton: Princeton University Press, 1981.

Welsh, Alexander. *Strong Representations: Narrative and Circumstantial Evidence in England*. Baltimore: Johns Hopkins University Press, 1992.

Zelnick, Stephen. "Ideology as Narrative: Critical Approaches to *Robinson Crusoe*." *Bucknell Review* 27, no. 1 (1982): 79–101.

Zimmerman, Everett. *The Boundaries of Fiction: History and the Eighteenth-Century British Novel*. Ithaca: Cornell University Press, 1996.

———. "Defoe and Crusoe." *ELH* 38 (1971): 377–96.

Zomchick, John P. *Family and the Law in Eighteenth-Century Fiction: The Public Conscience in the Private Sphere*. Cambridge: Cambridge University Press, 1993.

Index